FREE ASSOCIATIONS

FREE ASSOCIATIONS

Memories of a Psychoanalyst

ERNEST JONES

With a New Introduction by

Mervyn Jones

Routledge
Taylor & Francis Group
LONDON AND NEW YORK

Originally published in 1959 by Basic Books, Inc., New York.

Published 1990 by Transaction Publishers

Published 2017 by Routledge
2 Park Square, Milton Park, Abingdon, Oxon OX14 4RN
711 Third Avenue, New York, NY 10017, USA

First issued in hardback 2018

Routledge is an imprint of the Taylor & Francis Group, an informa business

Library of Congress Catalog Number: 89-20491

Library of Congress Cataloging-in-Publication Data

Jones, Ernest, 1879-1958.
Free association: memories of a psycho-analyst/Ernest Jones; with a new introduction by Mervyn Jones.
p. cm.
Reprint. Originally published: New York: Basic Books, 1959.
ISBN 0-88738-833-7
1. Jones, Ernest, 1879-1958. 2. Psychoanalysts–United States–Biography. I. Jones, Mervyn. II. Title.
RC438.6.J64A3 1990
159.19'52'092–dc20 89-20491
CIP

ISBN 13: 978-1-138-52379-1 (hbk)
ISBN 13: 978-0-88738-833-0 (pbk)

Contents

List of Illustrations

David Beddoe = Margaret
1710–1782 1713–1791

Thomas Beddoe
1735–1807

William Beddoe = Rebecca

Thomas Jones = Rachel
1803–1865 1785–1860

John Rees = Margaret David
1780–1864

Joseph Beddoe = Elizabeth Rees
1803–1852 1808–1889

John Jones = Ann Beddoe
1829–1882 1831–1925

Thomas Jones = Mary Ann Lewis, *q.v.*
1853–1922

Ernest Jones (two sisters)

Thomas Lewis = Lettis
1785–1872

Jones = Ann Morris
1804–1838

Benjamin Lewis = Ann Jones (eldest of ten)
1827–1892 1830–1906

Mary Ann Lewis
1855–1909

INTRODUCTION TO THE TRANSACTION EDITION

Mervyn Jones

IT was in the spring of 1989 that an unexpected letter from Paul Roazen invited me to write an introduction for a new edition of my father's autobiography. I accepted without hesitation. Thirty-one years had passed since the spring of 1958 when, in the aftermath of my father's death, I prepared the manuscript of *Free Associations* for publication and added an epilogue. This epilogue, which readers will find appended to the present edition too, explains why the book, written in 1944, was never completed and brought the life-story of Ernest Jones only up to the year 1918; and it gives an outline account of the remaining forty years of his life.

I realised at the time, and I can certainly recognise on re-reading, that my epilogue was brief and summary to the point of being scrappy. I was living through the busiest year of my life, when I was working for an understaffed weekly paper and playing an active part in the newly launched Campaign for Nuclear Disarmament, while also winding up my father's affairs, seeing to the sale or distribution of his personal possessions and his large library, and consoling my mother in her grief. My preoccupations mounted almost to absurdity when my three young children underwent, in total, three cases of chicken pox and one of measles, a broken leg, and a suspected appendicitis. But there was a deeper reason why I could not attempt either a rounded appreciation of my father's personality, or any kind of reflective comment on his work and achievement. The shock of his death–and it was a shock, although expected through the final months–had knocked me off balance, making it impossible for me to think calmly about him. Freud once said that the most important event in any man's life is the death of his father, and so it assuredly was for me. I mourned my father deeply, and I mourn him still. It will be understood, therefore, why I was grateful for the opportunity provided by Dr. Roazen's letter in 1989 to write about Ernest Jones as I could not write in 1958.

I had, in point of fact, written about him fairly recently in the first chapter of my own autobiography, which was published in 1987 with the title of *Chances* – a title that my father too might have justifiably chosen, since his life, like mine, was sharply affected by sudden and unpredictable happenings. In the context of my difficulties in my relationships with my father when I was a boy, I said that I never knew at any given moment whether I should be confronted by the conventional or the unconventional Ernest Jones.

He was informal in his manners, he detested pompousness and artificial formality, he enjoyed startling people with daring remarks, and of course he was opposed to what were generally regarded as "respectable" beliefs in the fields of religion and patriotism. On the other hand, his tastes in art, literature, music, and the decor and furnishing of his home were–by the standards of the 1930s, when I became concerned with such matters–distinctly old-fashioned. While the reproductions in the homes of my friends were of Renoir or van Gogh, or even Picasso, those in my home were of Raphael or Botticelli. He avoided sexual topics in everyday conversation, and never swore. Although he was a kindly father, he took his authority in the family for granted and never tried to "be a pal" to his son–an attempted relationship which was considerably in vogue at that period. Today, when people ask me what it was like to be the son of Ernest Jones, I have to disappoint them by replying that in most respects it was like being the son of anyone else.

What gives this little pen-portrait, I hope, a more than personal interest is the fact that it could also be a portrait of Sigmund Freud. Peter Gay, in his recent and admirable biography of Freud, comments with some amusement on the emphatic conventionality of Freud's personal habits, social behaviour, and artistic tastes. Freud it is true, was a generation older than Jones; but either Freud or Jones could have been seen, superficially, as a figure from the generation preceding his own. I should conjecture that it was the shared conventional persona (or perhaps one should say the conventional streak) that made it easy for the two men to establish a rapport as soon as they met and–generally though not invariably–to trust each other implicitly thereafter. Both of them used the word "gentleman" in a straightforward and unembarrassed way, as expressing an understood standard or ideal, with Freud using the English word for which there is no precise German equivalent. In this book, Jones records Freud's disapproval of Jung's ungentlemanly conduct, which played a not insignificant role in the parting of their ways.

One scarcely needs to point out that there is a strong contrast between, on the one hand, these conservative and traditional attitudes on the part of the pioneers of psycho-analysis, and, on the other hand, the innovative, indeed revolutionary, and for most people truly shocking character of the doctrines that they were expounding. Was it really credible, some may have asked, that men who believed that little boys had sexual feelings directed toward their mothers could also wear stiff collars, smoke good cigars, and require their associates to be gentlemen? Thus, however, it was. One explanation comes readily to mind. In view of the ignorant and malicious attacks on psycho-analysis that were being made in Germany and Austria, and to a milder extent in Britain and the U.S.A., Freud and Jones must have found it advantageous to demonstrate that they didn't wear eccentric clothes, dance the Charleston, or indulge in "free love." It is certain, all the same, that the conventionality was more genuine than calculated, and we can add that it was shared by other leading analysts such as Karl Abraham and Max Eitingon (though not by the exceptional oddball like Wilhelm Reich). The conclusion must be, in my view, that the conventionality of Freud and Jones–and in particular their prudery in the discussion of sexual matters outside the professional context–was a psychologically necessary compensation for the boldness and candour of their speculations within that context. To put it another way: for someone to write books advancing these highly unorthodox ideas, and treat patients in the heart of Vienna or London by these unorthodox methods, and also to have an unorthodox personal life, might have been more consistent, but would have involved an almost unbearable strain.

In no sphere does the contrast, or inconsistency, appear in more striking fashion than in the attitudes of these men toward women. As my readers will doubtless know, a great deal has been written on this subject since the rise of modern feminism. The publication of Freud's letters to his wife (especially those written when she was his fiancée) provided grounds for regarding him as the worst kind of male chauvinist–though Gay's careful analysis shows that the question is not quite so simple. The assumptions of masculine dominance and masculine leadership were generally accepted in the epoch covered by the lifespans of Freud and Jones (despite being questioned by Ibsen, Shaw, and others) and we can therefore see the acceptance of these assumptions in practice by Freud and Jones as an aspect of their conventionality, or rather this reluctance to make a bridge between their psycho-analytic understanding and their everyday attitudes. Central to the traditional outlook was the concept of the monogamous, faithful, lifelong marriage. I agree with Gay that the allegations of an affair between Freud and his sister-in-law is unproven and improbable; and as for Jones, while he certainly enjoyed a wide-ranging sexual life so long as he was a bachelor, I should find it hard to believe that he was ever unfaithful to either of his wives. In such marriages, it was the husband who implicitly exercised the more authoritative judgement, especially in intellectual matters. It does not at all follow, however, that either Freud or Jones regarded women in general as inferiors, intellectually or otherwise. The contrary is clearly the case, as we can deduce from Freud's close friendships with Lou Andreas-Salome and other women, and Jones' respect for such colleagues as Melanie Klein, Joan Rivière, and Sylvia Payne.

It is against this background that we can look at the most surprising episode in Ernest Jones' life: his marriage to Morfydd Owen. Love, we generally believe or try to believe, rises above incompatibilities, and certainly he loved her. Nevertheless, the incompatibilities were glaring. Music was the heart of her life just as surely as psycho-analysis was the heart of his, and in that sphere he scored very low in both knowledge and appreciation. Her social (including her musical) life was enclosed by Welsh loyalties and affiliations; he, although he was always proud of being Welsh, was glad to have escaped from Welsh provincialism and to have a number of English, European, and American friends. (He never considered making his home in Wales, even in the last phase of his life when his only occupation was writing.) Above all–or, if you like, worst of all–she was deeply and sincerely religious, while he viewed all religious belief as a harmful illusion, and was especially hostile to the narrow Welsh Nonconformity which he could recall from his childhood. Typically enough–I can hear my father's voice and see his smile–he claims that Morfydd was "gradually and painlessly" coming round to his outlook. Whatever may be the truth of this, the process cannot have been painless (Ernest Jones could sometimes be very insensitive). It seems to me unlikely that she would ever have renounced her religion, considering that it was bound up with her musical achievement–her lasting fame rests on her hymns–and must therefore have been emotionally precious to her.

We can all cite examples of successful and happy marriages in which each of the partners makes a career in totally separate fields. I don't think, however, that Ernest Jones was temperamentally suited to that kind of marriage or that it would have satisfied him. He needed a wife who would learn from him, assist him in his work when required, and devote herself to creating and maintaining a comfortable home environment for him. In my mother, he found the wife who fully met these qualifications.

A photograph of Morfydd–showing her haunting, mysterious beauty to full advantage–hung in my father's dressing-room, a room which my mother seldom entered. (It strikes me as I write that to have a "dressing-room" was another illustration of the old-fashioned persona.) He did not often speak of her. I felt that, with the passage of time, she had become for him a romantic and tragic memory–the "lost love" *par excellence*–rather than a real, accurately remembered woman. I thought, and I think now, that if she had lived the marriage would not have lasted. But he never forgot her. When I introduced my father in 1948 to the woman whom I was about to marry, and mentioned that we hadn't yet bought a wedding-ring, he immediately produced one. It was Morfydd's; it luckily fitted Jeanne's finger, and she has worn it ever since.

Let me now return to the theme of the relationships between Freud and Ernest Jones. Jones writes in *Free Associations*–and indeed I heard him say many times–that it repeated the relationships between Darwin and Huxley. This comparison must have pleased Freud, who was a devout admirer of Darwin; and since Jones, as he tells us in this autobiography, had admired Huxley since his youth, the idea was congenial to both of them. Huxley, of course, had ranked below Darwin in creative originality and had filled the role of the faithful and indispensably useful follower, and Jones saw himself in this light. He was clear in his mind that, while he was a man of exceptional intellectual ability, Freud was a genius–which is something else. This thought was also gratifying to Freud who, while remarkably free from ordinary vanity, had a core of pride deep within himself.

The comparison held good in a further sense. While Darwin was extremely retiring by nature and averse to public controversy, Huxley relished it. Freud was similarly retiring and reluctant to make public appearances. He could seldom even be persuaded (partly, it is true, because of his cancerous affliction and his speech difficulties) to mount the platform at a psycho-analytic congress. But Jones thoroughly enjoyed presiding over congresses, speaking, lecturing, and debating. He had the Welshman's ready tongue, the Welshman's spirited combativeness, and a zeal for converting others to his beliefs that may perhaps have been inherited from his Baptist forebears. In *Free Associations* he endorses Freud's view that proselytising for psycho-analysis was useless because of the profound psychological resistances that it was bound to encounter, and that psycho-analytic truths should be "placed at the disposal of anyone who manifested a desire for them." No doubt this was what he thought in his calmer moments, but when he saw an opportunity to reach the unenlightened he seized it, or even fought for it. In the 1920s he waged a persistent battle for the right to broadcast on BBC radio, eventually overcoming the veto imposed by Sir John Reith, the rigorous Scots Presbyterian who was Director-General. I well remember his triumphant return home after his fifteen minutes at the microphone. It is hard to imagine Freud consenting to speak on the radio, let alone–perish the thought!–on television.

Combativeness, within the ranks as well as toward the outer world, was a very evident characteristic of the psycho-analytic movement (or "movement") in its early years. The hostility shown by Freud's followers toward Jung, as renegade and traitor, plainly resembled–and was often compared to–the hostility of loyal Communists toward Trotsky. We catch the overtones of that hostility in Jones' allusions to Jung in this book, although his attitude as I recall it was rather one of pitying sadness–"after all," he explained to me, "the poor chap was just a Swiss pastor." Today, when Freudians, Jungians, Kleinians, and other schools of thought can confer amicably and admit that they can learn from one another, it is hard to credit the bitterness of past antagonisms. (In England, as one might expect, the token of reconciliation was a cricket match between Freudian and Jungian teams.) I don't think that Ernest Jones, if he could come back to life, would regret the burying of the hatchets. The acrimonious "controversial discussions" of the 1920s filled him with a melancholy weariness.

What he would think of the formation in France of an organisation called *Psycho-Analyse et Politique*, whose banner I have seen carried in marches through the Paris streets, is quite another matter. The question of the relationships between psycho-analysis and politics–I am of course thinking of politics in the high sense of attempts at social amelioration, not in the low sense–has been insufficiently studied. In these recollections, Jones tells us of attending Fabian Society meetings in the pre-1914 years. He is evidently anxious to play down the extent of his youthful sympathies with the political Left, and to explain that he was attracted only by projects that had a valid scientific basis, not by aspirations fired by emotion. I am not sure that the distinction was so clear-cut. A man is known, among other things, by his books, and my father had the excellent habit of noting on the flyleaf the date when he bought a book. Among those I have inherited are Upton Sinclair's *The Jungle*, bought in 1906 (the year of publication), and William Morris' *News from Nowhere*, bought in 1907. These are both brilliant works of Socialist advocacy, but they are nothing if not emotional.

We may reflect, too, on his attitude to his lifelong friend and brother-in-law, Wilfred Trotter. I knew my Uncle Trotter (thus he had to be addressed, because he detested the name of Wilfred) only in his later years, long after the "great change" described by Ernest Jones. What I remember is his caustic wit; this book includes several examples of it, and I will add another. In connection with Freud's book *Moses and Monotheism*, which my mother had translated, my father endeavoured to convince my uncle during a stroll in the garden that monotheism was a historic advance from polytheism. Trotter listened patiently and then pronounced: "The improvement is purely mathematical."

Having encountered Trotter's cynical wisdom, I could hardly believe my father's assertion that in earlier days my uncle had been an ardent and impatient revolutionary. It must have been so, and it must also have been true that Trotter had effected the change in a definite and open-eyed manner. What leaves one somewhat puzzled is my father's attitude. Since he believed (and this he certainly did believe) that social or political change was futile without a psychological reconditioning of human beings, it would have been logical for him to approve of Trotter's progress into realism, good sense, and maturity–instead of deploring, as he does in these pages, Trotter's cautious (the implication is almost "cowardly") abandonment of idealism. One feels that the change in Trotter had robbed Jones of something of himself – something of his youth.

Fundamentally, the question of the choice between social revolution or reformation and psychological (or biological) evolution is one that so far as I am able to see, cannot be resolved. The experience of the Soviet Union since the 1917 revolution has shown us, clearly enough to convince all but the willfully blind, that political action cannot be relied on to deliver the results that it promises. It would be unduly pessimistic, I think, to assert that a social revolution necessarily leads to the horrors perpetrated by Stalin, Pol Pot or Ceascescu, but it is undeniably true that no such revolution has fulfilled the hopes of idealists. The skepticism of Ernest Jones has, thus, been justified. Yet the other side of the argument presents its own difficulties: we have no solid evidence for believing that we can build a better society through the understanding and the progressive improvement of human psychology. Given that sadistic cruelty and flagrant injustice are as common in the twentieth century as they were in the remote ages of history (more so, it can be argued), this improvement, if conceivable at all, must need be a very slow process. Even the psycho-analysis of an individual takes years, its success cannot be guaranteed, and relapses into the original neurotic condition cannot be ruled out. Hence, long before we could hope to renovate the world by this route, we could all fall victim to nuclear war, or to the destruction of the ozone layer through human wastefulness and folly, or to some other cosmic disaster. As a political activist with a Freudian inheritance, I have been concerned all my life with these problems and doubts. Like my father, I have reached my sixties without arriving at any conclusive answers.

It has always been difficult, in fact, to situate psycho-analysis at a precise point in the political–or, more broadly, ideological–spectrum. Insofar as the Freudians were children of the Enlightenment, pleaded for tolerance of human frailty, and rejected the values of enforced social discipline, automatic respect for constituted authority, and dogmatic religion, they could be seen as aligned with the Left. But insofar as they pointed to the fallacies and false hopes nourished by radical revolutionaries, they provided support for the Right. Moreover, an aspect of the old-fashioned outlook to which I have referred was a distrust of governmental interference with personal life, even if it was well-intended and designed to advance progress or welfare. My father believed–as, no doubt, his father had believed–that the best government is the one that governs least. In earlier times this had been a tenet of liberalism, but in the present century it had become a hallmark of conservatism.

Almost a century has passed since Freud formulated his fundamental discoveries, and yet there is no agreed estimate in the intellectual world of their significance or value. Indeed, an illustration of this disagreement is that some would query the word "discoveries" in the preceding sentence and replace it by "theories," or even "delusions." If we try to identify the major changes over the past, say, 150 years in the way in which intelligent people think about the world, we can relate them to the work of four men: Darwin, Marx, Freud, and Einstein. The curious thing is that, while the objective importance of all four is admitted by common consent, they are by no means regarded in the same way. Two of them, Darwin and Einstein, are accepted as teachers who gave us a body of knowledge which it would be ridiculous to question. (In saying this, I set aside the "creationists" flourishing in some parts of the United States who, to the bewilderment or amusement of Europeans, are still battling against Darwin.) But the doctrines propounded by the other two, Marx and Freud, still provide fuel for acute controversy, and many critics–few of whom can be dismissed as eccentrics–have sought to attack them, to disprove of them, or (at best) to show that they had some validity when first advanced but are now outdated and useless.

All four of the men I have named claimed that their ideas were grounded in scientific truth (this being the accepted litmus test of any idea in the late nineteenth century) and the arguments relating to Marx and Freud turn on the question of whether this claim can be sustained. Marx drew a firm distinction between 'scientific' and 'utopian' socialism–the former, of course, being *his* socialism, while the latter was ascribed to such figures as Fourier and Proudhon. (Though, as a matter of fact, Fourier and Proudhon thought that they were being scientific too.) Not many people nowadays–even Marxists–would uphold these definitions with the same confidence as Marx himself. If the hallmark of science is its predictive power–its ability to say that, when the given conditions are *a* and *b*, *x* will occur–it can easily be demonstrated that Marxism lacks that quality. This does not necessarily detract from the value of Marxism as a method of social analysis, nor from its importance as a system of thought – to use a word that here becomes relevant, as a philosophy.

What, then, of psycho-analysis? Its claims to scientific status ought to be more sustainable than those of Marxism, if only because Freud and his disciples, including Ernest Jones, were well-qualified medical men and had carried out valuable scientific work of an orthodox kind. Freud never doubted that he was a scientist and that his discoveries (if I may allow myself the word) were of a scientific order, and readers of this book will see that Jones made this assumption too. Yet these discoveries were never subjected to the testing processes that are customary in the scientific world, such as a survey of a substantial number of cases with a corresponding number of controls. Freud was ready to make universal generalisations from his observation of a single patient, and this has furnished his critics with much of their ammunition. It may or may not be true that all men are born to grapple with the Oedipus complex, but Freud was content to detect it among the bourgeoisie of Vienna without asking whether it was as clearly present in proletarian Glasgow, let alone among the Yoruba or the Navajo. (However, if Freud and Jones were right in seeing the Oedipus complex as the key to the problems of a Danish prince called Hamlet, this does lend force to their assertion.)

It is possible, as a matter of fact, that Jones was more of a scientist in the accepted sense than Freud. Freud's cast of mind was boldly speculative–herein, indeed, lay his claim to greatness or to genius–and became more so as he grew older. To cite a well-known instance, Jones was startled by Freud's announcement of the concept of a death instinct and had considerable trouble in accepting i, since it lacked any demonstrable biological basis and contradicted the essential characteristics of all living organisms, as defined by biologists. Yet the concept helps us to understand many forms of human behaviour that would otherwise remain inexplicable.

An interesting book entitled *The Standing of Psycho-Analysis*, by B. A. Farrell–he is an Oxford logician–examines psycho-analysis by methods that might be applicable to other schools of thought. Farrell finds that psycho-analytic theory fails in large part to meet the requirements of logic; that psycho-analytic explanations of this or that neurotic condition are less than fully proved; and that its record of therapeutic success would not pass muster in the medical world. Despite these fairly devastating conclusions, however, Farrell does not dismiss psycho-analysis as fraudulent or valueless. He considers (and, what is more, he contrives to demonstrate logically) that it has made a great contribution to our understanding of the human condition.

We derive this understanding from two sources: from scientific knowledge and from philosophical speculation. (I should add, but am not here discussing, a third source, the insight of reactive art.) The two are not divided by any Chinese wall, and indeed have often interacted with each other. Some philosophers have also been scientists, or have progressed from science to philosophy. Aristotle, the father of western philosophy, codified existing knowledge of physics, biology, and other sciences, sometimes in ways that are still valid. We classify Descartes as a philosopher, but he also devoted himself to elucidating facts about *inter alia*, the nervous system. These examples encourage us to regard Freud as, perhaps, a similar figure, bridging the frontiers of science and philosophy. Nevertheless, a caution is in order: we should not go so far as to suppose that science and philosophy are the same thing, or that the latter is simply another name for the former. Scientific knowledge must be accepted as knowledge (until it is superseded, as Einstein superseded Newton). Philosophy does not serve us in the same way, since it is obvious that philosophers such as Hume, Kant, and Hegel cannot all have been equally 'right' or 'accurate' in their assertions. By the same token, however, philosophy is not subject to being disproved of or superseded. It is important and indeed precious to us as a guide to our thinking. Few of us, after all, are capable of thinking effectively about the problems that concern us without guidance of this nature.

I am suggesting, therefore, that we should do well to value psycho-analysis as a philosophy more than as a science. (We might well say, incidentally, that the death instinct is a philosophical rather than a scientific concept.) In this light, most of the criticisms of psycho-analysis for its deficiencies as a science can be set aside as irrelevant, for they proceed from judging it, inadequately, as though it were a discipline like histology or crystallography. If all philosophy is an interpretation of the world (as Marx impatiently remarked) we can say particularly that psycho-analysis is an interpretation of the human mind, and consequently of human action. There can be, and there are, other interpretations; but one can reasonably say that no other is more enlightening, or in the simple sense more fascinating, than this which we owe to Sigmund Freud.

More than a science, probably, a philosophy is shaped and coloured by the personality of its progenitor. A great man, just as much as an ordinary man, has his inherited intellectual equipment, his preferences and prejudices, his habits and tastes, his quirks and oddities; and Freud certainly had his full share of all these. A biographical, and still more an autobiographical, account of such a man–especially of his early years–cannot fail to be both valuable and absorbing. Freud wrote only a limited autobiographical sketch, and one of his odd quirks was his violent aversion to being the subject of a biography. Two very full biographies, by Ernest Jones and by Peter Gay, have nevertheless been written. Jones, the leading figure in psycho-analysis after Freud, set out to write an autobiography, and we must regret that it was not completed–although much of the material that would have been included in the later chapters did, naturally, find a place in his life of Freud.

The eleven chapters making up *Free Associations* are interesting, I think, on several counts. They give us evocative pictures of Wales in the days of the oil-lamp and the pony-cart, of London as it was explored and enjoyed by a medical student at the turn of the century, and of the rigidities and formalities of the professional hierarchy. They tell, thanks to certain startling events, a dramatic story of success and failure. Above all, they show us what kind of young man it was who–uniquely in his place and time–responded to the new and strange ideas of Freud. I am heartily glad to see the book republished and to commend it to a new generation of readers.

Preface

ANY reflective person who contemplates writing an autobiography must take some interest in his motive for so doing; an infliction of oneself on the public seems to call for some apologetic explanation, even if this is itself one more imposition. On putting the question to myself as sincerely as I could, the rather unexpected answer came: "Gratitude for life." Where I have not enjoyed life as fully as the opportunity offered, that has been because of recognisable limitations and deficiencies on my own part. Life itself, in spite of all its hardships, I have always known to be such a rich, a good, and a beautiful thing that I experience a deep need to say so, to tell someone so, to thank someone—obviously those to whom I owe it. And even if they are now dead, and I indulge in the illusion of prolonging that life by printed pages that may survive a few years beyond my bodily dissolution, why! I find both these wishes entirely natural in the circumstances.

Yet these, although they furnish the deepest motive for my impulse to write, could not in themselves justify the gratification of it. It happens, however, to have fallen to my lot to have assisted at certain scientific events to which I am persuaded history will ascribe a very considerable importance in the development of human thought, and it would seem becoming on my part, and in itself an expression of gratitude, to record something of them while they are yet alive in the memory. I refer to the evolution of Freud's work and ideas. It may also, in that connection, be of some interest to know what kind of person it was who attached himself to that work at a time when it was otherwise unknown in English-speaking countries.

In what I have had to say about my sexual and love life I have been entirely truthful, but I should be less than candid if I did not confess that the record is incomplete. I doubt if any other than a pronounced masochist or exhibitionist ever publishes a full record of such details, and, anyhow, they are for the most part not very interesting.

For my husband on the first anniversary of his death

Festal was the core of his beginning;
Cymbals clashing and the sirens singing.

Joyful was his youth carried before him,
A proud banner when the angels bore him.

Then the unimaginable, crushing,
Cast its shadow—with the world hushing.

Unimaginable horror bringing,
Crying, weeping, threatening, ever clinging.

Dragons in eternal circles rising,
Laughing, loving, hating and despising;

And his limbs turning to poisoned sliming,
Paralysed they felt the creatures climbing.

Yet he rose, with wild eyes terror staring
Pounding heart against the horrors daring

All his being 'gainst the creatures pitting
They, that now were poisonous honey spitting;

And his lameness and his horror fighting
Through the darkness, thunderous, alighting

On he went through murk and terror striding
Till he saw—and heard—and felt abiding

What no eye, no ear, no sense was sounding
But his heartbeat and his blood was pounding.

So the dragons cringed, their fangs now bending.
So he brought the deed to glorious ending.

Then the terror was at last receding
And he fell from many red mouths bleeding.

And there burst forth in cheerfullest eclipse
A cry of joy from his exalted lips.

Chapter One

Origins

I WAS born, the first child and only son of my parents, on the first of January 1879, in the parish of Llwchwr, in a village called Rhosfelyn; the Great Western Railway had in 1852 rechristened it Gower Road, a name my father later got changed to the hybrid Gowerton. It is situate in the centre of Gwyr (Gower), the ancient kingdom between Swansea Bay and Caermarthen Bay, and is about six miles away from both Swansea and Llanelly, though the direct road between these towns does not pass through it.

It is the common experience of psycho-analysts that a patient intimates in the first hour of the treatment, and often in the very first sentence, the most important secrets of his life, although this is done in such a veiled way that it may take months or years of arduous work before it is possible to read the inner meaning of them. Were I in the position of such a patient, the opening sentences of this book could be put to a similar use. I know that the essential story of my life lies hidden in those sentences, though they need a minute examination to decipher it or even discern its elements. Let me see; it may prove worth while to follow this train of thought; to do so should at all events illustrate the psycho-analytical attitude of mind.

* * * * * *

Much of life consists in the gradual taming of the grandiloquent hopes and fantasies of infancy. Poignant lessons teach us of what little account we are in the scale of things, and much of increasing wisdom consists in the proper assimilation of them. How well Browning described this process: ". . . little by little he sees fit to forego claim after claim in the world, puts up with a less and less share of its good as his proper portion; and when the octogenarian asks barely a sup of gruel and a fire of dry sticks, and thanks you as for his full allowance and right in the common good of life,—hoping nobody may murder him,—he who began by asking and expecting the whole of us to bow down in worship to him,—why, I say he is advanced far onward, very far. . . ."

One of my first lessons concerned my birthday. The blasts on the factory hooters at midnight, which I was always roused from sleep to hear, together with the general jubilation of New Year's Day, seemed to me to be an appropriate recognition of the event; and I still recollect my shamefacedness at the age of four or five on learning that the world in its greeting was concerned with thoughts transcending my self-important personality. An after-echo of this came some ten years later when I observed that the date of my coming of age would make me one of the "first men" of the twentieth century—to paraphrase Heine's similar remark about himself and the nineteenth century. Alas for the narcissism of childhood! Fortunate are those who can replace it by more solid grounds for self-satisfaction. To be the favourite child, as I felt I was—and my sisters showed much generosity in subscribing to this privilege—gives one much to overcome, and yet provides deep sources of confidence that help one in the task.

My mother had wished to give me the name of Myrddin, but my prosaic father cavilled at this and chose instead to name me after Queen Victoria's second son, Alfred Ernest, Duke of Edinburgh. It was a decision not easy to forgive, and when I grew up I at least discarded the first of these unwelcome royal appellations. In compensation and in loyalty to my mother I called my eldest son, now a novelist, by the anglicised name Mervyn. But the name Ernest seems to accord well with my serious temperament.

My parents were both of pure Welsh descent. My mother was in every way Welsh, but my father knew little of the language and took a decidedly English view of life. That I should find worth mentioning his converting the name of my birthplace into an English hybrid is no doubt an echo of every child's resentment at the fantasy of his father desecrating his mother; and I must confess to have never entirely succeeded in achieving a detached attitude towards the callous English acquiescence in assaults on the Celtic language and culture.

Gower itself played its part in my early thoughts. That ancient kingdom, then extending far beyond its present peninsular limits, once divided Glamorgan from Caermarthen, and it happened that my father's ancestors came from the Glamorgan side of it, my mother's from the Caermarthen. Gower has never been entirely absorbed by either county. Although it appears on the map as part of Glamorgan, and counts as such for parliamentary and legal purposes, having been joined to it in the sixteenth century, still it belongs (or did until a few years ago) to the diocese of St. David's, not to that of the Glamorgan city of Llandaff, and registration of personal events took place in Caermarthen, not Glamorgan. My own birth, for instance, was registered in Llanelly, not Swansea; I was thus able to obtain a Caermarthen county scholarship at a public school and subsequently a Glamorgan county scholarship at the University.

I was deeply attached to both my parents and regarded myself, indeed rightly so, as a bond of union between them. In our sitting-room I used to sit on a little cane chair between them, symbolising both the desire to unite and, no doubt on a deeper level, to separate them; the chair has survived to be used by my grandchildren three-quarters of a century later. It was a happy solution of the Oedipus complex that has stood me in good stead throughout my life, for it brought with it an unusual capacity for double loyalties, with little tendency to divided ones. Not only was I faithful to both counties, but also to both countries—indeed, I should find it hard to say whether I have loved England or Wales more.

My professional life has similarly been marked by intense devotion to both medicine and psycho-analysis, two disciplines I have always wished to be in amicable relations with each other. I was born to be a doctor, and could not easily imagine myself in any other capacity. Medicine, with its intimate contact with humanity, has always seemed to me the meeting-point of scientific and humane concern, the centre of man's most praiseworthy activities. The impelling motives for the pursuit of its study sooner or later override all the obstructions to knowledge, including even the delaying superstitions that the urgent clamour for immediate help has so often generated. It is no chance that when the Greek genius faltered at the threshold of scientific thought by disdaining the experimental method and enmeshing itself in the quandaries of philosophy, it was medical study alone that forced it into some relationship, however strained, with reality. Although our therapeutic powers are still feeble in comparison with what they shall sometime become, they are already based on a much more comprehensive knowledge of human realities than any other profession has any experience of—that of the legal and political professions, for instance, is flimsy by the side of it. So, in spite of my later discovery that many doctors very imperfectly shared my ideals, my admiration for the goals towards which medicine strives has never abated.

As to psycho-analysis, that again is a focal point where all the varied activities of the human mind come together—a key to the understanding of every fleeting thought, childish fantasy, and grotesque dream, as well as of all the customs and institutions by which men have expressed or codified their interests and needs. But when Freud proposed to separate psycho-analysis from medicine and to establish it as an independent discipline—in many ways a seductive idea—I successfully opposed this course by insisting on the reasons why it would lead to an impoverishment of both. On the contrary, by relating psycho-analysis more closely to medical biology, and by extending medicine so that it comprehends the mind as well as the body, we shall, in my opinion, arrive in time at a happy synthesis that will beneficially affect the most diverse fields of human activity. Perhaps indeed, in centuries to be, the medical psychologist may, like the priest of ancient times, come to serve as a source of practical wisdom and a stabilising influence in this chaotic world, whom the community would consult before embarking on any important social or political enterprise. Mere megalomania, it may be said. Perhaps, but it is my living faith none the less, and only our descendants will be able to say if it was a misplaced one.

Such threads run through life and affect small matters as well as great. I will trace this one in an entirely different region. One of the very useful vents my infantile curiosity found for its expression was a passion for topography. I do not regret it, since it resulted in my possessing a capacity for finding my direction and a knowledge of geography both considerably above the average. In my opening paragraph which serves as a text, stress is laid on several apparently trivial facts of topography. But they were not trivial to me. The identification of myself with Gower, as a unique province owing a double allegiance, fitted well into my world of fantasy, and the childish picture of myself as the Lord of Gower was as yet unclouded by the later discovery that this title was irrelevantly borne by at least two Scottish peers. The southern part of it was settled by Flemings, rapidly anglicised, in the early twelfth century—like Pembroke, it became known as Little England beyond Wales—and their descendants until quite recently kept within a sharply marked border, never intermarrying with the Welsh. This delectable foreign land of the south, with its entrancing bays and cliffs, gave me solace in my unhappy childhood days, which were many, and a sense of freedom from the pettinesses and restrictions I felt to be characteristics of Welsh life. From the age of nine I would often wander there with my dog for the whole day, and twenty to thirty miles was never too much to cover. Even more entrancing seemed the distant land of Devon (alike, even verbally, to Heaven), visible across the sea, and years later I could trace in my dreams the quaint wish that the Bristol Channel were narrowed to even less than its prehistoric river and would allow one to ford it to the Arcadian land beyond. Among these Gower cliffs, in 1823, the egregious Dean Buckland had discovered the first paleolithic skeleton in Europe, the so-called "Red Lady of Paviland". I knew the story in childhood from my father, and also the later anti-Biblical developments. I must owe to this young Aurignacian prince of 2,500 years ago, for so he now seems to have been, both the beginnings of my theological doubts and my lasting absorption in anthropology and pre-history.

A friend once remarked to me that he always wished to be both south and west of wherever he happened to be at any moment, and I can well understand that wish. Indeed, I once put it into practice in what later proved to be a significant action. Returning once from Devon to London by a circuitous route I drove from Hampshire into the *south-western* part of Sussex. Something in the scenery and topography seized me, and on reaching London I wrote to some agents asking if they had any cottage for sale somewhere south-west of Midhurst. They had one, an early Jacobean cottage at Elsted, where I now live. I was at once taken by both it and its position, but I remember that what clinched the matter was the vendor's remark that although otherwise in Sussex, Elsted was partly in Hampshire, its postal address being (then) "near Petersfield, Hants". A district with a double allegiance: just the thing. Years later I acquired a villa at Mentone, in the dream—now alas a vanished one—of being able to retire there in my old age, and I knew that I was largely influenced in my choice by the facts that Mentone was an ancient independent locality, still preserving its own peculiar language, and is now a frontier town owing attachments to both France and Italy.

It was not long before I discovered with what undeviating accuracy my intuitions had unconsciously functioned in the choice of my future home. (I need hardly say that I acquired also a cottage in Gower, though only as a *pied-à-terre.*) The more I looked about me the more evident did it become that The Plat, as I christened it—adopting the old Sussex name by which its paddock was known locally—was in all the respects that emotionally mattered to me the only house in the whole of England that topographically duplicated my birthplace at Gowerton. Here are the facts—all of course known to me at the time, though not consciously appreciated—that bear out this hardly credible assertion. Both villages are three miles from the western end of a county and situate at the apex of a triangle of which the other points, in every case six miles distant, are the market towns, one in each county, on which they draw: Swansea and Llanelly, Midhurst and Petersfield. A wild plateau divides both from the sea to the south, some dozen miles away. And, incidentally, I could never understand how anyone can live near a sea that is not to the south of them: how do they do without the sun's sparkling on it and the moon's mysterious pathway? Well, there are only five counties in England where one can find a village three miles from the next county to the west and where the sea is on the south; and in only one of them, Sussex, is there the necessary plateau from which to envisage the homeland on one side and the sea on the other—not to speak of the characteristic relationship of the towns. I will not go into all the other details, the house itself on the south side of the road and looking to the north, and so on. The whole thing would be uncanny were one not familiar with the unerring way in which deep emotions direct life.

ORIGINS

The stock from which I sprang is, I fancy, characteristic for those Welshmen who have managed to play a part outside their native land, so I will say something of it; what I have to narrate is based only on immediate knowledge, assisted, it is true, by several family Bibles in my possession, since I have never been concerned to institute any genealogical researches. Probably most readers will do well to skip these dry details. So far as I can judge, the direct influence of my parents seems to me more important mentally than what I can trace of hereditary agencies.

Of the patronymic sources I know little. My father's paternal grandfather, Thomas Jones, was in charge of a colliery's pit ponies, and migrated from Merthyr Tydfil to Swansea, where he worked in a livery stable, but, unlike Keats's father in a similar situation, omitted to marry his master's daughter; he was illiterate, as I know from the cross he affixed to his son's indenture of apprenticeship. His son, John Jones, whom I just remember, was a self-employed carpenter. I am told that he had the habit of taking refuge from his wife's tongue by immersing himself in the light literature, the counterpart of our detective stories, of the day, though, even so, she was apt to remove his "farthing dip" as an unnecessary extravagance, leaving the poor man in the dark. More complete, though temporary, escapes were afforded by embarking on long voyages, even round the world, as a ship's carpenter, and I recall my fondness for the souvenirs of those voyages, huge tortoise-shells and the like. My grandmother certainly had a vivid personality. I saw nothing of her reputed shrewishness—though my mother told me she was a thorn in her flesh in the early days of her son's marriage—partly because by then time had softened that aspect of her nature and partly because she allowed herself to show an affection for me which apparently she had been wont to check with her own children. The impression she left on me was that of an intelligent, kindly woman with a caustic turn to her speech and a devastatingly disillusioning vision of reality. She was given to expressing her views on life in proverbial sayings, a habit I seem to have acquired from her. She would, for instance, usually diminish the proportions of any family dispute with the words: "It will be all the same in a hundred years."

Her father, Joseph Beddoe, belonged to a branch of the Shropshire Beddoe family who had settled in Gorseinon (midway between Swansea and Llanelly) in the seventeenth century. At the end of the eighteenth century, one of them was drowned with his son when ferrying across the River Llwchwr; it always struck me as a particularly unmerited fate, since they were on their way to a chapel service to which they had piously walked several miles. Her mother, Ann Rees by name, came from Old Walls in the Welsh part of Gower. I well remember this old lady and the sponge cakes I used to buy for her as a delicacy in her toothless old age. She had been married to a weaver from Penmaen, also in Gower, but he had died at the age of forty-nine, so that she had to spend thirty-seven years as a widow; her daughter was to pass forty-three years in that state. Undeterred by her fate, she migrated to Swansea to be near her only daughter, whom my grandfather married in the same year, and took over the brewing department of the Red Cow in the High Street. Her mother, Margaret David of Llanrhidian, lived to be eighty-four, she herself lived to be eighty-one, and her daughter to be ninety-one. She was born in 1808, and so could relate to me memories of the Napoleonic wars. She of course never saw the great man herself but, incidentally, many years later I met another old lady who had—in Torbay.

Some of the Beddoe attributes appear to belong to dominant genes, for they have faithfully manifested themselves down the generations, and I have felt justified in giving the name to each of my sons. I did so in a vain endeavour to lessen the handicap my patronymic ancestry had laid on me. It is statistically demonstrable that the odds are heavy against anyone achieving distinction in life if he has to share his surname with hundreds of thousands of his contemporaries. Among the many handicaps that the Welsh share with the Jews, such as their outworn attachment to the Old Testament, not the least was the acquisition of surnames in unfortunate circumstances; and one can foresee a time when, if these attributes are to fulfil their proper function, an extensive re-naming will have to take place. To get back to the immediate theme: I have always fancied that if my father and I inherited an I.Q. higher than that of our relatives it probably came, via his mother, from the Beddoe stock. At one time I even toyed with the idea of hyphenating the name with my surname, but Freud dissuaded me on the ground of its being confusing.

My maternal heredity was almost as uninspiring. My mother's paternal grandfather, John Lewis, was a mason at Llandilo—the scene now shifts to the county of Caermarthen; he had come there from Llangefelach, once famous for its animal fair and now the site of an enormous steel works. Her father, Benjamin Lewis, who died when I was nine years old, had moved to Swansea. He was a competent architect and contractor, building railway stations, docks, and other constructions, and he tried to get me to follow in his footsteps by presenting me with his tomes on architecture. His biblical first name, so common in Wales, led to a curious contretemps in the time of the Nazi regime. His niece was married to a German in Berlin, the Herr Schmidt who managed the Adlon Hotel. The Nazis insisted that her maiden name, Lewis (like Louis, a corruption of the very Teutonic Ludwig), must be a corruption of Levi, and the fact of her grandfather being called David and her uncle Benjamin seemed to clinch the matter of her supposed Jewish origin. She had to appeal to me to verify her descent.

My grandfather was an attractive but eccentric person, with an all-or-nothing attitude towards life. He had a deep suspicion of doctors and their ways, and on the rare occasions when he was persuaded to listen to one he would say with a sigh of irritation: "Well, I'll give them another chance", and drink down the whole bottle of medicine at one gulp; the results at times confirmed his worst suspicions. Fifty years after his death his daughter, my mother's only sister, followed his example with a lethal result. She had been given some anti-thrombotic medicine for purpura in the skin, swallowed the whole of it, and promptly died of a pontine haemorrhage. Once my grandfather's wife commissioned him to buy some wallpaper for a bedroom that wanted repapering. In the course of the morning a van appeared and to her great dismay the unloading continued until one of their two living-rooms was chock-full of the material her obedient, or contumacious, husband had requisitioned—my earliest experience of sabotage. In his later years he took to drinking more than was good for him, and it became one of my duties—for I often stayed with these grandparents in their home in Swansea—to fetch him home from his haunts of revelry in the local pub—a summons he never failed to obey. This conduct saddened my saintly mother and, pursued by the fear, which had been increased by injudicious reading on the subject of heredity, that this trait would reappear in her son, she tried hard to bind me to total abstinence. Never having perceived in myself any sign of this dreaded inheritance, I saw no necessity for such an extreme measure. My grandfather and I were greatly attached to each other and my father must have thought he spoiled me. At all events, I recall his strongly disapproving what he considered the precocious proceeding of my grandfather replacing my petticoats by a pair of knickerbockers at the early age of four. My grandfather had a long stride and I evidently imitated him in this as well as no doubt in other ways, for I was much surprised in my early teens at being stopped by a stranger in a street in Swansea with the remark: "You must be a grandson of Benjamin Lewis, for you walk just like him."

My maternal grandmother was a Miss Jones, who married a Mr. Lewis, whilst my mother reversed the proceeding—not a difficult feat in Wales. She was gentle, refined, and had some aesthetic appreciation, but with a softer type of intellect than my paternal grandmother; she tried to instil into me various medical superstitions of the herbalist variety which my more robust Beddoe blood promptly rejected. She used to tell me tales of the Rebecca riots of the eighteen-forties and of the alarm felt when the rioting approached Swansea. Her family came from Llandybie, near Llandilo, and her mother, Ann Morris by name, was the only member of my immediate ancestry with some pretension to being "well-born"; the town of Morriston is named after her family. I was told that she had eloped with my great-grandfather, who was merely an employee on the estate. I possess a photograph of her in her fifties with her granddaughter, my mother, standing at her knee.

My maternal grandmother's father and brother, together with a friend called Davies, were drawn by the Australian gold rush of the 'fifties. On the way there they were wrecked on the coast of Ireland, and Davies, having had enough, went home and made a fortune in the tin-plate trade. His son became a fashionable London doctor and his grandson a distinguished surgeon, Morriston Davies, and a close friend of mine. We were entertained on discovering our ancestral friendship. The more pertinacious couple, however, proceeded on their way and apparently achieved their object, for a year or so later a cheque for £300 turned up as a first instalment of their gains. Then silence fell and no more was ever heard of them; presumably they were murdered or perished in some epidemic. My poor grandmother, not over-endowed with worldly wisdom, hoarded the cheque for a rainy day and was much distressed on discovering, more than fifty years later, that it was no longer valid. These were far from being the only adventurous members of my family: as a boy I used to exchange Christmas greetings with others in Canada, India, Italy, Natal, Australia, and the United States. But that particular family contributed its full share to the *wanderlust* that had led to their father's destruction. The eldest, Morris, became a farmer at Nelson, Ontario. The next, Richard, was the one who perished with his father in Australia. Then came my Uncle Tom, the only one to stay at home, whose son Herbert was in school with me. The next brother, Herbert, spent his life at sea, and the youngest, Henry, settled in Ohio.

I come now to much more important people in my life—my parents. My father was twenty-five years old when I was born, and my mother twenty-three. My father, Thomas Jones (1853–1920), was tall, blond, handsome—evidently a Celt. My mother, on the other hand, was rather short, quite dark, and very pale—the "Iberian" type of Welsh. Theirs must have been a wonderful love-match, as I gathered from many hints my mother dropped about love-letters and the poetry they shared, and the marriage was a completely happy one. I never heard a cross or even impatient word pass between them. My mother was the more openly affectionate of the two, and had little of my father's noteworthy restraint of emotion. Save for some deep inner reserve, which probably no one ever penetrated, I should say he was as mentally "normal" as one could reasonably expect, and for a psycho-analyst to say this means a great deal.

My father had a good grasp of the fundamentals of science, and was also pretty well read in the main English classics of prose and poetry.

He underwent a notable change in character after his three children were born, one of which my mother by no means fully approved. As a youth he had been very serious and rather stern, with unusually high aspirations of a moral order. The eldest of a family of six, he had psychologically replaced his father as the responsible head of the family at an early age. I may quote an example of this attitude. His next brother, John, had enlisted in the cavalry, but complained bitterly at having to regroom his mount whenever the officer found a stain on his white gloves when stroking it. So my father, at the cost of postponing his wedding for a year, bought him out—a dubious piece of kind-heartedness. The week after, John enlisted in the infantry, where he served for many years in Egypt and India. I know, particularly from the time of his last illness, that there was a deep bond between my father and his mother, who survived him, but I imagine it never found expression on either side. She certainly brought him up severely, with no "nonsense", as she would no doubt have termed any sign of sentiment, and what she expected of him he expected of himself. He early became converted to Baptism—also my mother's faith, hence their meeting—by the great preacher of the same name as himself, Thomas Jones, the father of three famous sons, one of whom was Principal of the University College of South Wales in my student days there. Furthermore he insisted on having the rest of the family baptised, except the youngest who escaped on the score of age. Like most Welshmen of that generation he was Radical in politics and entertained lofty hopes of social brotherhood in the future. The first of the many later discussions in which I have had to participate on the old theme of relative importance of the inner and the outer world, of environment versus heredity, nurture versus nature—there are many variations of it—was between my parents, since my father believed in progress by means of material betterment while my mother pinned her faith to internal regeneration, of course in religious terms. My father was the more convincing at the time, but on looking back I wonder whether my mother was not the nearer to the truth; I will not, however, embark on this theme, which would demand a book to itself.

Well, such was my father at the time of my birth. Shortly before this they had removed from Swansea to Gowerton, as it is now called, and that meant trudging six miles each way—there being then no Sunday trains in Wales—to attend the Sabbath service. In the village there were at least four chapels, among them a Baptist one, but the services were all in Welsh, a language in which my father was far from proficient. (My mother knew it well, and thereby hangs another tale. She had been sent for a year or two to a remote farm in Brecon to perfec it. And when, more than seventy years later, I engaged a teacher in London to gratify my little daughter's wish to learn Welsh, what was my amazement to find that she came from that very same farm!) Admittedly this was a severe strain in wintry weather, and my father fell from grace. Perhaps marriage, providing a solution of the sexual problem, had something to do with the relieving of his rigid principles, as may have also the "hardshell" intolerance of the local Baptists. Be that as it may, fortunately for us he took to attending the Church of England service and we children were brought up under that aegis.

I remember, however, being somewhat shocked when, at about the age of nine, I learnt of this apostasy of my father's. I had been delving into some of his Baptist literature and had been persuaded of the propriety of their two main contentions. One of them turns on the Protestant view that the moral responsibility of the individual cannot with advantage be shifted. Put anthropologically, it is plain that baptism, like circumcision, tattooing, and other similar rites, is an initiation ceremony that belongs to puberty, not to infancy. Or, in more modern language, sin is a personal matter that must be dealt with at a suitable age and cannot be dispelled at birth on the plea of its being inherited. A friend of mine, wishing to visit Sweden, bought a conversational manual in the hope of being able to deal with porters. The first sentence in it was the unexpectedly mandatory one: "Do not implant a prejudice in the mind of a child", and I do not fancy he ever had the opportunity of using it in his capacity as a tourist. Now the ceremony of christening, with all it implies, decidedly contravenes the Swedish exhortation, and some people think that it takes an unfair advantage of the plastic mind of the child. The second Baptist contention is less interesting, though it seems logical enough, if somewhat pedantic: it is simply that, if one holds with following the actual teaching and example of Jesus, one can hardly deny that he believed in the efficacy of total immersion of the body in sanctified water as the best means of purifying it of its sins.

Though it never occurred to me to be baptised, I exploited

the idea when in school to avoid being confirmed in Church, alleging that my parents were Baptists and wouldn't like it; it greatly annoyed the headmaster, who in the most materialistic fashion was roping into the "confirmation class" all the boys he could with the obvious aim of making a good impression on the ecclesiastical authorities; he became a bishop not long after. As a result of all this I have never passed through any religious ceremony, at birth, puberty, or marriage, and it is certain there will not be one when I die.

To return to my father. His backsliding proved a turning-point in his life, since it was followed by a notable change in character. He began with being strict in his attendance, and ours, at Sunday morning service, but it took me only a couple of years' pleading before I got at least let off the Sunday school in the afternoons. He was never a member of the Congregation, and so never communicated, but that did not prevent his being made a churchwarden. The previous one, an apparently very pious old gentleman, had purloined the church funds, and the authorities apparently came to the conclusion that honesty possessed certain advantages over orthodoxy. Whether this piece of cynicism finished my father or not, he evidently felt that strict attendance to his new financial duties absolved him from the need for further Sabbatarian obligations, much to the relief of all of us except perhaps my mother. His religious beliefs faded and he must have been a complete atheist after the age of forty.

Two modes of expression remained for what was left of his former ideals and principles. One was the faithful pursuit of social activities: School Board, Parish and District Councils, and the like. He took charge of the higher education of the neighbourhood, and I remember a series of examiners dining with us on their way to the South Kensington Science and Art examinations that were then the vogue; I attended some of the courses myself on steam, electricity, and other technical subjects. The other expression was the highest level of integrity in business matters. On one occasion he and a friend spent four long evenings in chasing through numerous ledgers in pursuit of an elusive twopence whose absence marred the perfection of the annual balance sheet, nor were they to be deflected by the bribes offered by their distracted wives. I was brought up to believe not merely that "business is business" and must come first before all other human considerations, but that such dictates of the Manchester school were the only sound basis for civilisation, chaos being the alternative. I remember at the age of eight being disturbed at hearing that the great firm of the neighbourhood, of which more anon, made a present of a turkey to each employee at Christmas. It seemed an irrelevant intrusion into what ought to have been a definite "business" relationship: what would happen to a clear-cut scheme of the universe if that sort of thing were allowed to go on? I need scarcely say that my father was highly amused at finding me adopt his business principles so literally.

The change in character to which I have alluded consisted essentially in an all-round relaxing and softening of various previously rigid attitudes. He became more tolerant, less strict, and in general more easy-going. On the other hand, and this was the aspect my mother regretted, he became less idealistic, less serious, more mundane, and perhaps more commonplace—more bourgeois. This tendency increased with the years as he rose in the world until at the end he could be distinguished from the average industrialist only by a certain air of distinction, a specially high standard of integrity and general trustworthiness, and a rare tender-heartedness. The change in question clashed with the idealism that naturally accompanied my own adolescence, so that I found his conversation less and less interesting, whereas in my childhood it had been inspiring. It was he who gave me my respect for science, and my devotion to its ideals.

I have said nothing so far about my father's career. Although he was a man at ease in every social *milieu*, his beginnings were humble enough and he was throughout a self-made man. He began life as a clerk in the well-known coal firm of Messrs. Cory; at the end of his life he took over the estate where his former chief had lived. He studied hard—I still possess his books from those days on astronomy, navigation, and other scientific or technical subjects—qualified as a colliery engineer, and was at the time of his early marriage the manager of a colliery near Gowerton. Soon after my birth he took the post of accountant at a large steel works, Messrs. Wright, Butler & Co., where he was before long made the general secretary. The firm, which is now an important constituent of the Baldwin amalgamation, had many ramifications; it possessed collieries, and also iron-ore mines in Spain and Italy, which my father had often to visit, so that his work was far from monotonous. In the late forties, in pique at not being granted the partnership he had been promised, he retired, but before long immersed himself in fresh undertakings, chiefly in his first love—coal; his last years seemed to be spent passing from one meeting to another of various Boards of Directors in Cardiff and London. Altogether a typical Samuel Smiles hero, and one of the better products of the "liberal" industrial era of good Queen Victoria.

Two of his failings were specially destined to deepen the inevitable rift between son and father. They were a difficulty in admitting that he could ever not be in the right—which of course gave me no chance of ever being so myself unless I accepted his every opinion—and the belief that young people should be kept very much in their place—a decidedly subordinate one; I was far from being the only youth to suffer from this latter characteristic, his younger brother being another. In fact, my father's retirement from the firm was induced by his resentment at being passed over by a callow youth, Charlie Wright, who, however, possessed the advantage of being the son of the senior partner. Being a specially argumentative youngster myself, I was in for trouble; and it came to a head when I was about thirteen. It began with an acrimonious argument about the theory of the siphon pump, and to this day I do not know which of us was in the right. I am afraid my sharp and perhaps impertinent retorts caused my poor father much pain; he had no recourse but to withdraw somewhat from me for a time, though he always retained a deep affection for me. His own characteristics did not change much, but I could afford to be amused when at the age of forty I was informed that I had travelled to Paris by the "wrong" route.

Of my mother, Mary Ann (May), *née* Lewis (1855–1909), I shall say less. A mother's influence, though more profound, is less tangible. My mother's influence over me did not continue much beyond the age of eight, and it made no direct contribution to my intellectual development, whereas my father's certainly did—between the age of eight and thirteen. She was a most tender and affectionate mother, and completely devoted to me. Yet she did not spoil me; indeed, she often enough remonstrated with my shortcomings, particularly my argumentativeness, and I can still see her warning me by pointing at my tongue, which she maintained was "sharp as a needle". Its quickness of response has often got me into trouble, but I nevertheless sympathised when later on I read T. H. Huxley's remark in the same connection that in spite of its disadvantages he would part more readily with most of his gifts sooner than his mother-wit. I knew well enough, however, as she explicitly told me, that nothing I could do would ever forfeit her affection and sympathy. An early relationship of this kind, as Freud has truly remarked, provides an unshakable basis for self-confidence in later life, and that I have never lacked. The only difference of opinion that ever arose between us—and it was doubtless a grave one—did so involuntarily on both sides. When I was three months old she was taken with rheumatic fever and that of course disturbed our intimacy. Anxious to do what she could to remedy the situation, she obtained various patent and well-advertised milk foods, which effectively deprived me of all vitamins. In consequence I was a puny and ailing infant, with pronounced rickets and a not very happy disposition. She was the most thoroughly and yet unostentatiously self-effacing woman I have known, devoted to the interests of her husband, her children, relatives, neighbours, house, and garden. She was thought highly of in the neighbourhood for her good works and unfailing kindness. She worked hard and unceasingly, and was extremely competent. She had a shrewd judgment, and my father constantly sought her advice in his affairs; he also found her useful in the check she gently imposed on his somewhat impulsive tendencies.

On looking back I think my mother must have had a slightly snobbish outlook—though I am not using the term in Thackeray's sense of "meanly admiring mean things". She did, however, think it seemly to aspire to a higher social status. When I rejected, and quite decisively, her suggestion that I enter the Church and announced my intention of becoming a doctor, she reflected that those were the two people who had an *entrée* everywhere. My wish was certainly unaffected by any such consideration; it had far deeper roots. Nevertheless, in my youth I can recall having a somewhat similar attitude to my mother's, and I still find it hard to understand those of the younger generation whose aim is to ape the manners and speech of classes below their own in the hierarchy. Fortunately, belonging to a profession obviates the question of one's "class", and makes it easy to be on instinctively natural terms with all varieties of one's fellow-beings.

Living in the country in those days was a very different matter from what it is now. For light the poor had candles, the others oil lamps. One cooked meat on a spit before an open fire and the basting was an interesting ceremony. All bread was made at home and it was my task to fetch the "barm" or yeast. The barm came from a shop belonging to a grocer who had spent some time in America, so we always spoke of the "American shop". We acquired also in this way a familiarity with American slang terms, such as "gosh", which in the early 'eighties could hardly have been widespread in this country. Laundries were unheard of, so that washing, mangling, and ironing took up a great part of two days a week. We had a cask of rain water, but the rest had to be fetched from a well a mile and a half away. I commonly accompanied this expedition through the woods; the servants of several houses would join together for the opportunity of gossip and to heave the heavy jars on to each other's shoulders after climbing stiles. Later on my grandfather was called in to build a reservoir in the hills and supply the village with water—a great event. I have retained a distinct memory of the prices of certain provisions my mother used to buy from vendors who brought them to her house. Eggs, for instance, were sixpence a dozen and would no longer be bought at the time of year when they reached the exorbitant price of tenpence. Butter, brought on cool cabbage leaves, was ninepence or tenpence a pound.

To complete my description of the domestic life I should say that the house consisted of eight rooms. The downstairs ones were in my early childhood labelled in order kitchen, dining-room, back parlour, front parlour. When I was about six or seven, however, my parents invested in a modern enclosed cooking stove, and that altered the nomenclature to scullery, kitchen, dining- and sitting-room, drawing-room.

My mother retained her piety longer than my father, and we would occasionally discover her rather shamefacedly reading the Bible. She was a faithful reader of the *Christian World*, though I suspect it was more for the weekly epitome of current events than for truly religious reasons. She would dole out to us items of stale news from this source for days afterwards. She was so easily shocked that when one spoke to her she at once put on a shocked expression in preparation for what might come. This reaction, though habitual, was fairly superficial, for it was seldom followed by any condemnation: she did not sit in judgment on her fellows. She had a very anxious temperament, and in my later boyhood it became related to constant illness and pain. She suffered from a gynaecological affection. This was finally cured, at a time when I was in my hospital studies, by an operation performed by Sir John Williams. It was an occasion for my having an interview with the famous man who brought two kings of England into the world; I had heard him lecture from time to time at the hospital, although he had by then retired to the consulting staff. He did not make any great impression on me, but I revere his memory, since few men have done more for their native land than John Williams did in his years of assiduous collecting of priceless historical manuscripts, the basis of the National Library of Wales which he subsequently founded. I had one more interview with him, in an agreeable *viva voce* examination, after which he awarded me the M.B. Gold Medal and Scholarship in Midwifery.

After this operation my mother enjoyed good health, and more affluent circumstances, combined with release from the upbringing of children, enabled her to devote herself more to the pleasures of gardening, a taste which all her three children have inherited from her. She died suddenly of cerebral haemorrhage at the early age of fifty-four, when I was thirty, and my father survived her for thirteen years.

The servant who acted also as nurse deserves a word of mention. When she came to us she knew no English, but I was foolish enough not to profit by the fact and learnt very little Welsh from her. We were fond of each other, but she must have been an anxious and rather bad-tempered woman, and my mother had a deal of trouble with her. She inspired me with a dread of what was euphemistically called "the burning fire", and this aspect of religious training was only partly countered by the interesting Bible stories I heard at my mother's knee.

One incident bade fair to make me think there might be some truth in her doleful predictions about my future fate if I did not obey her implicitly. The burning-fire threat alternated with that of the "Pen-y-ceffyl" (horse's head) which was to come and seize me in similar circumstances. And sure enough one dark night it did appear. In through the window came a horse's skull on a pole shrouded in a white sheet. My terror may be imagined. Fortunately it was followed, through the door, by a few youths who were making use of this old Welsh Christmas custom to collect a few coppers, and when I fully appreciated this my respect for my nurse became mingled with scepticism.

One of my memories of this nurse was that she taught me two words to designate the male organ, one for it in a flaccid state, the other in an erect. It was an opulence of vocabulary I have not encountered since.

Chapter Two

Boyhood

PSYCHO-ANALYSTS and other investigators have repeatedly deplored the absence of data concerning childhood sexuality in biographies and autobiographies, so that it would be most unsuitable for me to pass over this important topic. Some of the early infantile experiences had been forgotten until resuscitated by analytic work, and these are mainly of technical interest only. The practice of coitus was familiar to me at the ages of six and seven, after which I suspended it and did not resume it till I was twenty-four; it was a common enough practice among the village children. When I was seven a slightly older boy enlightened me on the subject of procreation, which hitherto I had known only unconsciously, and expressed his wish to sleep with my young mother for the purpose. I was of course shocked at this idea. I cannot remember from that period of my life a child who was not fully informed on such matters. Of the language habitually used I will quote only one example, and I admit it was an extreme one. A boy of nine, rolling on the floor with acute belly-ache, groaned aloud: "Oh God, it hurts so much I don't think I could f——k a girl if she was under me at this minute." The same youngster asked me once if I believed that men ever thought of anything other than their c——k when they were alone. He was the son of a prominent minister.

With such experiences behind me it may be imagined that in later years I found less of the usual difficulty in accepting that part of Freud's theory that postulates the existence of childhood sexuality. Nor was it easy to be patient with those who—as still do certain of the academic unco' guid—asserted that the sexual impulse first shows signs of life at the age of puberty, or even of marriage. The dishonesty of the world *in rebus sexualibus*, whether conscious or not, was evident.

Two other semi-analytical episodes I will relate in this connection. When I was three or four years old I used to sleep between my father and mother, a custom I certainly cannot recommend. One night I was awakened by the sensation of something hot and hard in contact with my leg. After some puzzlement I divined what it was, and immediately there came the curious reflection that I had known that long ago and forgotten it. So an unwelcome idea could be "repressed"! Then at the age of eleven I had several sexual dreams about my sisters and was very puzzled at observing that while the theme was agreeable during the dream it was very repellent as soon as I awoke. I concluded that the more moral part of one's naturc slept more profoundly than more primitive ones. In this I anticipated an interesting part of Freud's celebrated theory of dreams, and paved the way for a readier acceptance of it when I subsequently encountered it than might otherwise have happened.

My conscious memories reach back very far. Here are some from the age of two. I recollect a field snake intruding into the kitchen, and this was later confirmed by the nurse. It was in our first home, which we left soon after I reached the age of two. My father built the second house, and I well remember watching the proceedings. I have no direct memory of my elder sister's birth when I was twenty-two months old, but I remember a little while later that when she was being suckled I used to evoke general amusement by my piteous and sadistic appeal to my mother to "put the baby down in the cradle *to cry* and nurse *me*". This jealousy I compensated on the occasion of my younger sister's birth another twenty-two months later, which I well remember, by adopting her as my own and singing her to sleep —I still know the song—while rocking her at the end of a cord that reached almost the length of the house.

I went to the village school at the early age of three. I distinctly remember the details of the "babies" class where one began: the sing-song tune in which we learnt our ABC so thoroughly that I could never be in any doubt about the order of the alphabet, the abacus for learning to count, and so on; I can even recall the first word I learnt to spell. The school was a mile away. Froebel and Montessori were names of the future, and we spent our time at our desks learning and nothing else. At seven one was promoted to the "big boys" school, and there

I made rapid progress. The headmaster, Mr. Edmunds, was a friend of my father's, and every Saturday afternoon we went for long walks, sometimes spending the night away from home. Later on he deserted us for the joys of cycling, at first with the old "penny-farthing" model, which I also learned to ride, and then with what struck us as the less dignified "safety". He used to tell me stories of the Napoleonic wars which he had from his grandfather, who had fought in them; on his return from Waterloo the sturdy veteran had walked in two days from Gloucester to Llanelly, a distance of well over a hundred miles.

Everyone went home for their meals, so there were no such things as dinner-parties. The only guests I remember, besides the numerous and always welcome relatives, were the evening science and art lecturers who partook of an evening meal with us while waiting for their train. Evening callers were also not numerous, the doctor and schoolmaster being the only frequent ones. I never recollect my father going out to call on anyone socially; he was very much of a home man.

Before I reached the age of nine it was suggested, probably by my mother's ambition, that I should go to school in Swansea. Mr. Edmunds tried to bribe me to stay by offering to promote me two classes higher, but in vain; the idea of travelling alone by train twelve miles every day, and to a mysteriously superior school in a large town, was too tempting. As it turned out, neither the journey nor the school were the simple joys I had expected; both necessitated a process of hardening, the benefit of which was not visible to me at the time. The other boys who travelled from neighbouring stations were a rough lot and, being undersized as well as young, I came in for a good deal of horseplay; many is the mile I had to travel either on the rack or under the seat. The only exceptions were Karl Dahne, the son of the German Consul at Swansea, at whose country house I occasionally went fishing, and Charlie Wright, since Sir Charles Wright, Bt., Director of the Steel Industries of Great Britain in both wars; he was the son of Colonel Wright, the local magnate, at whose house children's parties were impressively formal affairs. School in Swansea meant, of course, the whole day away from home, and I used to lunch once a week at each grandmother's and the other days alone at a tavern, my first experience of independent life. The Higher Grade

School itself, a very rough place, was not much of a success, but two boys from that school are still good friends of mine: Arthur Davies, of whom more presently, and Herbert Lewis, a second cousin whom I discovered there. My career there came to an end after fifteen months through my contracting a severe attack of scarlet fever. It was almost the only serious illness I have ever had—at all events, I have seldom lost a week's work through illness in the seventy years since. I was delirious for several days and must have been in a dangerous condition. My poor parents were distracted and nursed me most devotedly. It left me with a recurrent tendency to ear trouble—I have had some forty attacks of perforative otitis since—but since this has meant only pain and not deafness it has not mattered much.

After my recovery my mother insisted that I be sent to the Swansea Grammar School, a seventeenth-century foundation of good standing. Whether she believed that—because of some embedded association between poverty, dirt, and disease—a school of higher social standing would be safer from attacks of disease, or whether my threatened demise had, by increasing my preciousness, stimulated my parents to greater efforts of sacrifice, I do not know; but I remember that the promise of the new school was held out to tempt me to more rapid convalescence. There I met boys of a higher social class, including many English boarders, and was made very aware of my deficiencies in speech; it occasioned, for instance, my first use of an aspirate. The industries in my native village had been settled by workmen and foremen from Lancashire, Durham, and the Midlands, so that the prevailing speech was the oddest mixture of dialects in which the grammatical peculiarities of the Welsh language made themselves heavily felt; often it was not clear whether a given word or idiom was English or Welsh. When we boys wished to affirm something, instead of saying "yes", we said "Ay, mun" or "Ay, wus" (corrupted from the Welsh "gwas"). Traces of this confusion persisted into adult life, to the amusement of my English friends. Thus, when nearly thirty, I was surprised to discover that what I had supposed was a perfectly good English word "bool", meaning a round door-handle, was nothing of the sort, but was a Welsh word "bwl".

Two little incidents in these Swansea days revealed to me that an urban proletariat existed which differed from the friendly working class of my village. A couple of town boys rushed into the playground of the Higher Grade School one day and wrenched a peg-top from one of us. When the owner tried to recover it he was savagely stabbed in the face with the spike of the top, so that the rough pilferer got away with his loot. Later, on my daily walk from the railway station to the Grammar School I often had to run the gauntlet of ragamuffins who cried after me: "Quack, quack, grammar ducks." I never found out the source of this curious epithet, but it was evident that my school cap was a source of envious hostility.

Life in the old Grammar School was pleasant enough, and I can still count good friends from those days. There were two minor misfortunes connected with it. Since I went home on leaving school I was unable to share in the school games, which proved a hindrance later. It was only partly compensated for by the experience of being drilled by an old sergeant, possibly dating from the Crimean War. We did all the regular parade stuff with our rifles: slope arms, ground arms, stand easy, etc., and then firing practice. But the most exciting was the "fix bayonets", followed by "prepare to receive cavalry", front rank kneeling, next leaning forwards, last standing. My uncle had been through the real thing in Egypt, with the Fuzzies charging and occasionally breaking into the squares; in fact I owned his medals. My other misfortune was that I developed a certain aptitude in mathematics. I had mastered the whole of Euclid, where my pleasure was essentially an aesthetic one (to the bewilderment of one of my teachers), before I was twelve, and found algebra equally easy. So I got to the top form, and at thirteen I obtained a scholarship at Llandovery College, mainly in mathematics. This meant that less attention was given to the classics, which I have since had every reason to deplore. Latin grammar, of course, stuck after six years of it, but I never had enough vocabulary to be able to read fluently. Of Greek I learned less, but that was my own fault. After two years of it I got my complacent father to beg me off further study. So Xenophon, the New Testament, and the *Medea* were the only things I struggled through—but with little lasting benefit. It was certainly galling in later years to have analytical friends in Vienna quoting Latin or Greek passages and being astonished at my blank response.

In Gowerton, my father's position gave me the free run of the steel works, a foundry that he managed for the family of a dead friend, a tinplate works where my young uncle was on the way to becoming manager, and several collieries. All this was replete with interest and I gained a good deal of knowledge of industrial ways. This gave me a background in which later on I felt various friends of the Bloomsbury variety were deficient. I was acutely conscious of the ugliness spread by industrial activity—the coal tips, ash heaps, smoke, etc.—but my father must have been very insensitive to any such aspersion on "business", for when he saw my beautiful Sussex home under the chalk South Downs in later days, he made the monstrous suggestion that it would be a good place for a cement works! But I observed that the enjoyment of other children did not seem to be lessened in the same way. It enabled me to understand the remarkable and perhaps depressing fact that only a minority of slum-dwellers are made unhappy by their surroundings and rebel against them.

Then there were the accidents. Many was the time I was awakened by the sinister tramp, tramp of the colliers who followed the rule of abandoning work in respect for a comrade who had been killed (or in protest against the risk to their life). Nearly fifty years later, an elderly man from Gowerton came to consult me; he seemed not to know that we came from the same place. He was very astonished when I told him I remembered the circumstances and place of his father's death in a colliery locomotive, and how the village children had been awed by the sensational detail that a piece of his watch had been driven into his heart! Not that we were squeamish as children. The village slaughter-house was a favourite resort, especially on the days when pigs' throats had to be slowly cut amidst the most piercing squeals.

In the early days I used to earn a couple of coppers a week for fetching the firm's letters from the post office soon after six in the morning. This enabled my father to go through them before starting out for his office. It was then he was bothered by the delays arising from the confusion between our village, Gower Road, and Gower Street in Swansea, and so applied to the Post Office and Railway Companies to change the name to Gowerton. In those days my father also acted as accountant to the firm, and once a week I would accompany him to his office to watch the handing out of the weekly packets of wages; for a time this got him the sobriquet of "Cashier Jones" in the way the Welsh have of distinguishing people by their occupations. I used to admire the minority of workmen whose packet included a golden sovereign, and felt sure they were very superior people, which they probably were. But the general run was seventeen to eighteen shillings.

Thanks to my father I was early in touch with public happenings. My first memory of this sort was of being held up in a crowd to see the Prince of Wales, who had come to Swansea to open the public library. That was in 1881, when I was two years old. My Uncle John fought in the battle of Tel-el-Kebir when I was three years old, and of course events in Egypt were followed closely. I well remember the anxiety about Gordon and the grief when his fate was at last known. I have since read most of what has been written about that episode and have wanted, and still want, to write a book myself about it. The story seems to me perhaps the most perfect epitome of the tergiversations and complexities of cabinet government that our history can show, and that all the high endeavour should have miscarried through the petty episode of Lord Charles Beresford's developing a boil on the bottom at the critical moment* seems a fitting bathos to it.

I was six years old when the Home Rule campaign was at its height, and I was as torn then as I have been ever since between sympathy for the patriotic desires of the Irish and—well-founded!—mistrust of their loyalty to the Commonwealth—sentiments I have no difficulty in combining in the case of the Welsh. Mr. Gladstone made a great speech at Singleton Park, Swansea, which I was privileged to hear, and afterwards we all filed past to shake hands with him; my father, like the man of sense he was, motioned to me to be content with a bow and so spare the great man a tithe of his painful ordeal. I am sure that this lesson in considerateness was worth far more to me than a useless memory of having shaken hands with the G.O.M. Naturally I was brought up a Liberal, but when I grew older the doctrinaire and nonconformist features of the misnamed Liberal Party soon alienated my sympathy.

* Private information.

The first play I saw, at the age of eight, was *The Silver King*, and it was representative of the plays of that day. More enjoyable were the visits of the D'Oyly-Carte Company, and I became almost word-perfect and tune-perfect in most of the Gilbert and Sullivan operas which were thrummed out on our piano. Other operas were also available at times, especially Italian ones. There was no late theatre train, so these indulgences were paid for by a six-mile country walk at midnight, usually in a merry party of six or eight. At the Albert Hall in Swansea there were occasionally other treats: solo concerts by the world-famed Mme Patti, who owned a castle nearby, George Grossmith (senior), and so on. Living in Wales gave me ample opportunity for hearing singing, but I must have been nearly twenty before I attended an orchestral concert. My father had a fair tenor voice, though quite untrained, but I do not remember my mother ever singing. Before marriage the instrument on which she used to perform was, unexpectedly enough, the concertina, and a complicated enough apparatus it looked. They were eager for us children to learn to play the piano. My sisters became fair pianists, the elder even a good one, but my own endeavours bore no fruit. A teacher came from Swansea once or twice a week, I rose early and put in an hour's practice before going off to school, but all in vain. From the age of seven to nine I slaved away at scales and exercises (tunes were not taught in those days) and when I ran into a—to me—dismal composer called Michael Watson the strain was too much and I begged permission to give up. In the early days I had regaled my sisters—we slept together still—with tales of my future appearances on the concert platform, but the point of these had nothing to do with applause or fame but only with the sums of money I should earn and how we should spend them together and become independent of our parents.

There was the usual village cricket and football to watch, but, apart from occasional otter-hunting, the only exercises I partook in at that time were tennis and skating. How different was the latter from the refined performances at London rinks of later years! Most of it was in the dark—both literally and technically. Armed with torches of rope and tar, we would trudge two or three miles to the canal-like "pills" on a marsh. There much time was spent, and by no means only at the outset, with a gimlet; when the hole in the heel to receive the screw of the wooden skate got too large a fresh one was made. When the ice broke one simply went into mud up to the thigh, whereas when skating over a disused shaft the penalty might have been a drop of a hundred feet.

When we children were small my parents used to plan to get away alone for their annual holiday. Since, however, they were wont to leave late at night by excursion train I would detect their movements and make enough clamour to ensure my being taken along at the last moment. Of my first visit to London, at the age of three, I have a distinct memory of a tired child being carried round the Zoo by the schoolmaster friend of the family, as I have of my first hotel lift, at the age of five, at Derby. After I was six it became the custom for the whole family to go together for the holiday, most often to seaside resorts in Wales.

When I was nine years old I was again taken to London, where we stayed in Bloomsbury. The old toll-gate, I fancy the last in London, was just being removed from its position in Gower Street opposite to University College Hospital, around which my activities were for years to centre. We attended one of the opening nights of *The Mikado* at the Savoy, with the unforgettable George Grossmith as Ko-Ko, and also—rather to my mother's horror—a music-hall performance at the Pavilion, outside which I observed for the first time the institution of whoredom; it was my mother's reaction of disgust that made its meaning plain to me. My father adventurously made his first trip abroad, to Paris, and he found it safe enough to take my mother over the following year—to the great Paris Exhibition of 1889; in the last war I presented to the Free French soldiers for their amusement a huge illustrated album of the Exhibition that was a souvenir of that trip. In my father's absence on the first trip I was left in London with my mother and on one occasion I was of some use. She felt she was being "followed" by an evil man and was visibly alarmed, so I reassuringly took her hand and darted minatory glances back at the base pursuer—with obviously successful results. My mother's Paris trip was her only venture abroad, and with good reason. They had the misfortune to run into one of the worst storms the Straits have ever known; the crossing took twenty-four hours and included fourteen hours' anchoring on the Goodwins.

The Jubilee year of 1887 was a vivid one, with its beacon fires on all the hills, the processions, the tea picnic with its gift of Jubilee mugs, and the general excitement. The year was also noteworthy to me of being that of my one and only religious conversion, at the somewhat immature age of eight. The occasion was a Salvation Army appeal to children on the beach at Ilfracombe. It was a genuine conversion, so much so as to enable me to enter fully into the many descriptions I read later of such events, but all subsequent endeavours—and there were many—to recapture its sense of simple certitude proved unavailing. Its influence did not last, since on my return home my gesture of enthusiasm towards the Salvation Hall (opposite the church) was gently damped by my father's deprecatory attitude. His own earlier emotional expeditions had by now been replaced by a steady and cool commonsense gait, which was both moderating and helpful to one of my more ardent temperament. I recollect one occasion, for instance, when he came to my bedroom—perhaps I was five years old—to attend to my screams on awakening from some terror of the night. He asked what the matter was, and on my saying that I was afraid he inquired: "Of what?" in such a startlingly matter-of-fact tone as to leave on my mind the deepest impression of the difference between internal phantasy and external reality.

His scepticism of any mysterious intrusion from unseen worlds was confirmed when, walking over a lonely mountain path at midnight, he found himself followed by a sinister noise of rattling chains, which paused when his steps paused and then relentlessly continued. On turning round my father discovered, as he had no doubt expected, a donkey which had broken loose and was seeking company.

I suffered considerably from night terrors in childhood, but the only conscious phobia I developed was of wolves who might at night descend on me from the nearby woods. It was no doubt a projection on to my innocent father of some oral-sadistic phantasies, perhaps given some point by a habit he had of playfully snapping at us when we tugged his moustache. It left an echo in a permanent dislike of wolf-like dogs, particularly Alsatians, which contrasted with the fondness I have always had for most other breeds. On my first meeting many years later with Anna Freud's Alsatian, who was unfortunately called "Wolf", my fears were confirmed. He flew at me and tore a piece of my thigh. Freud, who was present, sagely remarked on how dogs instinctively recognise those who dislike them or are afraid of them, and at once treat them as enemies.

At that time the question of career occupied the minds of boys, and properly so, at a much earlier age than is now customary. Most children knew what they were going to be, and anyone over the age of puberty who did not was regarded as an oddity or at least as a person of a very undecided character. I have still not got used to meeting young men in the twenties who "haven't yet made up their minds" about what they intend to do with their lives and who sometimes even ask one to believe that they haven't thought about it! Well, that was not so with me. Brushing aside my mother's suggestion that I become a clergyman, and even side-tracking the usual engine-driver phase, I knew as far back as I can remember that I wanted to be a doctor. Apart from a rich unconscious motivation, which I was interested to discover in later years, my determination was without doubt powerfully influenced by the personality of our family doctor. He was the first doctor to come to the newly rising industrial village and, until he acquired a house for himself, he lodged with us for a year or two, so that I observed him and his doings at close quarters. He was a handsome dashing fellow, with lurid stories of his harum-scarum medical student days in Dublin, and an ardent sportsman who presented me with the first of my long series of dogs. The birth of my younger sister, when I was three, comes into conscious recollection, as do the sounds of my mother's pain in travail. Her story that Queen Victoria, an assiduous queen bee, had sent us the new baby did not at all tally with my observations of the doctor's activities, and it was plain to me that he was a very exalted person who could bring the results of my father's misdeeds to a happy issue. From that moment, since a doctor was superior even to a father, I resolved to become one.

When I was about eight, however, my hopes were dashed, apparently for ever, by our doctor's assertion that I was too "delicate" for such an arduous career. For the next three years I was like a fox without a tail. Even in those days people spoke of one profession after another being crowded, though heaven knows the situation in that respect was a paradise compared with what it became later. All such arguments my father consistently answered with the remark: "There is plenty of room at the top," one which I have since observed to contain much truth, despite the professional competition that penetrates even the highest ranks. To his credit, he always left me scrupulously free to choose any career I pleased, but on observing my distress he offered to give me the chance of following his own profession of mining engineering by sinking a pit so that I could watch the whole process from the beginning. Fortunately for me, though not for his finances, shale was found where coal should have been, and the enterprise came to an abrupt end. Also fortunately for me, the doctor who had formed such a pessimistic opinion of my stamina died about the same time—like so many other doctors, from an overdose of morphia; his children formed part of a large collection of wards whom my benevolent father brought up. His successor pooh-poohed his judgment about me —perhaps on principle, in the way that successors have—and my self-respect was re-established. I used to accompany him on his rounds in his dog-cart and haunted his surgery. The leading lights of his hospital, University College Hospital, to which I also went, thus became familiar heroes to me years before I saw them in the flesh, and I was well acquainted with their attributes and peculiarities.

My father possessed a set of the "Popular Educator" volumes, which were a source of much interest and instruction to me. Among much else they contained a course in Italian, and I was immediately struck by the beauty of the words, and systematically worked through all the lessons. To master Italian grammar at the age of ten was certainly an odd performance, and I think I kept it to myself. A little time after I read in a very romantic novel of an astonishing episode. The aristocratic hero and heroine were conversing in the twilight on the terrace of a country house and were so moved by the beauty of the situation that they "insensibly dropped into Italian" as a language more befitting to it. How wonderful that seemed! This remarkable story only stirred my linguistic ambition.

Unfortunately there was never an opportunity to put my knowledge into practice in this particular fashion, and in the stress of other occupations most of it faded. But on at least four other occasions in my life I renewed these studies, and a good deal has ultimately stuck.

One other incident and I have done with childhood days. When I was nearly twelve the secretiveness that so often heralds the approach of puberty combined with an always strong instinct of curiosity to impel me towards a passionate interest in ciphers, about which I still know a good deal. I devised one myself which I was satisfied would baffle any opponent; I must admit, however, that it would not have been a very convenient code for purposes of rapid communication, since it involved the interplay of so many sub-ciphers that it took the best part of a day to transcribe a sentence into it. The complex, thus allayed, was able to transmute itself into a more useful form and, together with a dawning interest in phonetics, led me to study Pitman's phonographic shorthand. In a furor I absorbed the contents of his three manuals, the *Teacher*, *Conversationalist*, and *Reporter*, to such good effect that after a week I was able to pass the official examination. I sometimes look back with amusement on that thrilling week when I hear of young people groaning at having to execute the same feat in a year or more. I have always found the accomplishment very useful, both for note-taking with lectures and patients and for helping my secretaries decipher their own shorthand.

Chapter Three

Adolescence

AT puberty one begins life afresh and yet not anew. One of Freud's most interesting discoveries was that in the years immediately following puberty one is engaged in both reproducing and re-creating on another plane the stages of one's earliest development, of the first four years of life that are commonly blotted out from memory. The direction of one's path is inflexibly determined by the now unconscious past; and yet one is granted the opportunity of re-making it along more suitable and stable lines, of correcting earlier deviations in it, and of relating it more definitely to the environment. The vague, fantastic and irrational attributes of the first development now have a chance, on its repetition, of becoming better adapted to the world of reality.

A rich inner life of phantasy in infancy, one kept apart from the realistic contacts that went on side by side with it, reproduced itself at puberty after an almost dormant interval when I had been mainly concerned with the world of people. This brought about an inner disharmony, a sense of strain, with some unhappiness. Instead of throwing myself wholeheartedly into the new school life at Llandovery I compromised by making quite good external contacts with the other boys, but regarding this not as real life so much as a concession that had to be made to enable one to continue any inner personal life of emotional speculation. The main fault I found with them was that they were "too young", that they never seemed to think of anything beyond the actual moment and its doings. The greatest trial was, therefore, as it often is in Army life, that one got little or no time to oneself, no privacy. I had previously been too much accustomed to the privilege of enjoying my own company on long walks alone, whole days far from home on cliffs or moors, and had not had the advantage that resident preparatory school life gives of getting used to the constant presence of others at an age when this is more natural and therefore easier than it is rather later.

As I look back I do not find the phantasy life of that time particularly interesting, since its flow of emotion, which after all was its chief value, had not yet produced much precipitate of definite ideas. The more romantic aspects of love received of course their due—I was indeed for a short time in a state of adoration of a very beautiful little girl—but for the most part it was a matter of the vague spiritual aspirations so characteristic of that time of life. It was only later that these found more definite expression in social and philosophical interests. The aspect of them that has lasted longest was that most seductive of all emotional attitudes which the Welsh call "hiraeth", a word only imperfectly rendered by the English "yearning" and the German "Sehnsucht". I still count it as valuable to the imagination that, in the healthy process of transforming subjective phantasy into real striving, some part may be yet reserved for the ineffable and the unattainable; without this, one's ability to transcend the visible present and to penetrate intuitively into the unfamiliar and distant suffers decided limitation. Although I have since developed a quite reasonable amount of common sense I am happy to think it is not all of the matter-of-fact variety.

Passing from Swansea Grammar School to Llandovery College meant, among many other things, returning from the English world I had tasted to the Welsh one, since with very few exceptions the boys were recruited from the Principality. All the masters, however, were from English public schools and they never let us forget their opinion of our native inferiority, from which our only hope of redemption was through emulating the *Herrenvolk* whose outposts they were. My own response to this attitude was by no means simply a resentful one, since I could perceive it had much justification: we were indeed an uncouth lot, among whom codes and ideals were few and far between. In consequence, I have always taken a considerable interest in the psychology of the English and have felt enough admiration for them to be able to feel their points of view and predict their reactions better than most of them, with their remarkable inarticulateness, are able to express. The English are notoriously hard to understand—they really are a peculiar people—and I must be one of the few foreigners who have entered into their arcana.

As, I suppose, in most schools, the boys' predominant interest was in games. For myself I came to the conclusion that cricket was a game to be watched, not played. Football, on the other hand, was decidedly a game to play, and I made a quite useful half-back. At that time Llandovery was the nursing-ground for Welsh Rugby, then in its prime, and sent to the universities a steady flow of future internationals who were of course our special heroes. It was quite ten years after leaving school before my interest in the doings of the various Welsh teams began to pall.

A special feature of the school was the opportunity it gave for magnificent walks in mountainous country. Then there was the River Towy, with which much could be done. A large natural bathing pool was reputed to reach the depth of forty feet—at all events no one ever got near the bottom—and the swimming test upstream against a torrent which threatened to dash one against rocks was a respectable performance, too much so for my limited powers. In one dry summer I conceived the fantastic plan of blocking the whole river where it was more shallow. I worked hard at my dams, one from each side, but of course never managed to stem the torrent that raged through the remaining two feet in the middle. No doubt this passion to control water had some dark source in my depths, and perhaps the same is true of the engineers who do successfully construct dams.

Above all there was skating, for I had the luck to pass there the superb winters of 1893–5. For months on end one could skate for miles up and down the river. This enjoyment fused in a curious fashion with the romantic phase of adolescence that was already developing. I conceived the idea that the most delightful experience in the world would be to waltz on ice with a Viennese maiden to appropriate music emanating from an enchanted island in a lake. Nearly forty years later this youthful dream came close to fulfilment, and in a way that illustrated the precariousness of such dreams. At one of Baron Frankenstein's famous musical receptions at the Austrian Embassy, I beheld an entrancingly beautiful damsel standing alone. To my pleasure the secretary of the Embassy asked me to take charge of her. Our conversation, after ranging over various topics, came round to that of skating. She was an enthusiast and had brought her skates to London in the hopes of some enjoyment. I had by now learnt to dance on ice, and we arranged that the next day I should introduce her to our rink. On the way down, however, it turned out that she knew only more modern dances and could not waltz!

That reminds me that a lady used to travel from Swansea to Llandovery once a week to hold a small dancing class in the school. The polka, schottische, lancers, and quadrilles I knew from hops at home, but there was thorough drill in the steps of waltzing, which have never deserted me. But a tendency to giddiness prevented my ever becoming a devotee of dancing.

Study life, with its camaraderie and its evasion of house-masters, ran its accustomed course. The feat the boys most enjoyed was swarming down, and afterwards up, a rope let down some thirty feet from our window in the tower of the college. The purpose was to gather mushrooms in the dewy dawn, which in the evening were duly cooked over a fish-tail gas jet. One of the boys was English and once when he had hit his head badly he groaned: "Oh! it does hurt so." I remember being greatly impressed by his perfect command of English even in an emergency, as one is at hearing small children abroad talking French fluently; we others should certainly have said: "There's hurt it does!"

I have a vivid memory of all the masters. There were only two we respected: the Rev. McClellan, who taught us Latin, preached matter-of-fact sermons, and stood no nonsense; and T. J. Richards, the chemistry master, who was too reserved to be a suitable object of hectoring. He disappeared over the mountains once for a couple of days and we were told he had been driven to this act by severe toothache; I have thought since there were probably other reasons. I remember his excitement when he told us of Lord Rayleigh's recent discovery of argon in the atmosphere, though he could not have guessed how it was destined to revolutionise chemistry. Our house-master, a Cambridge wrangler, had the unfortunate habit of putting his hands into the pockets of pretty boys, which ultimately led to his departure; a school friend of mine found him years later begging on the streets of a northern town. There were two brothers on the staff. One of them I met not long ago, when he was over eighty, and he said gleefully: "Ah, many's the time I've swished you on the bottom." It was pure wish-fulfilment, for I never underwent any corporal punishment in any of my schools. I am grateful to his memory, for he took a prominent part in a redeeming feature of the school—the annual production, usually an excellent one, of a Gilbert and Sullivan opera. His brother used to ooze ethical platitudes in a way that never won conviction, nor did his harangues after he was ordained pass among us for good sermons. Later on he developed religious mania and shot himself. The classical master could never have been a boy; I shall never forget the inexpressible effect he produced one evening during "prep" by announcing that "cachination must cease in the north-east quarter of the hall". Then there was Berry, who taught us French until, at the age of forty-five, he decided to enter St. Bartholomew's Hospital as a medical student. When I look back on it, I feel that mental stability was not a prominent feature of the teaching staff.

Six months after going to Llandovery I passed what was then called the Lower Oxford and Cambridge Board Examination, the successor to which now exempts you from the London matriculation. A boy who had won the first entrance scholarship when I won the second achieved the remarkable feat of obtaining eight distinctions in the Board examinations. He was in my class and I knew and liked him well. But he was a dreamy youth, who hardly noticed the outer world. Somehow I divined that he could have no father and must be very attached to his mother. I was interested when I next met him forty-five years later, after he had retired from a high position at the Board of Education, to find that he had no recollection whatever of my existence—indeed very little of his school life at all. He confirmed my early diagnosis by telling me that he never woke up at all till the age of thirty when his mother died, whereupon he promptly got married.

The following year I pursued the natural course to the Higher Board examination, and then the question of career had to be decided. My unfortunate powers in mathematics led the authorities to put me in the sixth form in that subject with the object of training me for a scholarship at Cambridge. I was only fifteen and baulked at the idea of hanging about in school for another three years. Also, I had the wit to perceive that my mathematical ability, such as it was, was petering out—elementary and advanced mathematics appeal to very different types of mind—so after a term or two, much to the headmaster's disapproval, I decided to renounce the University plan and to aim at the London matriculation so as to proceed as soon as possible to my medical studies. That meant a change of curriculum in a direction alien to the tradition of the school—where it was *bon ton* to despise London matriculation—and arranging special classes in chemistry, Anglo-Saxon and other unfavoured subjects. My only colleague was my life-long friend Arthur Davies, who passed the examination with the sixth place in Great Britain and has since risen to the highest position in Somerset House.

We proceeded to Cardiff for the examination and my immature appearance there was such as to provoke the disgusted comment from someone who was up for the examination for the fourth time: "My God, I didn't know they allowed babes in arms here." I passed, however, in the first class. It was a strenuous time, and on returning to school for the last month there I was disgusted to find that the headmaster expected me now to turn to and revise subjects for the purpose of passing the Higher Board examination for the second time. By dint of specialising in this examination, and pressing the boys to pass it three or four times over, he had made the school attain an amazing rank in this respect in comparison with other public schools who took such matters more sensibly. I did not sympathise with his sharp practice and, knowing I was to spend the holidays working for a college scholarship, flatly refused to humour him, whereupon I was read a sharp lecture on my disloyalty to my school, an indictment which made little impression on me. If I did feel any pang of conscience at the "disloyalty" it would have been thoroughly and most unexpectedly dissipated some half a century later, when the Warden publicly hailed me as the most distinguished pupil the school had ever produced.

Two things I learned at Llandovery that helped to prepare me for my further psychological work: the depths of cruelty and of obscenity to which human beings can descend. I had no particular propensity to either myself and so could afford to note the phenomena fairly objectively, except of course when I was a personal victim. The remarkable callousness that boys intent on amusement can display towards the sufferings of a victim, and the way in which these, so far from arousing pity, can heighten the excitement, made the doings of Nazi concentration camps less inexplicably unfamiliar, when years later I came across them in detail, than they would otherwise have been. A favourite sport, for instance, was to lay a boy on his back, lie across him face downward and then get six or seven others to add to the weight by doing the same. All would go on breathing except the victim, whose chest was immobilised and whose only hope of escape from the intolerable sense of panic lay in being able to hurt one of the tormentors in a vital part and thus transform the scene into one of general confusion. Less popular, but revolting enough when it happened, was the practice of lowering a victim head first into one of the far from privy latrines. But I will not dilate on these mirthless jests. It should be plain how I came to entertain few illusions concerning the undiluted goodness of human nature; one might rather wonder how it comes to be as good as it naturally is.

As for the obscenity, I can best convey my point by a story. In the course of later studies I came across a series of portentous tomes, which bore the name of *Anthropophyteria.* They were edited, and mainly written, by an Austrian anthropologist called Krauss, evidently a simple soul, who was so impressed by the proliferation of obscene jokes and anecdotes among the Balkan peasants that he collected and recorded them in detail. I cannot pretend to have read all this conglomeration—I don't suppose anyone could—but I will say that wherever I dipped into it I failed to find any topic in the field of sexology, recondite sexual perversions, *et hoc genus omne*, on which any Balkan peasant could have enlightened the boys of Llandovery, or have related any joke that would not have been familiar to them.

Apart from mild "affairs", homosexuality appeared to have no serious vogue in the school. I never heard of an instance of pederastia, and even mutual masturbation was strongly frowned on. Emotions were perhaps not pent up enough to need compulsive outlets.

Two lasting grudges I bore my school, especially in later years. One was that Welsh was not taught there—or taught so surreptitiously that I never heard of it—at *the* leading public school in Wales! I thus never had the opportunity of acquiring a literary knowledge of what should have been my native tongue. The other was that one heard not a word of the extraordinarily rich Roman remains and associations for which the neighbourhood is famous—camps, battlefields, goldmines, roads, etc.; such information would have been a useful stimulus to my archaeological imagination, which had to lie dormant for many years. The present Warden of the College, I am happy to add, tells me that both these defects have long since been remedied.

* * * * * *

As I had expected, the vacation after leaving school had to be spent in coaching for a county maintenance scholarship (free education and £40 a year), which according to my father was necessary before I could proceed to my medical studies at the University College of South Wales, Cardiff. It was my first introduction to electricity and other branches of physics, none of which were taught at school.

Having taken this fence, I was able to register as a fully-fledged medical student, and also found that my London examination exempted me from the corresponding Welsh one, so that I became an undergraduate of two universities—those of London and Wales. I had the ambition of taking a degree in science in the latter, which meant extending my knowledge of mathematics very considerably. However, I desisted from this extra work after six months so as to make sure of passing my first medical examination. This decision caused me much regret and remorse for many years after, and I used to dream I was successful in acquiring that coveted degree. The regret was unexpectedly alleviated many years later when the university bestowed on me an honorary Doctorate of Science. There are not many people who remain an undergraduate for sixty years before completing the curriculum.

To enter university life at Cardiff at the early age of sixteen was a most heartening experience. Being emotionally precocious, I had the pleasure of finding myself among equals instead of among children. Rather unexpectedly this enabled me to feel free to be young and enjoy physical exercise and other aspects of life. I was, I think, popular and I certainly made good and lifelong friends there. The studies were engrossing and increasingly attractive as they advanced to the medical curriculum. Had it not been for my adolescent conflicts, which took mainly a religious form, the three years spent in Cardiff would have been wholly delightful.

The staff were men of parts whom with very few exceptions one could respect, one of the many changes from school life. The Principal was Viriamu Jones, F.R.S., who also occasionally lectured to us in physics. He was a handsome man with a suave and diplomatic manner, but he trimmed his sails so nicely that he did not give us the impression of being the kind of man one would completely trust. Selby, the Professor of Physics, was adequate but aloof. Parker, the biologist, had the name of being one of Huxley's many favourite pupils. (H. G. Wells was known to be another, which gave him an aura in my eyes. Huxley himself had died the year before.) He was a good teacher and a pleasant man with a sense of humour. He conveyed to us something of the scope and import of biology that Ray Lankester (who, incidentally, examined me in the subject) was at that time so magnificently expounding at University College in London. His assistant in Botany, who later became Principal of the College, remains in my mind especially for one remark. We were surreptitiously using H. G. Wells's *Textbook of Biology*, which had been skilfully written for the express needs of London University examinees. On his coming across this book on my desk he disdainfully delivered himself as follows: "I gather that his zoology is poor, I know his botany is bad, but I am told that he writes quite passable novels."

Thompson, the Professor of Chemistry, was another suave gentleman who, lolling in an easy chair, poured out his lectures with an extraordinary fluency but in such a conversational and casual fashion as to leave little impression on our minds. We never saw him apart from this, and the laboratory department was managed, or mismanaged, by a very tedious German, Perman by name, who was interested only in his private researches. In the second year, when it came to a difficult part of organic chemistry, we were so disgruntled that we made some sort of protest, and there was a joint conference between the Principal and Professor on one side and the students on the other, at which some plain speaking took place. Thompson must have been a small-minded man, since he took his revenge where he could after this. I was one of the victims. Taking advantage of the fact that I had been absent for a couple of days from illness and had neglected to supply a medical certificate, he stressed my "irregular attendance" in the term's report to such effect as to get my scholarship temporarily suspended, which led to a rather unpleasant scene with my father.

Nor must I omit to mention among the staff Paul Barbier, the Professor of French, whose charming daughter Marie, now a grandmother, was the belle of the college. Barbier was straight out of the Second Empire, curly top-hat and all, and his all-pervasive *bonhomie* made him an admirable ambassador for his country. I cannot recollect how I got included in his circle—probably through Marie's friends—but I greatly enjoyed the delightful parties he gave and I cherish a warm memory of him.

Towards the end of the first year's work two of us decided to take a six weeks' course of intensive coaching at the University Tutorial College in Red Lion Square. Here I first saw H. G. Wells, who was just finishing his career as a teacher of biology. My companion was J. F. Jennings, a man who later on, after just failing to achieve a career in surgery, became an excellent and fashionable doctor in Mayfair. He had many qualifications for this, apart from his very sound knowledge of medicine. He was very gifted socially, and was one of the two or three best raconteurs I have ever known. We struck up an odd but lasting friendship. He admired what he called my self-confidence; I respected his inner integrity and his wide knowledge of life—he had been in the business world before taking up medicine.

London in 1896 was very different from what it has since become. Golders Green was not, and an active person could well walk out into the country, at least northwards. Troglodyte travel was confined to the minute City and Waterloo tube, unless one counted the sulphurous Inner Circle. It was a point of honour among the young to leap from or on to an omnibus whatever its pace; to wait for a stopping-place was a sign of decrepitude. The trams also were of course horse-drawn, and had not yet desecrated the Embankment. When many years later I told my young son of this he showed his disbelief by countering with "Yes, and I remember the trams being drawn by elephants." The Admiralty Arch was a thing of the far future, as was Kingsway; so the Strand had not yet been impoverished by the dispersal of "Booksellers' Row" (Holywell Street) or the Lowther Arcade; I was surprised recently by someone inquiring in a newspaper where the Lowther Arcade used to be, since I was only vaguely aware of the disappearance of such a familiar landmark. Tottenham Court Road debouched into what is now called St. Giles' Circus by two mouths, one for traffic, one for pedestrians, and Charing Cross Station was more important for foreign travel than either Waterloo or Victoria.

We lodged in Mornington Crescent, overlooking the grounds now occupied by Messrs. Carreras' factory; incidentally, I was an early devotee of Carreras', when the old man kept a modest shop in Wardour Street, known only to the elect. We could seldom afford bus fares and tramped staunchly to Red Lion Square, as well as to theatres, Hyde Park, or wherever else we explored. This reminds me of two examples of my erstwhile callowness, which may be the occasion of a smile. One was my unwillingness, in the very parlous state of our finances, to enter an ABC shop lest being in Regent Street it might prove too expensive. We were, it is true, on very short commons and did not taste a potato in the two months we spent in London. The other was when we embarked on an expedition to the Oval. Following, as I thought, the example of my fellow-passengers, I held up a penny and uttered the word "Oval"; upon which the conductor sarcastically inquired: "Wouldn't like to buy the bus, would yer?"

Ah, that dry Cockney humour, how it delighted me! The withering scorn of the bystander when a policeman shook a man in the gutter, saying, "Come on, you're drunk," and had to listen to the comment, "Garn, he ain't drunk; I saw 'is 'and move." But jokes about drunkenness are no longer the vogue. Then the costermonger whose cart upset and whose apples wandered down the road, leaving an expectant audience to look forward to a lurid exposition of his emotions; instead, aware of his failure to rise to the situation, he dismally commented: "No, governor, there ain't no words for it." Or the sarcasm of the hansom cabby who, on being handed the exact fare in the form of a sixpence, a threepenny bit, two pennies, a halfpenny, and two farthings, turned on the country visitors with the remark: "And may I ask, ladies, how long you have been saving up for this little treat?" I once heard a cabby in Piccadilly call out, when a harlot was badgering a reluctant client, "Come on, governor, make up yer mind." On another occasion I overheard a lady of that profession reproach a rival whose skirts were being held above her knees, ostensibly because of the mud, "Play the game." But where is one to end with this rich theme?

At the end of the six weeks we felt like old Londoners and enjoyed initiating our other colleagues who came up from Cardiff for the examination (in the days when the University of London was ensconced in Burlington House!). I remember one of them, now a distinguished London surgeon, stepping out of the train at Paddington, gazing around, and exclaiming to our amusement: "So this is London!"

The next term we entered the Cardiff medical school proper, with a roomy dissecting-room whose window sills served as a lounge, and even with visits to the local hospital to learn practical dispensing. The first Professor of Anatomy we had was A. W. Hughes, a competent teacher and also a courtly gentleman who would have made an excellent country squire; the four-in-hand turn-out which he drove to the college every day was most dashing. Parties at his country house were great events, and how we enjoyed the singsongs during the couple of hours' drive back in the wagonette late at night. After a year Hughes left us for King's College in the Strand, where his coach and four, still in being, must have made even more impression. He died of typhoid in the South African War, where he was in charge of a surgical unit, and is commemorated by a statue at Corris in North Wales. I mention the statue because many years later a friend of mine related to me as a queer experience how he came round a corner and suddenly came upon a statue of an anatomist; I still can't see why an anatomist shouldn't have a statue if his friends want to erect one.

Hughes's successor was Dixon, a red-haired Irishman with a habit of blushing. I recall inducing one very painful blush when, in answer to a question, I said that the direction of the vagina was upwards and backwards (instead of the more respectable downwards and forwards). He was a gifted pupil of D. J. Cunningham of Dublin, then the most inspiring of anatomical teachers, for whose text-book we were admiringly grateful, and

today it is physics, tomorrow it may well be psychology. It would seem that minds bent in the direction of astronomy, of botany (!), of mathematics or of physics can more often tolerate an antinomy between religion and science than those whose interest is biology, chemistry, geology or physiology, who dislike the coexistence of disparate modes of thought. At the time of which I am writing, those who spoke in the name of science on philosophical, social or other general matters were predominantly biologists, or at least men extensively influenced by biological doctrines. To the plain man, "science" had long meant biology, with perhaps geology and paleontology as well. This influence would have been immensely more powerful than it was had it been accompanied by the knowledge, since afforded us by totalitarian political conduct and psychological investigations into the infantile mind, of the closeness of the human mind to the animal mentality; man is not so far away from his primitive origins as was supposed in the civilised nineteenth century. Even so, a medical student handling the human brain and illumined by evolutionary perspectives found it increasingly difficult to picture the mental apart from the non-mental, whether this be described as simply "matter", as electronic waves or particles, or as mere mathematical equations. And with that go all the beliefs in discarnate deities and spirits concerned with our doings, as well as beliefs in personal or impersonal immortality.

It was plain to me thus early that the central problem of philosophy—and therefore ultimately of science, which pursues philosophical problems, converting them one by one into scientific ones—concerns the so-called relation of "mind" to "matter". Hume long ago warned us against postulating a metaphysical entity, whether called "mind" or "soul", to explain the simple phenomena of mental processes, but his teaching is still often forgotten. Our conceptions of matter itself keep changing, and in that era we had not got beyond the grossly atomic one. Whether mind and matter coexist on parallel planes, whether mind is the primordial substance that informs matter (Bergson) or even the only one—matter being an illusion—or whether mental processes are simply manifestations of certain material changes, it is hard for any student of medicine not to regard them as *functions* of the latter (in either the physiological or the mathematical sense of the word). The jest of "no mind, never matter", following Berkeley, could scarcely be taken seriously by any geologist or biologist, whereas the complementary "no matter, never mind", far from being a jest, represented the most serious fact of all experience, to be denied only by those who are carried away by their wishes. Such was the fundamental conviction I won at the age of seventeen, and the one to which I have since adhered. I had in fact become a confirmed atheist, not of course in the popular sense of someone who denies any possible existence of a deity, but of one who sees no good reason for believing in the concept.

I should not hesitate, therefore, to describe myself as a philosophical materialist, were it not that the term, having been so extensively employed for purposes of abuse, must necessarily carry with it erroneous connotations. But I would say that in the realms of both thought and action the distinction between men who believe that mental processes, or beings, can exist independently of the physical world and those who reject this belief is to me the most significant of all human classifications; and I should measure any hope of further evolutionary progress by the passage of men from the one class to the other more than by any other single criterion.

The echoes of the great controversy over evolution had recently been reawakened by Huxley's famous debates with the Duke of Argyll, Mr. Gladstone, and Dean Wace, and to buy one by one, after carefully saving up the three shillings and sixpence, the volumes of the Collected Edition was one of the notable events of that period of my life. These volumes turned the scale. Even more trenchant were Kingdon Clifford's incisive essays on ethics, which his friend Leslie Stephen had edited. Only recently I was re-reading Bertrand Russell's penetrating essay on Clifford's other volume, *The Common Sense of the Exact Sciences*, and it revived my boundless admiration for that diamond-like mind that glances straight through what are to ordinary people obscure mysteries. It is those rare beings who arouse an awe of amazement at the species to which we belong.

The decisive point was reached when I gave orthodoxy its last chance by attending a lecture entitled, "Why I gave up Agnosticism", by Dr. Rendell Harris, a famous Biblical scholar who died only in 1941. To my disappointment, which turned to scorn, it proved to be the cheapest kind of missionary revivalism, which made it plain that the lecturer had no idea what agnosticism really meant and was merely bent on drowning thought with floods of emotion. I should say that Huxley—apart of course from my father—was the only man who ever influenced my mental development. Even he did not mould it so much as make my innate trends clear to me, since, pretentious as it may sound, I must unconsciously have identified myself with him. Indeed, in later years my relation towards Freud, whom I appropriately designated the Darwin of the mind, was not altogether dissimilar from that of Huxley's towards Darwin; we were both "bonny fighters".

From religion one passed naturally to philosophy, ethics, and sociology; many writers—Comte, Herbert Spencer, and others —dealt with all these fields together. At that time, and of course in later life, I read widely and deeply on them, but I cannot truly say that I have greatly benefited from my endeavours. Time and again I have emerged from a course of reading in philosophy with the conviction that the authors were really avoiding specific problems by converting them into tenuous sophistries that had little real meaning. Then after a while I would feel that this was an unfair judgment on what were obviously great minds, and that it was much more likely to be due to my limited powers of intellectual apprehension, which indeed have always been unmistakably deficient in abstract fields. So would follow another attempt, and the same thing would happen. I should formulate my mature judgment on philosophers rather as follows: they are people who have been impelled to deal with various personal problems in their unconscious by making serious efforts to think consciously; they have intellectualised the emotional conflicts. To my mind this is a high compliment, since I hold that extraordinarily little real thinking is done in the world, and not much even attempted; what commonly passes for thought is mostly a much more primitive process. That even philosophers do not often succeed in this difficult task no longer surprises me, nor does it diminish my respect for them.

But the real reason why so few philosophical questions have received a definite answer in all the centuries they have been pondered on, and why there is such an astonishing contrast between the diversity of philosophical opinions and the widespread agreement in scientific work, is that the questions have more important subjective origins than has been hitherto discernible. The result of this is that the questions are mostly not well put; it takes great insight to put a question well or fruitfully. Most of the questions will for this reason never be answered; they will turn out to be questions that should never have been put. Science has already by-passed some of them and will surely by-pass more by showing that, strictly speaking, they are not real questions. The question of free will, which lies at the root of the most central problem of philosophy, is a striking example of this. What will be asked in the future is: why is the illusion of free will insuperably strong, and why is it of such vital importance to the mind? Descartes, who strove so hard to maintain this illusion, inadvertently came very near to the truth when he slipped in the word "only" in his passage: "The power of the will consists only in this, that we so act that we are not conscious of being determined to a particular action by any external force."*

Sociology and ethics I found simpler matters: I mean, not in themselves, but as regards the books written on them. It was always so evident that they lacked the necessary basis in biology and psychology, that they could for the most part be summed up as merely fumbling attempts to gather together descriptions of facts with little appreciation of their significance, or else as attempts to lay down *ex cathedra* points of view derived from subjective attitudes. Unfortunately this is nearly as true now as it was sixty years ago.

In respect of social and political questions I was immature or uninformed. I cannot recall much feeling of resentment, such as might have been far more in place then than now, at the injustice and inequalities of society, nor was I seized with indignation at the economic oppressions and exploitations that the younger generation sees everywhere nowadays; I probably took social and economic differences very much for granted. What concerned me far more than the cruelty of mankind was its apparent irrationality. It was only many years later that I was able to perceive the relationship between the two.

* The word "external" should of course mean external to the mind, not to the whole organism.

For the next ten years I was drawn to Socialist doctrines; this was more for the orderliness and efficiency they seemed to promise than for the remedying of social injustice. It will thus be understandable that the planning of a Saint-Simon or his successor Comte meant more to me than the diatribes of a Fourier; I even encountered Comte's English follower, Frederic Harrison. The practical Robert Owen also made his appeal. It is strange that in the years of youthful rebelliousness I was not more affected by the appeals to individual freedom made by the Mills, Bentham, Adam Smith and other writers. I read widely in those years and became familiar with the lives and doctrines of the various brands of Socialists, from the Abbé Mably (the first real Marxist) through Babeuf, Proudhon, Karl Marx, Lassalle to the more anarchistic Bakunin and the vague but exciting Tolstoi. Not that I really ever accepted any of the slogans and panaceas so profusely and persuasively offered. I always had a conviction that the arrangements of society were highly unsatisfactory, but also an equally strong one that the reasons for this were much more complex than given in any single formula. More than half a century later I am as far as ever from dogmatism in this field, to which I have devoted most of my life, and can still only recommend further research and cool investigation as the necessary prerequisite.

All these preoccupations naturally interfered with my medical studies and took away many an hour from those that should every evening have been devoted to them. It was not surprising that I did not do so well in the Intermediate examination and for the only time in my medical career had to be content with a second-class pass. Although the concentration imposed a considerable mental strain at the time, I certainly do not regret it now. I have not found in life that people to whom a point of view comes easily adhere to it so tenaciously when put to the test as those who had to win it at a cost. The philosopher Croce once wrote: "A thinker who does not suffer his problem, who does not live his thought, is not a thinker; he is a mere elocutionist, repeating thoughts that have been thought by others." The experiences of those years made me find myself and discover the values that were to guide me through life.

Foremost among them I should put the preciousness of honesty in thought. I will admit that it does not emanate, as one might easily claim, purely from a disinterested moral or aesthetic love of truth for its own sake—a sort of ethical or religious substitute—but also from the sense of security that the pursuit of truth gives. I have always thought it simply foolish of anyone to contend for an untrue point of view, for what was inevitably the losing side. Theologians talk about sinning against the light; this is not only fighting against the light but being stupid as well. It might be said that this begs the question of the difficulty of knowing what is true or untrue, but I have specially in mind the numerous cases where a little courage in overcoming blindness of emotional origin, or the illusions of wish-fulfilment, is the equivalent of the virtue of honesty. My attitude was bound up with a curious intolerance of illusion. Once I had been able to tear aside an illusion that had previously dimmed my vision, once I had "seen through" something, the insight thus gained was never lost. In psycho-analysis one has the constant experience of patients who see a point, apparently clearly, one day and not the next; the progress in insight is not evenly continuous. Still more remarkable have been the cases of analysts preserving an apparently lucid insight into the depths of the mind and then losing it again, sometimes for good. Such a process is so alien to my temperament that it has always needed an effort to comprehend it, to understand how one can be deceived over again—strong though I knew the wave of inner resistance against the insight to be. One of the very greatest surprises in my life was when Freud related to me what was happening to a well-known analyst, Jung, the first event of the kind; it took a great effort to apprehend it, to believe that such a thing was possible—and, as it turned out in that case, lastingly so.

When I gaze back, through the mists of more than half a century, at that youth of seventeen I am persuaded that the picture I conjure up is not very far from the truth. It is that of a youth who, though bright, quick and intelligent somewhat above the average, had no special endowment of facility, aptitude, or mental powers; he had to work hard for everything he acquired. Outwardly merry and friendly, inwardly he was over-earnest for his age. There was a good supply of self-confidence, still more of hopefulness, but stronger still was a deep sense of duty—not so much of obligation towards the world as the benevolent desire to do something for its good. This desire, or ideal, was surely the dominating influence in his nature, one that must have been transmitted, in different forms, from both parents. It had, of course, its narcissistic components as well. There was the confident belief that he had it within him to achieve some lofty aim and, further, the worldly ambition to reach some position in life that would give him the necessary opportunity for influencing his fellow-men. But these components were harmonised with the altruistic ones, to which they were definitely subordinated. Clearly a nature exposed in an unusual degree to the inevitable blows and disappointments of life, but one with enough resilience not to be broken by them. And so it proved.

He was poorly enough equipped for the purpose of making any mark in the world. Ill-educated, lacking in any particular mental endowment, destitute of any cultural refinement, with all the rawness of which youth is capable, he was especially hampered not so much by his belief in the essential goodness of humanity—for that is tenable enough—as by a naïve disbelief in the significance of evil and in the difficulties of coping with it. This feature, till remedied by the experience of life, was bound to pervert judgement as well as to invite painful disappointment. Yet one peculiarity distinguished him from most of his fellows, one that was to run through later life. It was a scepticism concerning any nostrums—political, educational, ethical, or others—that simply appealed to the emotions, and a preference for action based on a previous investigation of the biological factor in the situation. This meant taking a long view—often a very long view—of any sociological problem, the displacing of categorical solutions in favour of thorough studies that would disclose conclusions having some measure of stability and permanence—in short, scientific conclusions. This attitude, I would maintain, is the only true revolutionary one.

On looking back I am astonished to reflect what little thought we ever gave to the future, though that seems to be characteristic of the adolescent age; it is no doubt better "to greet the unknown with a cheer" than with anxiety. The middle of the twentieth century seemed far too remote to be concerned with and I recall very few thoughts about it. That it would be a more electric age, with much less steam, smoke, and dirt, was an aesthetic wish that has come true. That also we should have to fight Germany some time and in the end defeat her conformed with *The Battle of Dorking*, an exciting novel of the 'nineties, and later with H. G. Wells's *War in the Air*, but no one then had any glimmering of the immensity of the effort and horror that victory would cost, nor of its unfortunate consequences. As to the division of society, I must have assumed that in spite of the illusion of "democracy" the fusion between the "Rulers and the Ruled" would never be complete—a law that Russia has over-emphasised in the last forty years—and also that the more altruistic professional class would receive its due recognition and continue to be distinguished from any other upper or middle class.

I turn from such weighty topics to narrate some of the lighter aspects of the period of my life I am describing. Life was free and easy in those late Victorian days, in the emancipation from the early Victorianism that modern writers persist in miscalling Victorianism *tout court*. The college was a mixed one, and the days of chaperonage belonged to the past. Love affairs of all kinds were common enough, and I underwent my baptism of fire in one of an exceedingly romantic and adoring order. It came to a sad end, the lady after a year or two wisely concluding that I was not a very eligible *parti*, but when I met her some thirty years later, *en secondes noces*, we agreed that we could have made a perfectly good marriage of it had matters gone otherwise. Cruder relationships I knew of only by hearsay, but there was enough on that topic related in the dissecting-room to provide a liberal education.

There were many advantages in the non-resident system of the university and in the total absence of supervision, proctorial or otherwise. At the age of sixteen the freedom of being able to return to one's rooms at any hour of the night was a welcome change from the absurd discipline of school, with its childish "bounds" and the rest. For the envy of modern students I may mention the cost of accommodation in those days. For the munificent sum of six shillings a week one could have a comfortably furnished sitting-room, a bedroom, and bathroom, with all service, including cooking and waiting; the actual food consumed was bought for one and entered on a separate bill. My mother had secured my first rooms for me, at the exorbitant rent of ten shillings a week, and I was so reproached at supporting this increase in the normal cost of living that after a year I compromised by finding for myself another place at the rate of eight shillings.

To my great regret I neglected athletics, and confined myself to cycling. Of this there was a good deal, either alone or with a girl companion, and many times I rode to Newport and back (24 miles) before breakfast. There was of course the world of theatres and music-hall. Cardiff was well equipped in the latter respect, in the days when such artists as Marie Lloyd and her sister, Vesta Tilley and the rest, were star attractions. The only music was a choir to which I belonged, conducted by Dr. Joseph Parry, one of the leading musicians of Wales. He was both inspiring and patient, but a singing voice was one of the Welsh attributes that was not vouchsafed to me.

Most enjoyable of all were the unforgettable smoking concerts the medical students organised every term, of course in the familiar dissecting-room. There was a remarkable display of talent, and the rousing choruses belong to my warmest memories. My own contributions consisted in recitations of Kipling's Soldier Ballads. I acquired enough reputation in this field to find my services in request in many other places, but there came a time when over-confidence led to a painful downfall. Essaying a new poem with, I suppose, insufficient preparation, I found that my memory failed me. The audience—a large one, of two thousand, in the Park Hall—encouraged me by clapping, and I moved on to the next verse. When I broke down in this also they lost their sympathy and the rest of the recitation didn't go down well. On only one other occasion in my life have I frankly bored an audience, at my first after-dinner speech, which I turned into an over-serious lecture. But I profited much from each of these failures.

During my early student years there were two intense aesthetic experiences—both to do with scenery—that exercised a lasting influence on my enjoyment of life. My father and a number of friends decided to go by an excursion train to Portsmouth to see the Naval Review that played an important part in the Queen's Diamond Jubilee, and I joined them as they passed through Cardiff. There was no sleep that night: the train was crowded, and men smoked or played cards. I decided to stand in the corridor and enjoy the freshness of the June night. The English countryside was new to me, at least that of southern England; I had seen Derbyshire dales and Exmoor uplands, but they were not startlingly unlike parts of Wales. Now I was to witness a revelation. When dawn came we were passing through Wiltshire with its swelling curves and beech copses. The fragrance of the early morning air was intoxicating. Coming from a sterner and rougher land, I had not known that a countryside could be so gentle and mellifluous. The love of chalkland country then implanted has never left me, and I am grateful now that I dwell amidst it.

The expedition proper was moderately interesting. We went round the Navy in a launch, saw the Prince of Wales embarking to review it, and watched the display of naval illuminations and fireworks at night. There was a truly British absence of organisation. The visitors ate Portsmouth out on the first day like locusts, and on the second there was no food to be had. After two days and nights without lying down we tried to find a train home, but the officials at the railway station were distracted, and even the engine drivers to whom we appealed told us they only wished they knew where they were going to! But above and beyond that excitement and confusion there stayed with me, and for ever, the remembrance of a fragrant dawn in a tender countryside made to be loved.

The other impression, if less breath-taking, was richer and more splendid. In August 1898 my father decided to take me on a tour abroad. Perhaps he divined it would be my last long vacation for some time to come—indeed the next proved to be a quarter of a century ahead—or perhaps he simply wanted to reward me for having worked well. At all events I am very grateful to him for a precious gift. I had reached the age of nineteen before ever going out of this island, and the result was so successful that I determined not to take my own children abroad until they were of an age to benefit to the full from the experience. As with so many resolutions of the kind, this one was changed by circumstances: my little daughter had flown to Paris and visited Vienna before she was six, and at the age of nineteen my elder son had seen more of the globe than ever I have.

I used the word tour just now—not "trip" or "holiday"—

Chapter Four

Hospital Student Days

THE twenty months in London before I obtained my medical qualification, at the early age of twenty-one, were crowded ones; they were, incidentally, the only ones after the age of thirteen when I was entirely supported by my father without any contribution, however modest, on my part. There were the life and amenities of London to absorb as well as the novel impressions of hospital work and studies. Jennings and I agreed to share "diggings"; we found them in Lansdowne Place, which overlooked the old Foundling Hospital. That reminds me of our German waiter who, gazing one evening from one window at the pre-territorial Volunteers drilling in the grounds of the Foundling, made the oracular comment: "In Germany drill all day; in England drill after tea." Foreign waiters were much exploited in those days. They worked for practically nothing, and lived in revolting conditions; this one, for instance, slept in a dark cupboard under the stairs. And the landlady took us to task for chatting to him, since, as she explained, he would leave as soon as he had learnt English: this regardless of the fact that the poor wretch was submitting to the unpleasant life for no other reason.

The choice of suitable lodgings in those days was very wide, so it took us some time to make a final decision. I recollect that my first excursus into print was an article on this topic I wrote for the Cardiff College Magazine.

I had the advantage among those proceeding from the universities outside London of having friends already scattered in other hospitals, and I made ample use of it. One got smuggled into a friend's hospital to attend some special lecture or to see some special operation or demonstration. That broadened one's knowledge of the methods in use in other schools than one's own, and also gave one some acquaintance with famous teachers (and examiners!) elsewhere. Of these, the man who made the deepest impression on me in St. Bartholomew's, where Jennings studied, was Dr. S. J. Gee—I wonder if anyone nowadays reads his famous book on *Percussion and Auscultation.* I see now his stocky figure, hear the peculiar indrawing of the breath that accompanied his speaking, and recall his masterly sureness in the examining of his patients. Then there was the inimitable Mr. Lockwood, perhaps one of the last to use the old smart phrase "huntin' and shootin' ". His surgical contempt for physicians was such that he would threaten confused students with the dreadful fate of becoming mere "doctor-men". His endeavour to reason clearly degenerated very often into an obsession for definitions—"patients don't break down; cabs break down," I once heard him tell a terrified student—and his caustic tongue inspired general fear. Once, however, I knew him meet his match. A student had used some colloquial phrase that roused Lockwood's ire and he demanded to know what exactly it meant. "I should have thought that obvious to the meanest intelligence," drawled the student to everyone's astonishment. But the best is to come. A few days later in the operating theatre Lockwood encountered the student and addressed him jocularly as "Mr. meanest intelligence". "Oh, still rankling, sir?" was the unperturbed reply. Then there was the famous surgeon-historian, Sir Anthony Bowlby, whose son is now a colleague of mine.

Nor, of course, did one meet only Welsh colleagues on these occasions; my first acquaintance, for instance, with Lord Horder, then an earnest young house-physician at St. Bartholomew's Hospital, was made over a ping-pong table. These experiences were all the more valuable because in those days—I do not know if it is still so—the ten medical schools of London certainly held more aloof from one another than did German universities situate hundreds of miles apart. Among the latter the promotion of a teacher from one to another was a complete commonplace, whereas in London a teacher who was appointed to the staff of another hospital than his own often spent twenty years as an outsider before he was finally accepted by his colleagues and students. Proud traditions were strengthened through this attitude, but at the cost of considerable isolation and delay in assimilating improved techniques that had been devised a few streets away.

The experience of wandering from one's own hospital in this way encouraged one to be on the look-out for special lectures in the medical world, at the Royal College of Physicians, Huxley Memorial Lectures at Charing Cross Hospital, and the like. In this way I was privileged to listen to, among others, Hitzig, the discoverer of cerebral localisation, Virchow, the doyen of pathologists, and the great Lord Lister himself. One naturally approached with awed interest the man whose insight and courage had been the means of saving far more lives than anyone else who has ever lived. I was more surprised then than I should have been later to observe what a simple and direct personality he possessed. At the Hitzig lecture I met a German student, later a well-known neurologist in Berlin, who was to come into my life twice later, after intervals of ten and forty years respectively; I refer to Dr. Otto Maas.

Our nearest friend was H. S. Ward, and since both Jennings and he were "Bart's" men it was natural that I saw more of that hospital than any other alien one, and that my powers of repartee were severely tested in defending University College Hospital against their contemptuous boasts. But it was another U.C.H. friend who was saucy enough to inform a Bart's audience whom he was addressing that their acknowledged superiority was due not only to their having been founded by Rahere in the twelfth century—being thus the oldest hospital in England—but still more to their steadfastness in retaining a mode of thought so nearly contemporaneous with that of their founder.

Bertie Ward had no parents and had been brought up by an uncle, who had a small butcher's shop in the poorest part of Cardiff. This reminds me of a startling experience of his in London where at some dance he met a young Scottish aristocrat. On hearing that he came from Cardiff she said: "Oh, then you must know my friends the Butes. Their place marches with ours in Scotland." Ward had to confess that somehow he had never encountered the Marquis—that grandee who built and owned most of Cardiff—on his occasional visits to Cardiff Castle, but we never heard what the girl thought of the strange person who could live in Cardiff without knowing the Butes. It was of course not the last we let him hear of his friends, the Butes.

I just now used the word "smuggling" about these surreptitious visits to other hospitals, since actually they were against the rules. Perhaps the most impudent was when, after procuring our regulation white jacket, I smuggled Ward into the out-patient surgical clinic where I was at the time working, somewhat to the surprise of the surgeon-in-charge who must have thought his memory for his "dressers" was failing. The occasion was, it was true, a rather special one. A pretty young actress had come, accompanied by a friend, for a minor operation, and I had mentioned the fact to Ward, who insisted on turning up. The following Sunday, accoutred in silk hats and frock-coats, we most improperly paid a professional visit to their rooms, and dressed the wound. Naturally we got to know them and learnt a good deal from them about stage life—that glamorous world that used to fascinate the youths of that day. The patient herself died of pneumonia not long after, but her companion, Winnie Brook—daughter of a more famous mother—remained a serious friend for many years.

My Welsh associations lasted for five or six years only, but for that time they were pretty active. The old Cardiff students met for an annual dinner and smoking concert, at which my Kipling recitations were still appreciated; on one occasion I got Wilfred Trotter, of whom more anon, to make one of his inimitable after-dinner speeches. We later broadened it into an annual Welsh Medical dinner society, of which I was secretary while it lasted. I joined the Swansea Society and helped to convert it into the Glamorgan Society; I was vice-president of it at the time we transformed it still further into the Welsh Club—I think about 1904—and then my interests drew me into other circles. After a time I almost ceased to be a Welshman, but in later years two circumstances—my first marriage and my children—reawakened my interest in the institutions, language, and scenery of Wales. It would be appropriate here to say all I have to on the subject.

I am not prone to generalise on national characteristics, and am well aware of the fallacies in doing so, but I am here concerned with subjective, not objective, judgements. One thing in particular draws me to Welsh people, and one thing in particular takes me away from them. The first is their quickness in personal response, their quickness of apprehension, and their ready reaction of friendliness and helpfulness. Where in England would you find a farmer, as I have in Wales, rushing forward to help open a gate and apologising for its stiffness, when you were engaged in trespassing on his crops? Then to understand and be understood instantly is a pleasant relief from the tortuous and circumlocutory social contacts of the English, much as one appreciated the respect for the personality of others, and reluctance to intrude on it, that constitutes the obverse of their attitude.

The negative quality of the Welsh, at least so I feel, is the remarkably parochial or even petty nature of their interests, despite the vividness of imagination they display in certain limited spheres. Possibly this is a necessary defect in all small nations—I have felt the same with the Dutch and the Swiss in particular—but whatever the reason it undoubtedly becomes tedious after a while.

The first wider circle was of course that of medical students, who certainly in those days had—and presumably still have—attributes of their own. Perhaps the most characteristic was levity, which may well be a reaction against the grim aspects of life with which they are brought into contact at an age when they are emotionally unprepared for it. Later on they develop other defences against having their feelings stirred in ways that might interfere with their professional capacities, just as no doctor would dare to treat a member of his family who had a serious illness. One touches here on a problem that has much occupied me in later days; the exceptional difficulty of teaching psychology to medical students, whose whole training strengthens their natural defence against facing deep emotions—namely, "flight into the material". Much of my life has been spent in trying to get doctors to face the mental sufferings of their patients instead of either treating them as non-existent ("imagination") or else due to indigestion. I have found this hard enough, and am sure the difficulty would be even greater—though not insuperable, given sufficient tact—with frivolous medical students. Desirable as it is for them to have some knowledge of psychology, I have been sceptical about the wisdom of incorporating it into their curriculum so long as most of the teachers available are, as at present, unfitted for the purpose. The result might well be to mislead the students into the belief that they had acquired a knowledge of the subject, and to provide them with further inner defences against the emotions that have to be faced before this can be attained.

Nevertheless, the positive aspects of student levity have their undeniable attraction, and not only in youth. Their ebullience of spirits, their pseudo-cynicism about worldly matters, and their ability to deal humorously with serious topics, especially to relate excellent witticisms on such themes: all these I shared to the full. And how we loved London for providing us with such a rich life! Jennings, Ward, and I took an oath never to leave it. The other two are buried there and I expect to be as well.

Often of an evening we would come together, indulge in a "pub-crawl" that revealed many sides of night life and of London characters, and spend the rest of the evening chanting songs and choruses in one another's rooms; when a piano was not available, a banjo served well as accompaniment. At least once a week we dined out and we became thoroughly familiar with every restaurant in Soho. The lowest price for a four-course dinner was a shilling, at Roche's, and I have shuddered since to think where the food could have come from. At Pinoli's and others the price was eighteenpence, while on grand occasions bang would go half a crown at such superior places as the Café Marguerite. Gambrino's beer cellar, the Café Royal, and the lounge of the old Empire were also favourite haunts, but usually only for drinks. We were all of us free and easy in our intercourse with strangers, and so gained in these ways a considerable experience of the manifold variety to be found in London life.

Dinner over, we would scrutinise the evening paper to decide which theatre or music-hall should receive our patronage. In those spacious days it was not necessary to reserve seats or even to wait in a queue, except of course for a first night or some special performance. Those were the great days of musical comedy, in which I underwent a thorough course before I began to reach towards serious drama. Daly's, the Shaftesbury, the Lyric, and the old Gaiety in the Strand—how we regretted the erection of the later edifice in Aldwych, which in its turn is now disappearing!—were all favourites, and we became word-perfect in piece after piece. Jennings once told of a friend who, when invited to go and see *The Geisha*, replied that he had already seen it; Jennings replied: "My dear fellow, I've seen it thirty-three times." Then there were the first Gilbert and Sullivan revivals at the Savoy, still instinct with their original spirit before later players arose to debase them into burlesque or even farce; I am merely sorry for, and cannot blame, the present generation that affects to despise such sources of beauty and merriment. We saw the music-halls at their apogee, with Dan Leno, Albert Chevalier, T. E. Dunville, Harry Tate, Chirgwin, and the young George Robey at their zenith. Several times we were the witnesses of Marie Lloyd's ribald, and unfortunately unprintable, impromptus, and we collected many other—perhaps *ben trovato*—examples. Incidentally, I would express the opinion that, whatever the average may be in the two sexes, that indefinable quality called "vitality" reaches on occasion a higher pitch of intensity, amounting to true genius, in the female sex than it ever does in the male: Marie Lloyd, Pauline Chase, and Gaby Deslys, not to mention the various re-creations of Carmen, are examples that come to my mind here.

I do not propose, however, to compete with the professional theatre-goers who have recorded at great length their memories of the stage of the 'nineties, nor even to record personal impressions—of no special originality—of famous players like Henry Irving, Beerbohm Tree, George Alexander, Charles Wyndham, Coquelin, Eleonora Duse, Sarah Bernhardt (who seemed to be always saying "Go home, little girl, go home"), Ellen Terry, Mrs. Kendal, Mrs. Patrick Campbell, Lily Langtry, Réjane, and so many others whose characteristics have been fully described elsewhere. I only wanted to indicate that for several years I was an exceedingly ardent and catholic theatre-goer, who missed little from *The Belle of New York* to the Ibsen and Shaw plays that were just then captivating intellectual London. The end of it was my joining the O.P. Club, then dominated by the great singer, Sir George Henschel, in the old Covent Garden Piazza, whose after-dinner cabarets always revealed a dazzling selection of talents that was only palely reflected in the fare available to the general public.

There is little doubt that the art of the drama is second only to that of poetry in providing material for the study of the emotions, which play such an important part in the dynamic psychology to which my life has been devoted, and I remain indebted to the many exponents of it who afforded me pleasure and profit combined.

On Sundays there were occasional jaunts up the river; I have always been very fond of sculling and punting, and at one time or another I have acquired a knowledge of the whole length of the Thames that only regular devotees can excel. Those were the great days of Boulter's Lock at Maidenhead, and the revelry at Skindles Hotel until the special late train to London; sixty years later I had the opportunity of describing these scenes to the present owner of Skindles as we flew to Naples, his ancestral home. The crowds of actresses with their sweeping summer costumes and gay cartwheel hats obliterated the sight of all the lawns as well as most of the river, and we took it for granted that their smart cavaliers were all members of the Horse Guards. It was at all events a world we could gaze at from without.

More often the day was spent in Hyde Park. In the afternoon there were the military concerts—replaced in the winter by ballad concerts in the Queen's Hall—and the ever-interesting *va-et-vient* that went on around them; it was said that a quarter of a million people used to promenade in that little area, and there were many pretty faces among them. After it was over we regularly proceeded to the Marble Arch, which we did not often leave till after midnight. The three of us took an active part in the debates there, and we became known among the habitués as the " 'Oly Trinity". It was a wit-sharpening experience, and to it I must owe some of my later reputation for readiness in debate. Our two topics were religious and medical. The hunger of many Londoners for enlightenment on the former was much greater in those days than it now seems to be; I remember once bringing tears to the eyes of a country clergyman by describing a poor collarless man's concern over the possibility of passages in Josephus' letters being forgeries. The discussions over the niceties of theological data were almost Scotch in their intensity and thoroughness. We three were none of us biased, and would always take sides against whichever disputant was the most prejudiced; we were interested in the appeals and arguments of both parties. On medical matters, on the other hand, we knew our own minds. Anti-vaccinationists and anti-vivisectionists were met with a barrage of figures, facts, and awkward questions. When they held special meetings, in

St. James' Hall or elsewhere, a rally of medical students ensured that they never had it all their own way, while the attempts of "chuckers-out" to purify the assembly led only to rowdy scenes.

Nor was the opposite sex neglected all this time. When I have heard since from lonely and timid patients how hard it is in London to get to know anyone of the opposite sex, my own experiences assured me that their difficulty was a subjective one, since I cannot believe that London girls have become more coy in the course of the present century. In the 'nineties they certainly were not, whatever may be said of the much maligned Victorian age. It is true that we confined ourselves to a little dinner, a theatre or outing—for instance a day up the river—and some embracing, but that was our own choice. A young and attractive nurse, whom we had known at Cardiff, in some miraculous fashion got made matron of a small hospital in London in her early twenties, and this hospital was regularly sent four theatre tickets. Ward and I would be invited to make a foursome; after dinner and the theatre we took a hansom back—girls on our knees—and in the small hours, after trains and omnibuses had ceased, we would trudge back on foot from Ealing to the depths of Bloomsbury. Some six miles of pavement with the prospect of a short sleep and a long day's work ahead seemed little in youth.

Anti-vivisectionist meetings were among the occasions when large bodies of medical students would collect for special purposes, a message being sent round beforehand among the various hospitals. One of these was when the first London Regiment, the "C.I.V.s", were leaving for the Boer War. We decided to occupy the whole gallery of Daly's, where they were playing *The Greek Slave*. I really cannot recall the relevance of this proceeding, or even whether any of the troops were in the theatre; I don't think they were. Streamers hung across the theatre and we dominated the play, of course joining in every refrain. Young players who had only a line or two to say or sing were to their embarrassed gratification wildly applauded, and were not allowed to continue before rendering an encore—their one and only experience of such a thing. I was told afterwards that Huntley Wright, some of whose jokes were embroidered from the gallery, was furiously angry and wanted to get the police to clear us out, but that Rutland Barrington shut him up with the query, "Were you never young yourself?" After the performance Ward and I swarmed up some pipes into the Green-room, where a crowd of young actresses thanked us for the show and forced a pair of tights on each of us as a souvenir. Little did we think at the moment that these garments would have to serve us as a pillow that night. When we got back to the street we found our crowd trying to storm the Café de Paris—with a strong force of police shoving them about in all directions at once. On our appearance some police for some reason called out: "Let's get the leaders!" and immediately we found ourselves being frogmarched to Vine Street police station. A desperate attempt at rescue in the middle of Piccadilly Circus failed. An hour later an old school friend of mine, Forsdike, to whom I owe many a good turn, appeared at the police station with the request that they release at least "the little fellow" (myself) because he was very delicate: to my gratification I learned that they contemptuously replied: "Yes, bloody delicate; it took three of us to hold him." So came about the first of three nights I have spent in a police cell—not counting "temporary detentions" by Nazis and Fascists in later years. In the morning we were escorted in a black Maria to Great Marlborough Street, where an eloquent speech by Ward resulted in our being discharged with a caution.

Then, of course, there was the great day of Mafeking in May 1900, when all London lost its head for the only time in its history. I was two days and three nights in the streets, and many was the prank we played. To begin with, four or five of us wrenched loose the chains that bound Phineas, the Scotch life-sized figure adorning the hospital tobacconist called Archer. We mounted him on to a crowded lorry and hauled it to Grosvenor Place, where Baden-Powell's mother lived. Then on to Buckingham Palace, the War Office, and other suitable localities. It was the start of Phineas's celebrated career. He became a mascot of University College, and therefore the envy of King's College students who made many surreptitious raids to abduct him. Sometimes they succeeded, sometimes not, but he was the cause of many a vigorous scuffle. In vain was he sold to Catesby's in the Tottenham Court Road; I think he is now the private possession of the college.

Many of the upper classes who ventured to go to the theatre

that evening had an enjoyable experience. On emerging they found that their equipages were no longer their own. Some students climbed on the roofs to wave flags and then we hauled one brougham and landau after another *backwards* up Regent Street, to the extreme bewilderment of the plunging horses and to the alarm of the be-diamonded *grandes dames* within. On the second night the police, who had hitherto stood aside, intervened to restore order. One of them had his helmet mischievously knocked off and, turning round, arrested two of my friends who were quite guiltless of the offence. Ward and I went along to Vine Street to testify to their innocence, but the only reward of our protests was that we were locked up too. In the morning an order came to liberate all those arrested, and thus ended my second night in the cells.

The period I am writing of is nowadays referred to as the Naughty 'Nineties. I cannot judge how appropriate the term is. At the time the words used by the younger generation were "*fin de siècle*", which meant smart and sophisticated, and by the older, "decadent". I had no *entrée* to society, and was only on a very distant fringe of the intelligentsia of the day. One subscribed to the *Yellow Book* and the *Butterfly*, and so learned to admire Aubrey Beardsley and Ernest Dowson, who seemed to be the brightest stars. Oscar Wilde's downfall was not long before, and I can testify to the horror his name evoked; I recollect even ten years later seeing an old gentleman thump the table as he rose and vehemently announced that that name was not to be uttered in *his* house. The famous Whistler case was also before my time. I had not yet heard of the Fabian Society, and H. G. Wells and Bernard Shaw, though known, had not yet achieved the extraordinary domination over the mind of youth that they were to gain in Edwardian times.

All this while, I have said nothing about my own hospital, which was, after all, the centre of my life during the period I am describing. I must have been, it is plain, a high-spirited youth at that time, doubtless making up with more boyishness than is normal at nineteen or twenty for the undue seriousness of my earlier days at school and at college. Most of it indicates elation at triumphing over earlier conflicts—or, more strictly, over the exaggerated conscience that occasioned them, since the conflicts themselves were only partially solved. The serious-

Grandmother Lewis with Ernest Jones' Mother

of his life actively. In a private interview with him—and I had very many—he would concentrate on the topic as if nothing else existed and no one else mattered, as if time was of no importance: but, the business done, there was no delay. He organised the day with automatic ease and perfection. Foreign visitors—and he had many—were invited to breakfast, and little did they know that it lasted just as long as was necessary to develop certain photographs their host had arranged the moment before they arrived. He was swift in all his doings. Once I was present when Christopher Heath—whose assistant he was —was abusing him for the way he neglected his hospital work. Horsley was amusedly listening to the harangue, leaning lazily on the mantelpiece as he did so. Heath continued: "At this moment, for example, when it is two o'clock, here you are lolling and your out-patients expect you at half-past one. Why aren't you with them?" "I've seen them all already," was the crushing response.

At operations, also, while not a minute was lost, there was no sign of haste. His great operations for trigeminal neuralgia took from two to three hours, and every step was carried out with infinite patience. His assistants had, it is true, occasionally to suffer from the strain. He was by nature ambidextrous, and seemed to expect others to be so too. On my first day as his assistant I had to use my left hand to clip a bleeding artery with a forceps, and a not unnatural fumble led to the comment: "I must have your eyes examined for astigmatism."

Horsley never lost time on preliminaries. Harvey Cushing told me once of his first visit to Horsley, in 1900. He decided to spend a few minutes with the pathologist while Horsley was cutting through the skull in the operation he wished to witness. Soon he returned to the operating theatre—and was told that Horsley had just removed his *second* cerebral tumour. I can still hear the gruesome sound of Horsley's bone-secateur scattering chunks of skull about the floor. It seems extraordinary that a man with all his exquisite delicacy and knowledge of electrical technique should not have made the obvious next step to an electric cautery and restoration of the bone flap.

Among Horsley's characteristics was an attractive masterfulness. Without any personal conceit, he was convinced that what he was engaged on was so valuable—in religious phraseology, he was the Servant of the Lord—that other people could do nothing better than attend to him and his needs, and that without a moment's delay. In the laboratory, the operating theatre, the nursing home, this was very successful, since those about him liked and admired him and so shared his point of view. But it didn't always go down elsewhere, and Horsley told a good story of how he once overreached himself. He had just landed at Quebec on his way to attend the British Medical Association meeting at Toronto. It was, I fancy, his first visit to the American continent. Calling a porter, he commanded with his quiet princely air: "Now, come along, my man, this is mine, and this, and this." The porter, unaccustomed to his devoted adherence being taken so for granted, simply put down his pack and asked: "And who the hell are you, anyway?" Horsley had an ultra-English personal reserve, and was unable to appreciate the open equalitarian candour of Americans, of whom there were always some watching his great operations. I remember one of them buttonholing him as he left the theatre and opening a conversation with the question: "And how old may you be, Sir Victor?" Horsley replied shortly: "Forty-five," and, turning to me, said in a very audible voice, "Aren't these Americans dreadful!"

The biography of Horsley by Stephen Paget is no doubt an accurate record, but it does not bring this remarkable personality to life. Trotter once remarked that the only way of doing so would be to depict a number of short sketches of him in various situations: fishing in Cumberland, addressing a political meeting, absorbed in laboratory research, and of course in a surgical ward and operating theatre. The lectures and letters published by the *British Medical Journal* on the occasion of Horsley's centenary, April 1957, gave a very adequate idea of his outstanding personality and achievements.

Of the resident staff at that time, one made a special impression on me: my own house-physician, Ivor Tuckett, a man who subsequently had the remarkable career of being first a Professor of Physiology at Cambridge, then a farmer in New Zealand, and then an ophthalmic surgeon in the south of England. House-physicians did most of the real teaching in those days. After supervising our ward work all day, they finished by giving us tea, followed by an hour's grind, in the way of a private tutor. Tuckett was a very sceptical and highly scientific thinker, demanding close evidence for all opinions; I would almost call him cynical in his attitude to official teachers, but that he had a genuinely kind nature. I came to hospital, after passing the examination in pharmacology, rather puzzled to know how doctors made their choice among the numerous drugs at their disposal for curing various diseases; their range with bronchitis, for instance, must have been forty or fifty drugs. My naïveté received a smashing blow in the first week when Tuckett calmly stated that in the whole Pharmacopeia only four drugs could claim to have scientific evidence for any therapeutic effect at all. And so he went through the whole of medical teaching, sifting traditional beliefs, pious hopes, and superstitious opinions from the definite basis of tested knowledge. It did me a world of good, and I never lost that perspective of the probable as compared with the possible. He was otherwise a slightly eccentric personality with a high power of self-control. One Saturday afternoon, when dressed in white to go up the river, he was signing a number of important legal documents which I was to witness, and the ink-bottle upset over them all. He gazed with increasing horror as the ink trickled over his sleeve and trousers. When it was all over he turned to me and said: "How very trying!" Once I observed that there was a small hair attached to the hands of his watch, and called his attention to it. He informed me that it was one that had annoyed him on his face, so he had plucked it out and condemned it to revolve eternally!

Of my own work in those brief student days there is little of interest to record. My lot was cast in a good vintage year of fellow-students—the years certainly vary in that respect—and that gave a stimulating environment; several of them later attained very distinguished positions in the profession. I worked hard and successfully, feeling very happy that I had so definitely found my *métier*. I discovered a special flair for clinical work and felt I could achieve a mastery in that field in a way I had never thought possible with any of my previous subjects of study. To pass the qualifying examinations in nineteen months after going up to the hospital was a matter of no difficulty—indeed most of us did so—and there I was at the age of twenty-one with the field of medicine open before me.

The most novel experience was naturally midwifery. Nowadays, I believe, medical students learn this work in well-conducted hospital wards with everything to hand. We had the rawer experience of having to go out—"on the district" as it was called—and attend the patients in their own homes. This was a salutary test of a student's self-reliance and presence of mind, since not only had he to face this test alone, but he might easily encounter an urgent crisis that would require all his coolness. Some students rose to the occasion, others didn't. I was one of the former, and so greatly enjoyed the adventurous life. We had, of course, been somewhat prepared beforehand, but not always encouragingly. I remember, for instance, the following gruesome maxim on the subject of bleeding: "If the blood soaks into the bed all is well; if it bumps on the floor, be cautious; if it runs downstairs, send for the obstetric assistant." This mission was usually carried out by the anxious husband, but to send to Harley Street for the obstetric physician in still more serious cases was a matter of chartering a cab, this being in pre-telephone days.

Midwifery practice among the poor brought one close to the bedrock of human existence. London was at that period much nearer to eighteenth-century squalor than it is now. One penetrated down alleys that policemen would enter only two abreast, but the doctor's black bag was an infallible passport and neither doctor nor nurse had anything to fear. But I had never before seen such overcrowding in a basement cellar, not deserving the name of room; the elder children would be peering with awed eyes at their naked mother in agony, dirt, and blood, while between her groans she would vainly command them to avert their gaze and the lodger would from time to time interpose her person. Occasionally the only person to act as a midwife and procure hot water would be a child of ten or twelve. More than once I had to deal with a woman lying in a corner on straw or sacking without a penny to buy coal. Then the "doctor" would have to turn to, buy wood and coal, light a fire, and boil a kettle before proceeding to his professional duties.

There were of course the lighter aspects of it all to complete the picture of primitive humanity. Most of those were provided by the still Dickensian midwives who sat crooning by the fire, sometimes smoking long pipes. One of their tasks was to enliven the situation by caustic comments, such as, "It's no use complaining, my dear; you've 'ad the sweets, you must 'ave the bitters." But the patients also involuntarily contributed. One called out as the baby appeared: "Oh, doctor, is it a black 'un?" To foretell the sex was one of the things expected of the "doctor", and a colleague of mine acquired a reputation for this by descending to the following stratagem. He would announce that the baby was to be a boy and then write down "girl" on a slip of paper. In the former event there was no more to be said; in the latter he would dispute the patient's memory of his prediction and produce the slip of paper in support.

To go to bed with a buzzer at one's side and to know that for several weeks there was no chance of an undisturbed night was also an education—to one's sleeping faculties. We made the observation, which I pass on for what it is worth, that in such circumstances it is more important not to miss a hot meal than not to miss sleep.

The student period was broken by another holiday abroad, in August 1899. My father was arranging to buy for his company a concession in Portugal where iron ore could be obtained, and I accompanied him. We travelled direct by *train de luxe* from Paris to Lisbon, so that all I saw of historic cities like Salamanca was tantalising glimpses from the window. In Lisbon the local negotiators were evidently keen on business, for they entertained us royally. We drove to Cintra and the other local sights, and I enjoyed it immensely. It seems to me strange now that I never found another opportunity of exploring that lovely country, but it is far from being the only one of which I could make that remark. The transaction itself evidently had its oriental aspects, since I remember a discussion about how large the present to the King had to be to gain his consent, a proceeding which took my poor father rather out of his depths. I also was brought into the atmosphere of bribery, and one of the gentry invited me to accompany him to a chic brothel where I could taste what he called *le vin du pays*, an offer I politely declined, to his considerable surprise.

After a week in Lisbon we all crossed the Tagus and went up-country to view the estate in question, part of the journey being made by riding on donkeys through cork forests. While the others were talking business, I went for a walk and came across a derelict castle on the property. I climbed it, and was enjoying a lazy time in the hot sunshine when my gaze encountered one of the most hideous apparitions I have ever seen. Below me was a huge creature, naked to the waist, whose dark swarthiness, hairiness, and repulsive features made him look more like a gorilla than I thought a human being could. More than that, his face was distorted with rage and I soon perceived that he was uttering menacing cries at me which were reinforced by the waving of his club and the baying of his savage hound. It was a moment for a stout heart. French, the only foreign tongue I then had at my disposal, he naturally did not understand, so I desperately tried to appease him with attempts at colloquial Latin—hoping very much that the Portuguese language had not deviated so far from it as I had been given to understand. Somehow I managed to convey to him that my intentions on the property he was guarding were not maleficent, and his guttural speech gradually subsided to a growl.

On our return journey we stayed at Bilboa, where the company owned extensive mines and where we heard surprising stories of grand pianos being smuggled through the customs, and at San Sebastian. Then came Biarritz, where I learned the distinction between the English, German, and Russian seasons—there being apparently little left for the French. My relations with my father were by now becoming more strained—fundamentally, I suppose, because I was finding it irksome to be "taken" in tutelage to places I should have preferred to explore in my own way—and they came to a head by my commenting rudely on his refusal to allow a window to be opened in a small bedroom we were sharing in common. He decided to go straight home and left me to finish the journey at my leisure, which was a wise and generous gesture. So I pottered about with great enjoyment at such places as Bayonne, Bordeaux, and finally Paris.

The year 1900 saw me attain my majority on its first day, and six months later I was a qualified medical man with ample time ahead of me before having to decide on the particular form my career was to take.

Chapter Five

Success

THERE now followed three years of crowded experience, all imbued with the magic of glittering success: success enough to satisfy the most ambitious young doctor. Everything fell into my hand. I had but to wish and plan, and behold, it came about. A certain spoiltness in my nature, assuredly derived from my relations with my mother, a certain insistence on getting my own way—a tendency that persisted till well past middle age—was now amply catered for. I tasted to the full the illusion of youth that one can have command over the future, and was impatient with those whose life had gone awry: why had they not simply determined to plan it otherwise? I listened without understanding to such adages as "a young man dreams of what he will do with life, an old man regards with wonder what life has done with him". That at least would not be my fate, I said. And even an onlooker would probably have picked me out as promising to belong to that galaxy that constitutes "the ornaments of the profession".

But it was not to be. Fate hammered one hard blow after another in rapid succession, until all the dizzy early success and promise crumbled to dust; and the path I actually followed took me almost outside the ranks of my chosen and beloved profession—certainly to none of its recognised high places. Not that I ever gave way under the blows themselves. I fought back with determination and with unchanging resilience. What happened rather was that the obstacles arising in the original path coincided with a change in the direction of my own interests, so that the one I came to pursue remained still in harmony with my volition.

I look back upon those three exciting years with pleasure, without regret, and assuredly without bitterness. They have, however, a certain dreamlike quality that distinguishes them in my memory from the times before or after. This haze emanates no doubt from the wish-phantasies that fate was for the moment tantalisingly fulfilling, only to mock me when later I returned to the sternness of life. It is one of the many things known, but not adequately recognised, that few can tolerate success with equanimity. With most it brings about either a deterioration of character or a lack of confidence that often enough is equivalent to a neurosis. My success had stimulated both the less and the more laudable elements of my nature, and in later years I came to recognise that the former had played a greater part in my misfortune than I was able at the time to admit.

If he is engrossed in his work, there can hardly be any phase in a physician's life more wholly satisfying than that spent in residence as a house-physician; for my part I certainly found it so. Several fortunate features heightened this satisfaction. I was lucky enough to have a term of eight months instead of the usual six of those days. Rose Bradford had charge of the wards in the summer vacation and was to continue in charge, his senior retiring from the active staff. The latter's house-physician was incapacitated by illness, so I volunteered for the vacancy. It was not a legal procedure, since I was not yet qualified, but it was arranged that the resident medical officer should sign any death certificate, etc., which I could not. So I became Bradford's first house-physician. Many years later, alluding to this, he was good enough to add, "and I don't expect ever to have such a good one." And indeed it would not be easy to find one whose eagerness could well have surpassed mine; one must do well if one's whole heart is in something. I aimed at the highest standard of efficiency and went far beyond the usual routine. Then, I knew Bradford's personality so well that it was easy not only to provide him with the most suitable material for his teaching, but also to supply the most effective stimuli to arouse his somewhat spasmodic teaching impulses. I am sure we got the best out of each other in that time, to the benefit of both patients and students.

The only people who suffered were the nurses, who could not understand why life had to be lived at that high pitch and who must sometimes have felt that I was expecting of them more than was reasonable. This was the fly in the ointment. Although it took me some time to perceive it, my passion for the highest standard of work was bringing me more and more into conflict with those who did not share it and were merely incommoded by it, a situation that could only end in unpopularity. It was usually possible to inspire students and junior nurses, but I was less successful with older people—ward sisters and, above all, senior physicians—who doubtless regarded my efforts as the ambitious and perhaps impertinent strivings of a young man who needed to be kept in his place. Added to which, as I have remarked before, I had a tongue. And a young man may be so filled with righteousness that he can see no reason for restraining his tongue when his virtuous endeavours meet with opposition. That is my diagnosis of myself in those years, and I should not cavil if someone couched it in harsher terms—using such words as opinionated, tactless, conceited, or inconsiderate.

At the time, however, I was blissfully unaware of this growing danger, and sailed ahead on my path with gusto and enjoyment. Willing to assume any responsibility, feeling capable of doing so, and knowing I was trusted in the use I should make of it, I could only be extremely happy in my work. It was hard work, too. In those days a house-physician had not only the usual ward work to attend to, followed at the close of the day by an hour's teaching of his "clerks"—four or five students—but he had also to discharge the duties now carried out by a casualty physician, a medical registrar, and a pathologist. Nowadays it would be unthinkable that an important teaching hospital could exist without such officers, but so it was then. The house-physician kept all the case records; and blood-counts, together with less aesthetic pathological examinations, were carried out in the sitting-room between tea and dinner. The latter function, always a jolly one in which survivals of medical student boisterousness were allowed some outlet, was presided over by the resident medical officer, who had usually been qualified for five or six years. In my time this was Dr. Charles Bolton, a capable and lovable man, who has been a good friend to me; he was later physician to the hospital and University Professor of Pathology. After dinner one took advantage of the darkness to make ophthalmoscopic examinations, and of the absence of students to visit each other's wards to see interesting cases or consult with one another over difficult ones. Most of us were working for higher examinations, so that the day would finish with a couple of hours' studying, to be followed by a

Ernest Jones as a young doctor

Morfydd Owen

midnight round of the wards. My rooms and wards must have been among the last used in the old hospital, dating from the eighteen-thirties, and the present one was already taking shape with the munificent help of Sir Blundell Maple.

My first excursion into medical research occurred while I was still at this post. At a post-mortem, which of course house-physicians carried out in lieu of pathologists, we came across a remarkable plaque around the heart, a calcification of the pericardium, and Dr. Bradford suggested that I demonstrate it before the Pathological Society of London, reading a paper on any conclusions I should reach after studying all the pertinent literature on the subject. This I did, without too much trepidation, and it proved to be the first of my contributions that text-books thought it worth while to incorporate. Though a very minute pebble, it was still an addition to the edifice of medical knowledge—the edifice to which it was my life's aim to add something permanent, however little.

In spite of all this work I managed to get off one afternoon a week to continue my work with Dr. Beevor at Queen's Square. It was about this time that I first played a somewhat active part in a clinical observation. Following the French neurological periodicals, I came across an astonishing recent find by Professor Babinski. He had noticed that on stroking the sole of the foot what mattered was not simply whether the toes moved or not but whether they moved upward or downward. This seemingly trivial point turned out to be perhaps the most valuable "physical sign" indicating the health or disease of the nervous system, far transcending the old knee jerks, etc. Beevor was very taken aback to think of all the years neurologists had been testing this plantar reflex while overlooking such a simple observation. I collected cases illustrative of it, admitted them to my wards where they could be demonstrated, and read a paper on the subject before the College Society, thus contributing in a minor fashion to the acceptance of the new discovery.

I was also able at this time to make a very minute contribution to neurology. Beevor and Horsley, in their animal experiments, had detected a minute spot in the frontal lobe, stimulation of which resulted in a twisting movement of the tongue. I found the same thing clinically in a case of hemiplegia and recorded it in *The Lancet* (September 1901). I had long decided that what

I most wanted to work at in my profession was neurology. The diseases of the nervous system were themselves fascinatingly precise and, with the exception of purely hereditary ones, mostly of unknown origin. That they were singularly unamenable to treatment did not deter me. I did not suffer from the therapeutic obsession—the belief that treatment is the beginning and end of medicine—that produces so many poor doctors and holds up the progress of medical knowledge. On the contrary, I held —and still do—that the questions of prevention and cure will answer themselves provided only we understand enough about the nature of disease and the forces at work.

Then, there is no field of human phenomena where the problems of heredity can be so easily isolated as in neurology. Anticipating the later views of eugenists, I felt that social organisation could only be empiric so long as we were unable to distinguish accurately between hereditary and environmental influences, and I still believe this is a highly important goal of scientific research. More than all this, however, of which I knew nothing when I was first drawn to neurology in Cardiff days, I was under the spell of biological teaching, and realised that no stable or satisfactory solution could be found for any human problems, notably the social ones, unless it was based on a full knowledge of man's biological nature. This also is a view I still hold more strongly than ever. I was then under the illusion that this could best be studied in neurology, where it would seem that human impulses and the control of them could well be examined. (Most neurologists are still under the same illusion.) My mistake was in bringing "mind" and "brain" too close together, not seeing that, whatever the ultimate relationship of the two may prove to be, it may easily happen that phenomena can yield to investigation in the one field when they strongly resist it in the other. Not that I was in any way unaware of the philosophical problems involved. On the contrary, I even conceived the idea that a profound study of speech and language—the only mental function where some counterpart can be localised in the cortex of the brain—with their disorders would be the most promising path to investigating the relationship between mind and brain; with this end in view I did an immense amount of work in that field, which remained for some years one of my side interests. Incidentally, it has a certain irony that the only position I have ever held in the University of London is that of membership of the Board of Studies for Comparative Philology.

It might be thought that I have been reading back into the mind of a youth between sixteen and twenty-one thoughts and mental attitudes that must belong to a later age, but I am persuaded this is not so. Although immature in my emotionalism and impulsiveness, I was precocious enough intellectually. And I knew at the time that my interest in neurology had eventually a sociological origin, a fact that had an important bearing on my future.

So my path seemed clearly marked out: I had to achieve a position in neurology that would give me the opportunity to study and teach. Although surgery has had to accept many pure specialities—ophthalmology, gynaecology, etc.—where the exponents devote themselves wholly to one branch, medicine has always been more chary of according this liberty. However obscure and recondite the interests of a neurologist may be, he is expected to remain a general physician as well. The position of Dr. Risien Russell as Physician to University College Hospital, and acknowledged authority there on nervous diseases, and also as Physician to the National Hospital, Queen's Square, where he could delve into his more abstruse studies, was the perfect one for my purpose, and I proposed to myself in due course to succeed him. Since that day positions have been created still nearer to my heart, those of psychologist to both these hospitals; a former student of mine, Dr. Bernard Hart, was the first to hold them.

I fully agreed with the official deprecation of extreme specialisation, though how to combine adequate concentration on specific problems with a generously wide perspective of surrounding knowledge is a question that remains unanswered in every branch of science. So I determined to take advantage of my youthfulness and to spend a few years becoming familiar with departments of medicine other than neurology; there was no danger lest my primary interest in this fall into the background. The Resident Medical Officership of the U.C.H. was the regular stepping-stone to an appointment on the permanent staff, though when there was no suitable candidate for the latter it would be held by less ambitious people on their way to a country practice. I could afford to wait for it, so that when the time came I should have a serious standing through having exceptional previous experience. The resident medical officer had to supervise the whole hospital, and it was therefore desirable for him to have held more than one resident post. My next step was plainly to become a house-surgeon, and ideally to be house-surgeon to the great neurological surgeon, Sir Victor Horsley, which would give me experience of an aspect of neurology seldom accessible to physicians. University College Hospital, unlike some others, did not allow house appointments to go by personal favour, but insisted on a competitive examination—in this case a written paper followed by examination and discussion of clinical cases in a public forum. There were three other candidates, all of whom became distinguished surgeons later. My star was still rising, however, and to the general surprise I secured the appointment.

Being Horsley's house-surgeon had two special advantages. One was the special experience in surgical neurology gained by assisting at the diagnosis of and operation on obscure tumours of the brain with Horsley's marvellous technique. He would spend three hours lifting and dissecting tissues with infinite gentleness and patience. The other advantage was that he was very little interested in any other aspect of surgery (except the thyroid gland), prone to scamp other work, and only too glad to delegate it to anyone else he decently could. His house-surgeon, therefore, was left to perform a variety of operations that no other surgeon would think of deputing, and this no doubt was the reason why I had had such formidable competitors against me. Moreover, the surgical registrar at the time, Wilfred Trotter, was a man to whom Horsley could safely leave any operation whatever, and he did so as often as possible. So between us Trotter and I had unrivalled opportunities. I recall twice taking in patients with crushed legs, a double amputation through the thigh being necessary. Trotter would amputate through one thigh while I did the other; it is a pretty formidable operation, but both patients recovered. One of the two, I remember, had come to this sad pass in a peculiarly unfortunate way. He was what is called a "peeper"—that is, he achieved sexual excitement by witnessing some erotic scene—and, presumably unable to do so in any other way, the poor fellow used to haunt the Underground Railway (of course in pre-electric times), wait until he observed a likely couple in the separate compartments that made up the trains, and then in the tunnels creep along the footboard to catch the desired glimpse. It was a sprightly occupation, because he had to return to his own compartment before reaching the next station, but doubtless he knew the stretches well from experience and had become skilful at timing it. On the fatal day in question, however, the excitement overcame him; he lost his hold and fell on to the line, and a train came along from the opposite direction and cut his legs off. What effect this retaliatory mutilation had on his later mentality I do not know, but one can well imagine it to have been immense; it was a supreme example of a physical and a psychological trauma combined.

Wilfred Trotter was my best friend and—apart from Freud—the man who has mattered most in my life. This is an appropriate moment to introduce him in my narrative. I had known him casually in student days when he was working for higher surgical examinations—he was seven years older than I—but it was only in 1900 that I first got to know him well. We had had the habit of chatting for half an hour after lunch when I was a house-physician, and when I became a house-surgeon and he surgical registrar we naturally had much work in common. Later still we became intimate friends, and he will often reappear in my story.

His character underwent an important change about the time of his marriage, in 1910, to my sister, and those who knew him in the last thirty years of his life, or from the excellent memoirs the Royal Society and the medical press published of him after his death, while they will recognise many of the things I have to say about him, may be surprised at others. The change was essentially this. In the earlier years he was the most extreme, and even blood-thirsty, revolutionary in thought and phantasy that one could imagine, though there was never any likelihood of this being expressed outwardly. After the change he shut down this side of his nature completely; as he somewhat cynically put it to me, shocking me by the words, he decided to put security first. This resulted in a high degree of correctitude and constitutionalism in his deportment, a singularly detached relationship to the world, a fondness for private speculation, and, inevitably, some measure of inhibition. He became a commentator rather than a pioneer even in his own field; but what a commentator!

I have never known anyone who excelled Wilfred Trotter in the sobriety of his judgment; in the philosophic calm with which he apprehended experience, however arresting; in his penetrating understanding of human nature, both individual and general; or in his profound grasp of the essentials of the scientific attitude and its significance for mankind. It was my sympathy with this last-named feature that mainly drew me to him, together with the all-embracing scepticism it implies, a quality with which, as has already been observed, I was not over-liberally endowed by nature.

Nor do I happen to have known anyone with a wider knowledge of English literature, a more precise feeling for English idiom, or a greater interest in the niceties of English style. His influence here was invaluable to me. How he castigated my Celtic propensity to mixed metaphor and hyperbolic inexactitudes! I had no innate stylistic gifts myself—and such gifts cannot be acquired—but if I have learnt to avoid some of the grosser faults commonly exhibited by scientific writers it is entirely because of the way I took that influence to heart. How surprised I was when he remarked that if I were not careful I should find myself writing English like Bradford or Horsley, "and how dreadful that would be!" To have these godlike personages held before one as deplorable examples to shun was something to make an impression on a badly educated youth of twenty. But Trotter's iconoclasms were very far from being confined to matters of linguistics. They were constantly displayed as he wandered from one field of thought to another, from philosophy to medicine, from public affairs to religion. He told me once that his brother was a connoisseur in blasphemy, but in his own lack of respect for the supernatural he must have closely rivalled him. One day, examining the thigh bone of a youth who had just died from a massive sarcoma that enveloped it like a malignant mushroom, he remarked pensively: "If I ever get to heaven I should like to ask the principal Person there what He has to say about this." A succinct comment on the ancient problem of evil and suffering. Nor did the great ones of this world fare better. Rank, authority, veneration counted for nothing. They had to win respect by some quite unambiguous achievement or not at all. Mr. Balfour was "that precious nincompoop", H. G. Wells (after *Anticipations*) a "sensible little chap", and so they all got placed. Those who knew him only in later years will recognise remaining traces of this critical tendency, expressed in more refined and urbane phrases.

Trotter was exceedingly sensitive to the nuances of social relationships, and was always acutely aware of what the other person was feeling. To him the insensitive people who blunder or bludgeon their way through life, not caring or even knowing about the feelings of others, were in the highest degree repellent. His sensitiveness made him prefer a guardedly impersonal approach in a conversation, and he would always try to turn from the individual to the general. I doubt if he ever revealed his inner thoughts to anyone but myself, and naturally I have no wish to reproduce them. When hurt or depressed he would respond by cogitating over the experience until he could generalise it and condense the result into an epigram. I wish I had collected these, but I will quote a couple from memory. "English is very wasteful in its synonyms; it does seem unthrifty to keep 'Be reasonable' when we have already 'Be like me'." "Genius consists in an infinite capacity for enduring pain and for inflicting it." "You will observe," he added, "the sting of that remark is in its tail." The sadistic-masochistic trait in his temperament is evident here. It was a highly pronounced trait in his phantasy life, but though a sadistic love of mastery, even involving cruelty, was so prominent there, I never in my life knew of his doing or even saying an unkind thing, and the tenderness he could show to his friends and patients was of a rare order. His most cutting remarks were not wounding. There is no better example than the one Dr. Elliott quotes in his memoir of an incident when Trotter, driven to exasperation in the course of an operation, finally remarked: "Mr. Anaesthetist, if the patient can keep awake, surely you can." This was related to me many years later by the victim, then a distinguished Professor of Medicine.

Another epigram I will recall had more bitterness in it. It was based on his deep conviction that man is little more than a member of a herd, and that most of his behaviour emanates from social suggestion rather than from reason. "Physical courage is admired by everyone, hence it is universal (soldiers are by definition 'brave' even in a conscribed army): moral courage is admired by few, so it is rare: intellectual courage is admired by no one, consequently it does not exist."

Why Trotter selected me as his friend is not altogether easy to say, although our conviction of the fundamental importance of science, and particularly of biological science, was an obvious basis of common interest. He said once it was my capacity for imagination, but I suspect it was that I provided the sympathetic audience of which, in spite of, or rather because of, his general aloofness, he stood in need.

I could not relate the story of my life without saying something of the man who played such an important part in it, but it is time to return to myself. In the short interval between the house appointments, in April 1901, I took Dr. Beevor's advice to recuperate from an overworked state by spending a week or two in the Riffel Alp in the Valois. It was immensely refreshing and enjoyable, and two incidents stand out in my mind in connection with it. One was my first encounter with American speech. I was standing on the terrace enjoying the morning air when an attractive girl nearby turned to me with the remark: "My, ain't it good; you could just eat it with a spoon." This vivid new language naturally produced a prepossessing effect on me, which was confirmed by closer acquaintance with it in later years.

The other episode stays in my memory because of its bringing me nearer to death than I have ever been since (apart of course from air raids). I had been doing some amateur climbing, of which I had been proud as a boy, and curiosity led me to inspect an eyrie on the shoulder of the Gornergrat. The mother eagle's demonstrations, however, made it plain not only that it would be prudent to leave the spot but that I must choose another path than the one of my ascent. I soon came to the edge of a cliff where by letting myself down on to a narrow ledge I might hope to jump to a grassy slope below. Time being a prominent feature of the situation, I made no more ado and dropped on to the ledge, soon perceiving as I did so that there would be no means of retrieving my steps if I wished to. But the more I looked at the grassy slope the less I liked it. As, indeed, I subsequently discovered, it sloped sharply and was so small that I should almost inevitably roll off the edge of a precipice, beyond which there was nothing to be seen but the town of Zermatt some two thousand feet below. My ledge was too narrow to take more than one half of a foot and I had no hold for my hands, so I was fairly caught. Having a poor head for heights made matters still worse. I reflected that I had committed many foolishnesses in my life, but that this one was final. It was, however, essential to keep calm, so I deflected my anxiety by making some professional observations on my pulse rate. The end of it was that by digging my toes into the crack above the little ledge and by using friction to support me by pressing the flat of my hands against the sheer overhanging cliff above, I managed slowly to edge my way sideways. After what seemed an endless distance, I was able to climb to safety. There it was possible to recover equanimity and to reflect on the moral and philosophical lessons to be learned from the experience.

The examination for the Bachelorship of Medicine took place when I was still a house-surgeon, so that I had to keep my mind on two faculties at once. Feeling well prepared, I followed up the pass papers by taking the honours ones as well, and was gratified at obtaining first-class honours in both medicine and obstetric medicine. More than that, I won second place in the former subject, with a gold medal, and first in the latter, with a university scholarship and gold medal. An old friend from Cardiff, Charley Thomas, who later on attained the highest position in the school service of the London County Council, reversed my feat, being first in medicine and second in obstetrics; he was several years senior to me. I think the greatest pleasure I got from this success was the elation it generated in my family; my mother was of course delighted and my father broke through his reserve in the endeavour to express his satisfaction. But it presumably catered to my "omnipotence complex", which was beginning to be stronger than was good for me. There is no doubt that success of this kind is taken by the unconscious mind as a sign that fortune is pleased with one, that one is "all right", and that there is no need for further self-criticism or moral effort. Coming as it did after my earlier years of burning self-criticism, with its sense of guilt in the spheres of religion and sex, it necessarily put a considerable strain on my mental balance and harmony by inducing a swing in the opposite direction.

I had so enjoyed my two house appointments that I was loth to leave University College Hospital, where I felt so much at home, and so I applied for the only remaining resident post, that of obstetric assistant. It was six months taken away from my direct medical career, but it was interesting and I could afford the time. I was well up in the work, and on the occasions when my chief could not turn up I conducted the ward visits in his place, apparently with the approval of the students and visitors who attended. I supervised the birth of over a thousand babies, and when passing through the district nowadays I sometimes wonder which of these middle-aged men and women I had helped to bring into the world. During this post I passed the Bachelor of Surgery examination, another unnecessary proceeding, since in those days the M.B. examination itself, a qualifying one, included surgery.

Then came the move from the Alma Mater— as it proved, for ever. Before it, I had the opportunity of acting as temporary pathologist for a couple of months during the illness of the holder of this new post. I still wanted to broaden my general medical experience before specialising and—a fateful decision as it turned out—postponed the next logical step of a house appointment at the National (neurological) Hospital, before returning, as I hoped, to U.C.H. as resident medical officer. So I became house-physician at the Brompton Chest Hospital. My three chiefs there were Dr. Hector Mackenzie, a capable specialist, Sir Dyke Acland, a courtly member of the well-known Devon family, and Sir James Kingston Fowler, who was a really great physician, although—perhaps because of his reserved temperament—he never attained quite the preeminence his merits deserved.

Two of my fellow house-physicians were specially interesting men. One of them was F. C. Shrubsall, who later became an authority on mental deficiency in the service of the London County Council. I had known him in student days, since he was a friend of my set at St. Bartholomew's. Before proceeding there from Cambridge he had made a name for himself by anthropometrical researches, and in this connection an amusing story was told. When he was "clerking" to Sir Dyke Duckworth, a portly royal physician, both attended an International Anthropological Congress. The distinguished physician seemed to know no one there, and while he was disconsolately strolling about he espied his clerk engaged in an animated conversation with foreign anthropologists. Observing his chief's lonely plight the student dashed forward and offered to introduce him to some of the anthropologists. He spent all his spare time and holidays in a stance where he could observe the colour of the eyes and hair of the passers-by; a pinprick in a card would record the results. Despite a curious appearance and many oddities "Shrubbie" was a very likable person; we remained friends until his death. He was singularly honest-minded and very direct, but his controversial hits never hurt.

The other man was W. C. Acherson, who had been cursed with a Falstaffian figure that went ill with his serious and agile mind. He was one of the first people I met who knew what the name of Janet stood for, a name that was just entering my ken, and his intention—like mine—was to devote himself to the psychological side of neurology. He was also the first friend I had who was blessed with worldly goods, and to whom it would never occur to go to the theatre except in the stalls. He did himself well all round. I remember receiving an urgent message one morning to send in a hansom a day-suit of clothes because, after dining in evening-dress, he had spent the night at a lady's flat. He was a beautiful violinist, and he taught me to appreciate Brahms. When in earlier days he had worked at Pittsburgh trying to adapt himself to an industrial career, a time he described as a nightmare, he lived only for a chamber quartet there, of which he was a member. Periodically he was overcome by an irresistible urge to go off to Bordighera (and nowhere else), and no consideration affecting his professional career was allowed to stand in the way of it. In the end this exotic, promising, and altogether delightful person settled in Japan, of all places in the world, and from then on I lost sight of him. I can only suppose that he went native and became a god of good luck in an immense kimono.

Another unusual connoisseur at Brompton was Dr. Schorstein, one of the visiting staff. Seeing me at concerts, he kindly gave me tickets to several. We heard together a series in which Richard Strauss conducted his own works, another in which Fürtwangler conducted Beethoven's nine symphonies as well as many others of his works—rare musical feasts. In those days we also heard the Joachim quartet in the old St. James' Hall. Schorstein was, I think, at that time the only Jewish consulting physician in London, which differed immensely in that respect from Berlin and Vienna.

Cultural knowledge, however, could not have been evenly distributed, since there comes back to me the memory of a physician on the staff of that same hospital assuring me that Tolstoi was busily engaged at the moment in daily rehearsals at His Majesty's Theatre of the great play *Anna Karenina*, which Beerbohm Tree was staging. And I can recall the comment a member of another hospital staff made on it to me: "Fancy making all that fuss about a trumpery episode with a girl."

One piece of Trotter's scepticism that I had thoroughly assimilated was his doubt concerning the prevalent belief in the harmfulness of cold air. Evidence had accumulated to show that a large proportion of all physical illness, perhaps more than a half, was ultimately derived from air-borne infections, and yet the medical profession persisted in sharing the ancient dread of fresh air—actually the only means whereby one could be safe from such infection. It is true that the field of supposed danger was becoming more restricted. They no longer ascribed appendicitis, peritonitis, and kindred conditions to "chills striking inwards"; hepatitis was no longer due to a chill on the liver; nor could salpingitis (most often a sequel to gonorrhoea) be explained as proceeding from a draught that had by a devious route entered the womb when the lady was insufficiently protected during menstruation. But in the large field of respiratory infections, from pneumonia to rheumatic fever, the old belief held full sway, as indeed it still does; the test case is the common "cold in the head". Trotter and his brother had experimented by spending nights in wet ditches on the Brecon Beacons to see if it was possible to "catch a cold" in this long-feared fashion, and I repeated the experience myself in nights on the South Downs with similar results. It has taken the Research Unit of the Medical Research Council years to confirm these early conclusions. Once one begins seriously to doubt this prevailing belief, the evidence of it being founded on unreason rather than reason becomes more and more conclusive, and one perceives that some important superstitious tendency is present. Years later I had the opportunity of unravelling the source of this and of publishing an essay on the psychological significance of the false belief in question. In the flush of the discovery I became somewhat of an ardent pioneer. I remember going from Brompton to Cardiff to address the medical students there on the subject; I must have been very persuasive, since they interrupted the lecture to tear open all the windows—to the considerable discomfort of an elderly chairman.

Brompton itself was an interesting study in this connection. Semmelweiss had been interned in a lunatic asylum in Budapest for daring to proclaim that tubercular patients improved in an open-air regime, but his suggestion had been revived in Switzerland, where it was hoped that the dry mountain air was safe enough to try the hazardous experiment, and it was now being taken up in a gingerly fashion in England. The underlying attitude, however, contained some very confused thinking. Instead of seeing that contaminated air was apt to be harmful when re-breathed, so that it should be avoided, the view was rather the homeopathic one that the patient would be cured by varying the dose of the poison that had made him ill. Open air was still a powerful, and potentially dangerous, agent that could be administered as a heroic measure in the hopes of its "hardening" the patient and thus immunising him against its evil effects. I was amused to find that at the Brompton Hospital, the timid inspirer of the new treatment, my bedroom window had been built so as never to open, and I had to break a panel to obtain a modicum of ventilation. This particular folly of men is peculiarly unfortunate in its disastrous results, for it leads to conduct that greatly increases the very danger (in respiratory disease, etc.) it is supposed to guard against. I may mention here one practical consequence at least to which this train of thought has led. A good friend of mine whom I had recently come to know, Jack (later Major) Evans, happened later on to be in a key position when the question arose of choosing the form to be taken by the Welsh National Memorial to King Edward, and he consulted me on the matter. Referring to the late King's stirring words on the subject of tuberculosis ("If preventable, why not prevented?"), in which he had shown much practical interest, I suggested that the memorial take the form of a campaign against tuberculosis in Wales where, because of the specially strong dread of open windows, it is very rife, and the suggestion was adopted, with results that are now well known.

In August 1902 I was given a fortnight's holiday from Brompton. The first half I spent in Brussels staying with a Catholic family into which a hospital friend of mine, Sidney Bree, was proposing to marry; I was to be the best man, or witness as it was then called. It happened that the young lady had a sister who was also engaged, but to an unsympathetic partner, and we conceived a mutual attraction. Before entering what she correctly foresaw would be the reverse of Elysium, she made a dash at some happiness in my company. This led to the fiancé challenging me to a duel, a proposal which the girl's mother managed to thwart. When I left she came with me as far as Bruges, and there was a love scene at the top of its famous belfry. We then parted; she returned to her fate and ultimately became a grandmother. In later years I was present at the wedding of Bree's daughter, and we still see something of each other after so many years.

In the following week Ward and I spent a few days with my family, who had taken a house on the cliffs of Gower. Two girl friends of my sisters were there, and one of them confided in me so sympathetically about her unhappiness at being engaged to the wrong man—it was her fourth such attempt—that I was moved to relieve her distress by gallantly offering to take his place. Four years had passed since I had had anyone of the opposite sex to care for, and the amorous mood aroused in Brussels was doubtless also a factor. But it was a mistake which I had much cause to rue before long.

It was while I was at Brompton, two months later, that I came for the first time into close contact with death. My friend Ward was taken ill with an extremely obscure complaint, gradually became delirious, and died; it was only afterwards discovered that a minute focus of infection in a finger had set up blood poisoning and finally meningitis. His loss produced a blank horror in me. It may be measured by my being revolted at what I felt to be callousness when a friend of his sympathetically remarked to me on what a "ghastly business" it was; the phrase seemed to me so utterly inadequate and superficial. The memoir I wrote of Ward was the hardest I ever had to write of any friend, and it has been my lot to have to write a great many.

After Brompton, at the beginning of 1903, I became resident medical officer to the North-Eastern (since named the Queen's) Hospital for Children in Bethnal Green, hoping that experience gained in that position would stand me in good stead when it came to applying for the more important corresponding post at U.C.H. My surgical experience came in useful, since the distance from the consulting staff in Harley Street, and the absence of telephones, meant that I was expected to perform most of the emergency operations. I was supposed to operate the primitive X-ray apparatus of those days, at which I was not a success. I also had special charge of the Eye Ward, under Mr. Sydney Stephenson, and of the Diphtheria Ward, which in those days was always full. Tracheotomy was frequent enough and the wounds sometimes slow in healing; to facilitate this, and diminish the child's distress on the tube being withdrawn, I invented a special apparatus that has proved useful, my sole contribution to surgery. Altogether I had great respect for surgery, and never shared the sense of superiority that so many physicians evinced in regard to their colleagues.

Indeed, the beginning of the troubles I shall presently have to relate happened in connection with my taking a surgical view of a case in opposition to the physician in charge of it. A child had been very ill for some days, and from the physical signs and blood examination I was convinced there was an abscess in the chest. The visiting physician, on the other hand, insisted it was a solid condition in the lung. On one Saturday, when he would not be seeing the child for two or three days, the empyemal abscess I had suspected burst into the lung and the child was spitting up pus. An immediate operation gave the only chance of saving its life, and it was my duty to perform it. The physician, having been proved palpably wrong in his diagnosis, could not say anything, but his attitude to me made it plain that I had got into his bad books. Since he was on the staff of the National Hospital, Queen's Square, this had important consequences in my life.

My appointment was for a year, but it came to an untimely end after six months. One Friday evening I heard that the young lady to whom I was for a time engaged—the seaside affair that didn't last—was being operated on for appendicitis. Although it meant a six hours' journey, I naturally wanted to be with her. There was a rule against a resident spending a night away from the hospital without permission from the committee, but in the emergency the only person I could get hold of was the senior surgeon. He said rather vaguely he thought it would be all right if I was away till the Monday morning, so the next day I departed, leaving the two other residents in charge. But I had made more serious enemies than I had known, and had now given them a handle. Chief among them was the matron, whose hitherto unchallenged authority I had on several occasions braved; in a non-teaching hospital the matron often attains through her continuity a position that enables her to disregard these passing resident doctors, an attitude I had somewhat resented on finding prescriptions and instructions changed at her orders. The long and short of it was that the committee called on me to resign for breaking the hospital rules, and remained adamant in their decision. The surgeon was reprimanded for giving me permission when he had no right to, and —not being a fighting man—was not in a mood to put up much of a defence for me.

Such episodes do not cause heart-searchings to somewhat foolish young men: they can so easily be imputed to the tyranny of one's elders. So I was readily comforted by Trotter's dry comment that "to a hospital committee it is the unessential that matters", nor did I for a moment perceive that my ambitious dreams had met with a final check. I knew of a physician to a great London hospital who had been dismissed when a house-physician for kissing a nurse, a much more heinous offence than mine, and yet had recovered his position—incidentally, perhaps through marrying the girl.

So with a comparatively light heart I set forth to make good and spent the next month or two working hard for the M.D. examination, one which in those days comprised both medicine and psychological medicine. I came out first in the examination, with a heavy gold medal then worth £20 and since much more. The following month I took my Membership of the Royal College of Physicians, only a fortnight after reaching the necessary age, and thus attained the rank of a consulting physician. This is customarily followed in six or eight years by the grant of the Fellowship, but forty years had to pass before I was considered respectable enough to attain it. Nor was I made a Fellow of University College, which was the custom with students who won the M.D. medal; the Dean of the hospital at the time, Dr. Risien Russell, was a stranger to the hospital and did not seem to know of the custom. That omission, however, was remedied fifty-five years later!

So I ended this period of my life with a combination of great success and minor frustrations in circumstances which made it easy to attribute the former to my own merits and the latter to the demerits of others. I was to learn that life is not to be divided off into compartments as simply as that, and that the matter of estimating merit and demerit is a far more delicate affair. Heaven knows there is enough injustice in the world, but part of the art of life consists in learning to accept that unalterable fact as part of the game instead of exploiting it to protect one's *amour propre*.

Chapter Six

Failure

A LITTLE chastened—but heartened by the recent examination results—I cheerfully embarked on the next step in the programme, that of spending two years as house-physician in the sacred precincts of the National Hospital before returning to U.C.H. to continue my expected career there. The omens could not have been more auspicious. Beevor and Horsley, old chiefs of mine, were on the staff and would be sure to speak for me. No better-qualified candidate could ever have applied for the post; not only did I possess the highest academic qualifications, even the most senior obtainable, but I had already had the unusual clinical experience of five resident posts and in addition had served for two years as clinical assistant to the National Hospital itself, thus evincing a special interest in neurology. In the courtesy interviews one had to have beforehand with all the members of the staff I was received with an almost embarrassing welcome. I do not think anyone could have felt surer of the success of any undertaking than I did of obtaining that appointment, on which I had so set my heart.

Judge, then, of the blow it was when on calling at the hospital to hear the result, a seeming formality, I was informed that the appointment had been given to someone else, someone who, I knew, possessed none of my qualifications. I remember staggering out into the sunshine in Queen's Square, feeling quite dazed, for in some dim way I perceived that my whole future was now at stake. This was confirmed shortly afterwards when I learned what had gone wrong. The neurologist I had offended at the Children's Hospital—whose nephew, incidentally, was given the post in question—had spoken with emphasis of how "difficult" I was to work with—a sinister phrase in any service —and in proof of it quoted the fact that the committee of the hospital had had to send me away as an impossible person. The other members of the selection board could not challenge such a strong indictment, so they could do nothing but pass me over. There was, no doubt, a modicum of truth in his account, but I know my own good-heartedness and loyalty well enough to describe his version of my undeniable deficiencies as exaggerated. However, I knew that from now on I should have a bad name and be a marked man, a *mauvais sujet*, among the powers-that-be, and so it proved. The consulting medical profession in London constituted then, and probably still does, a relatively small club.

All this was evidently the response of a spoilt child to an unexpected reverse. On two occasions in later life I endured far more poignant blows, but by then I had gone through a good deal of hardening, so that they did not take me so by surprise. Situations of this kind are common enough, so that a psychological comment seems to be in place, especially since the factors in the present case are fairly evident. The roots of my excessive reaction lay far back in infancy. The premature weaning and early ill-health had combined with internal factors to induce a deep feeling of insecurity and inferiority, against which the life force (for I must have had somewhere an unusual amount of vitality) had reacted by building up a defence of the opposite extreme, an unwarranted belief in the omnipotence of my wishes which lulled me with the fatal promise that I should get whatever I wanted—provided I wanted it hard enough. This had then been fostered by many circumstances, by my being the eldest and (for my mother) the favourite child, the only son, intellectually precocious and thus winning admiration—and, of late, especially by the three brilliant, but deceptive, years of success I have described above. Now, however, after having been nursed by Fortune into both cherishing and trusting in that belief, I was hurled with a terrific bump into the world of reality, where I had to learn that such beliefs were nothing but delusions, that however strongly one might wish for, deserve, and expect a particular issue there was not the slightest guarantee that it would therefore come about; the world was simply not like that.

My main response to the whole affair was not one of depression, or even of indignation, so much as of bewilderment. It never occurred to me to take the reverse as a final defeat of my hopes, but I was for the moment brought to a state of perplexity about what to do next. I called on two or three of the hospital staff, who told me what had happened. One of them recommended me to set up as a neurologist in Cardiff. It was very sensible advice, and had I taken it I had every prospect of a worthy and serene existence; certainly a less stormy one than mine has been. But—as I think fortunately—my daimon was not concerned only with the sensible things of life. London had from childhood meant for me more than a place; it was the prime place from which life could best be explored, and no provincial capital, not even that of my native land, could serve instead. I naturally turned also to Trotter, and his philosophy probably epitomised the situation in some pithy epigram which I have forgotten. At all events his belief in me sustained my own fortitude, and I resolved to persevere in the face of what would now be grim obstacles.

Plainly I could not go back to another junior resident post even if I could get one—the post at the National had really been over-junior for one of my standing, but I was set on the neurological experience and prospects it held out. Nor could I with any hope apply to be resident medical officer at U.C.H. when that post next fell vacant in a couple of years' time, since the indispensable condition was an impeccable reputation for getting on smoothly and tactfully with every type of person—matrons, porters, nurses, patients, hospital staff, and—last but not least—lay committees. So any chance of reaching a staff position at my beloved Alma Mater became improbably remote, a "weaning trauma" it took me a very long time to overcome. Many years later when Trotter was senior surgeon there, I remarked wistfully to him on how wonderful it must be to be connected with an institution of such pioneering traditions, and he ungallantly replied: "Well, you know, I can hardly share your romantic illusions; you see, I married the lady."

Since I was without means—resident appointments had meant keep with a small salary—the immediate question was how to secure a livelihood. With that object in view I took a quarter-time appointment, at I think £250 a year, in the Education Department of the London County Council, where I was put in charge of the mental defective schools. To consolidate my position there I entered on a course for the Diploma of

Public Health. I chose the Cambridge one, since it held the reputation for the highest standard in bacteriology, and that would give me the best opportunity of improving my knowledge in that important subject, one in which I was specially interested. I must have written good papers at the examination, for at the *viva voce* the examiner surprised me by asking, as his first question, how long I had been a medical officer of health. He had reason for curiosity, since I looked decidedly younger than I was, and I was young enough in all conscience. One had in the course of the training to act as assistant to a medical officer of health, and that work I did in a Jewish quarter of the East End of London. It gave me much insight into foreign customs and modes of life.

I then had a moment to take a breath and look around at the prospects. I took a room in Ampthill Square, Camden Town, and found I could manage on my income, with other odd earnings. The D.P.H. course occupied most of my time, but I also took on clinical assistantships at the Hospital for Sick Children, Great Ormond Street, under the most famous children's specialist of his time, Dr. (later Sir Frederic) Still; and at the East London Hospital for Children, Shadwell, under Dr. Morley Fletcher of St. Bartholomew's. Morley Fletcher and I would meet at Baker Street, travel by Underground to Aldgate, and then very cautiously ride in a tram to Shadwell. No physician in those days could risk his reputation by travelling in a public vehicle, but we were never detected. I held a similar position at Moorfields Eye Hospital, under Mr. Marcus Gunn. Here I became in time one of the chief ophthalmic assistants. I had chosen to work under Mr. Gunn because of his special interest in the important connection between ophthalmology and neurology; my all-round training, centring on neurology, was continuing.

It was at Moorfields Hospital that I met Mr. Nettleship, the distinguished ophthalmic surgeon, a man whose character I very much admired. When the time came for him to retire, instead of seeing nothing left in life but bridge and golf, he conceived of a plan whereby he could use the remainder of his life in serving science in a way that was hardly possible except to someone who commanded leisure. Among the remarkable diseases that exactly repeat themselves in different members of a family, a certain number affect the eye. It is of great practical, as well as theoretical, importance to discover by what laws these hereditary complaints or defects are transmitted; but accurate facts are difficult to ascertain in mankind. The material does not lend itself to experimental breeding, the life-span is long, and the records are imperfect. It was this latter task that Nettleship now embarked on, and he lived long enough to make a valuable contribution to knowledge. He was handicapped, however, by living at a distance from libraries—at Hindhead, which I can witness was then far less like Hampstead Heath than it has since become—and still more by his ignorance of foreign languages, except for some French. When he invited me to assist him, at an agreed payment, I boldly volunteered to translate from any European language the material he wanted: and, what is more, I did so, from Portuguese to Polish. The task was easier than it sounds, since the technical terms used were recurrent, and usually similar in different languages; again, all that was needed was an abstract of the relevant data, not an actual translation.

The problems of heredity have always fascinated me, and I must have been one of the first to follow the leap from the sombre Galton-Pearson period into the bright day of Mendelism, de Vries being absorbed *en route.*

In the next four years I must have seen over 100,000 sick children and so gained, if not an intensive, certainly an extensive, view of their special complaints. Dr. George Carpenter, one of the physicians of the North-Eastern Hospital, was just then starting the *British Journal of Children's Diseases*, and enlisted my services to devil for him. I had charge of all the abstracting and reviewing work, wrote many of the editorial articles, and made myself generally useful. Messrs. Adlard, the publishers, were good enough to initiate me into the mysteries of format, types, and so on, and I thus embarked on an editorial career that lasted, with one scientific journal or another, for some thirty-five years. I had also the opportunity to publish a number of papers on children's diseases from the ample clinical material at my disposal.

Through Dr. Carpenter I got some insight into the shoddier side of consulting practice. He was one of a small number of people who set up in the West End as consultants without being on the staff of a teaching hospital—a custom that has become far more frequent since—and so were looked down on by the more reputable class who had staff appointments. It became my lot to have to do with a good many of them, and it was by no means a pleasant experience—particularly as it looked as if I might have to join them. There were a few brilliant exceptions such as Vaughan Harley, but for the most part they were the failures in the upper ranks of the profession and in any event were deprived of the inestimable stimulation a teaching hospital affords in keeping abreast of the latest researches and knowledge. Nevertheless I have the impression that their standards of honesty towards their patients were higher than that of the post-war generation. A few had good private practices, but the others had to eke out a living by shamefacedly disappearing into the City every day to work in insurance offices or in less reputable occupations, such as treating the venereal diseases of stock-brokers. Dr. Carpenter was, among other things, the medical officer of health for a small town in Kent—work for which he had no qualification and which in fact was performed by his sanitary inspector. He was a man with no scientific method and little learning, but he had a quite remarkable flair for clinical diagnoses. When in his last illness he rose from the table exclaiming: "My God, I have a cerebral haemorrhage," the outcome soon proved the correctness of this far-from-easy diagnosis. Trotter's comment on it was: "How very like Carpenter to have died guessing right."

Besides the comprehensive D.P.H. course, and all the school and hospital work, I was engaged that year (1904) on an arduous piece of research which Sir William Gowers had suggested to me. Gowers was one of the greatest neurologists of his age and his text-book was the standard one in several countries. He had a peculiar personality and was reported to suffer from attacks of megalomania; a priceless saying attributed—*ben trovato*—to him in one of these was that every day he conceived an infinite number of original ideas, any one of which would make the reputation of an infinite number of neurologists. But his real interest appeared to be in Pitman's phonographic system, a knowledge of which, so he seemed to think, would be the greatest imaginable asset to the medical profession; to this end he founded, edited, and largely wrote a medical periodical in Pitman's shorthand. At one time he induced Lord Lister and a few other enthusiasts to petition the General Medical Council to include a knowledge of Pitman as a compulsory subject in the entrance examination to the medical profession, but needless to say the deputation met with no success. When I interviewed him on the occasion of the appointment at the National Hospital he somehow became aware of my acquaintance with the system, probably through seeing me read his periodical in the waiting-room, and at once adopted such an intelligent person as a protégé; of course, all our correspondence had to be conducted in shorthand.

The research he proposed I should carry out was to investigate a large number of cases of hemiplegia, determine the relative frequency of various features accompanying the stroke, and thus facilitate the very difficult diagnosis of whether it was due to bleeding or clotting in the brain; the results of the research, really a gigantic piece of what the Germans call *Hosenarbeit*, have been incorporated in medical text-books. I began by searching all the case-books of University College Hospital since its foundation in 1830; I am probably the only person to have done this, and I was sorry to hear recently that the Health Service has ordered them to be destroyed. It made me familiar, incidentally, with the endless changes in medical practice and custom that had taken place in that time, and particularly with the ways of once-famous members of the staff of my old hospital; to read the notes of many historic figures was in itself a matter of great interest.

Next I visited most of the borough infirmaries—as they were called in those days—around and about London to examine any cases of the kind immured in them. Then I had to go through the vast literature on the subject in English and French, and in doing so was spurred on to a methodological problem. Memories of my schoolboy mathematics were revived, and I perceived that most writers on medical topics had no idea of the theory of probability, still less how to handle it. For example, they did not seem to know just how many observations had to be made before one could say that A was commoner than B; if A happened 15 times and B 10 times out of 25 possibilities, many writers would quite happily assert that A happened much more often than B, quite regardless of the problem of chance with such a small series. I was equally shocked by other evidences of laxity in this matter of series. Writers making collections for statistical purposes would unwittingly count cases twice over when they had been recorded more than once from different points of view, they would be oblivious of selecting factors that vitiated the possibility of their series representing pure samples, and so on. In addition to such crude and obvious fallacies I detected a number of subtler ones, and so was led on to make a thorough study of statistics in medical work. This produced several by-products in the way of papers illustrating the use of mathematics in medicine, including accurate and convenient methods for enumerating different kinds of cells in the blood and cerebro-spinal fluid. But I regret to observe that pathologists are still given to recording their differential count in the misleading percentage fashion instead of in absolute numbers, apparently not realising that, for instance, eosinophilia may be present with 2 per cent when the total count of leucocytes is 25,000.

A smaller piece of research went on at the same time under Dr. Bradford, who was then also superintendent of the Brown Institute. It was a study of the "Nissl granules" in the nerve cells of the pons medulla in hydrophobia, and it meant studying material from the last cases of that painful disease to occur in England. Mr. Walter Long had first stamped out rabies in this country—taking advantage of our being an island—on one of those rare occasions of a politician deigning to act on scientific advice; it was a brilliant piece of work courageously carried out against ignorant opposition.

When I was a small boy I startled my mother by telling her I knew what quality I most longed to possess. Instead of the spiritual one she hoped to hear, I said, "Energy." Somewhat doubtfully she acquiesced: "Yes, that's a good thing too." Well, that was a childhood wish the fairies granted me in full measure. Nowadays I look back with awe at the amount of work, thinking and reading, I was able to get through in the year 1904, and to be honest with myself I cannot say that it differed in this respect from the years before or the many after.

At this period I embarked on an unusual and arduous tutorial career. It began with my getting connected with a dry old character, Mr. E. S. Weymouth, who ran an extensive business of coaching for medical examinations by correspondence in a "University Correspondence College" in Red Lion Square. In a short while I became the tutor in all sorts of subjects, from forensic medicine to obstetrics. One mapped out in detail a course of reading, stating even the pages to be read each week, and got the candidate to answer weekly examination papers, which were then corrected and returned to him with a set of model answers. It was quite a good system. Naturally the initial task of organising the numerous courses—I think I had some seven or eight—was an immense work, and they all had to be periodically re-written to be kept up to date. More work was entailed in helping candidates with M.D. theses, advising on the choice of subject, providing a bibliography of it and perhaps even abstracts of what had been written on it, and so on. But I rather specialised on the higher examinations; very few who were not my pupils can have passed the M.D. in psychological medicine, for instance, in the first ten years of its being instituted.

Finding me useful, Weymouth got me to work at his office two afternoons a week—at of course a suitable payment—where I advised him generally and helped particularly in answering inquiries. I became in time a complete Bradshaw to the complicated regulations and conditions of examinations, and of the numerous qualifying bodies in the United Kingdom—there were more than twenty of them. It was a highly special piece of knowledge which I do not think anyone could have possessed in that comprehensive form, and it entailed a prolific correspondence with the registrars of the various universities and other examining bodies. It proved to be very useful, however, since candidates, learning of our being so well-informed, were inclined to expect a similar efficiency in our teaching courses. I proved very successful at this work and for the next ten years I had the largest "coaching" practice in the country; some of it continued for still another ten years until my wife firmly put a stop to it.

THE PLAN having gone so badly astray, I was in no position to form a new one, and could only vaguely hope that if I could make sufficiently notable contributions I might become known as a neurologist and possibly acquire a position in some less important hospital. For the next few years I regarded myself as primarily a neurologist, but now I come to the interesting passage from neurology to psychopathology and psycho-analysis. In 1904 I certainly should have been very astonished to know that in another half a dozen years I should occupy a chair of psychiatry.

My psychiatric experience had begun in 1902 when my friend Ward was a resident at an asylum outside London. I would visit him every Sunday and try to learn something from the cases we would discuss together. After his death I kept up this practice for some years, knowing friends at various institutions. There was Bernard Hart at Long Grove, Epsom, Stoddart at the well-known Bethlehem Hospital ("Bedlam") in London, and Charles Bolton's brother who was pathologist at the Claybury Asylum in Essex. F. W. Mott, F.R.S., the real father of the Maudsley Clinic, used to visit Claybury and would take me along; I always remember his kindness to me, then and later. His interests were centred in neuropathology, and he had little psychological aptitude. Not that his attitude was a negative one in the latter respect; he wrote me a letter in June 1910, when I was in Canada, congratulating me on "spreading the knowledge of Freud's valuable work".

Psychiatry at that time was at its lowest ebb in England, and no studies or observations were carried out in any of the mental hospitals. I remember a satirical friend of mine, himself an amateur psychologist, asking me once what alienists discussed at their meetings: "I suppose they read papers on an improved variety of Chubb lock." When I was holding a resident appointment at University College Hospital, an asylum superintendent whom I had met telephoned saying he had a vacancy on his staff. Could I think of anyone who would be willing to fill it? He added: "I don't expect him to be interested in insanity, but he must be able to play cricket with the patients." I understand that the terms of such appointments are considerably more onerous nowadays.

The only psychiatrists I can recall in private practice were those who had retired from the position of superintendent at Bethlehem, successively Sir George Savage, T. H. Hyslop, and Sir Maurice Craig. When consulted, they would sign the necessary certificates and often consign patients to expensive private hospitals where they would periodically visit them. Stoddart here was an exception. When his turn came he became a teacher at St. Thomas's Hospital and a few years later I got him interested enough in psycho-analysis to take up the practice of it.

Much more important motives than these, however, were driving me in the direction of psychopathology in its narrower sense, and took me a year later into the study of psycho-analysis. In those days psychopathology, or what we now call medical psychology, was in an even more abysmal state of ignorance than the study of insanity. It was entirely the prerogative of organic neurologists, who were naturally supposed to know all about "nerves", the popular name for all psychoneuroses. How they coped with such patients was always a puzzle to me, but I can quote one example. One of the most famous neurologists of his time advised a patient, who suffered from a severe obsessional neurosis, to take a trip to the West Indies to obtain relief from his distressing thoughts. On his return in the same state as before, he was sent off to the East Indies, and when even that failed to cure him he was despatched on a trip round the world. It was at that point that the disappointed patient came under my care. The pathology of such symptoms—when they were not regarded as entirely "imaginary", i.e. really non-existent—was considered to be a mysterious disorder of the cerebral cortex, so, since it was known that the nervous system contained rather more phosphorus than other organs, the correct treatment was to administer phosphates.

With hysteria an exception was made. Centuries of experience had apparently shown that this disorder, being due to a wandering of the womb—hence the name—could be counteracted by a drug, valerian, the odour of which was specially obnoxious to the womb. This went on even after an enterprising chemist isolated the valerianic acid which, being odourless, should have lost its specific powers. Something in me rebelled against these materialistic views and inclined me strongly towards a psychological explanation. It was an inner flair, perhaps sympathy with suffering, but it was strongly supported by what I was learning from my reading.

For some reason that we do not yet understand, conversion hysteria was far commoner in those days than after the First World War. Paralyses and anaesthesia were to be seen in every hospital, and most infirmaries could produce patients with astasia-abusia who had been bedridden for perhaps twenty or thirty years. Hysterical convulsions were similarly frequent, and apart from those seen in hospital I often enough had to minister to girls in convulsions met with on a stroll through the town. Trotter one day, in unforgettable words, advised me to try to unravel the mystery of these convulsions: "One sees only the blood trickling under the door, but we know nothing of what tragedy is being enacted within."

In the previous couple of years I had, despite other occupations, been able to read through the immense French literature on hypnotism, hysteria, and double personality. The names of the writers became such household words that even now many come to my mind: Azam, Barety, Beaunis, Bertrand (who in 1823 discovered the psychological nature of hypnotism), Binet, Briquet, Bourn, Deleuze, Despine, Durand de Gros, the Abbé Faria, Liébault, Liégeois, Mesmer, Marquis de Puységur, Noizet, etc. Then there were the early English surgical hypnotists, Braid (who coined the word hypnotism in 1843), Esdaile, and the unfortunate Professor of Medicine, Elliotson, on whose account the Council of University College passed the following rule in 1837: "That the Hospital Committee be instructed to take such steps as they shall deem most advisable to prevent the practice of mesmerism or animal magnetism in future within the Hospital." I wonder if this has ever been rescinded. Before long I was to get to know personally some of those leaders: Bechterew, Bernheim, Milne Bramwell (who had visited Bernheim in Nancy in the same summer of 1889 as Freud had), Fovel, Schrenck-Notzing, etc. There were also a few American records of multiple personality by William James and Morton Prince.

My interest in such problems was, however, by no means a passive one, as I shall presently relate.

Chapter Seven

Harley Street

TOWARDS the end of that year Trotter made the startling suggestion that we should "set up" together in Harley Street and join those residents, at that time fewer than two hundred in number, whose brass plates in that street announced their claim to be consultant physicians or surgeons. It was quite in place for him to do so—he was seven years older, though he had qualified medically only four years earlier, than I—but it seemed very presumptuous for a youth of twenty-five and almost brazen for someone with such bleak prospects as mine were; there was at that time only one physician in the street who was not on a hospital staff. However, sometimes the bolder course is the wiser one, and indeed there was no more feasible alternative. So early in 1905 my father bought the lease of 13 Harley Street from the widow of Sir William MacCormac (Surgeon to the King) who had recently died, and there we lived for a little over three eventful years.

Trotter's prospects of a successful surgical career were already excellent, although a more showy colleague, Rupert Bucknall, had forestalled him by being made assistant surgeon to University College Hospital in 1901. He deserves a word to himself. He had achieved fame among us by winning the Gold Medal at the M.D. and coming first in a billiards championship the same evening as the examination. He was assistant at the hospital to Sir Victor Horsley, so in 1902, when I was their house-surgeon, I saw much of him and was the first to recognise that the poor fellow showed the beginnings of general paralysis of the insane. Three years later this became manifest when he declared that he was the German Kaiser, and I remember Trotter remarking that if he ever fell a victim to the same disease he would not develop such a banal delusion but would imagine that he was Nietzsche. In the following year, 1906, Trotter replaced him on the permanent staff of University

College Hospital. A year before that, he had been appointed to the surgical staff of the East London Hospital for Children, Shadwell, so that by then he had ample clinical and teaching opportunities at his disposal.

Trotter and I had for the past year or more been in the habit of dining (always a steak at Frascati's) and spending the evening together several times a week—chiefly walking in Hyde Park and talking hard, and it was an inestimable privilege to have his constant companionship. We shared a large study together—our consulting-rooms were not much needed—and there we had constructed, so vast were our literary projects, what has been described as the largest desk in Europe, which I still use.* His irreverent brother tried to get us to decorate a frieze around the room with various blasphemous subjects, such as the Holy Ghost escaping through the window on Joseph's return home, and the like. There we did our work, in the intervals of making plans for the world. We were both devoted to poetry and read much to each other, but mostly we talked and talked and talked.

Trotter was endowed with what nowadays would prosaically be termed a strong Saviour complex: that is, he felt towards the world very much as Jesus did towards Jerusalem. He yearned to do great things, and felt he was destined to redeem mankind from at least some of its follies and stupidities. His rich imagination evolved the most poetical phantasies, in which the theme of self-sacrifice always played a part. In later years this love for mankind changed to a considerable scepticism about the species, his tenderness being renewed only for the individuals he had the opportunity of helping personally.

When I think of this later attitude I am amazed to remember his old flaming passion to arouse mankind from its slumbers, to communicate something of his intense desire for a richer life. In a letter of his, dated 1909, I find the following passage: "I don't find in the attitude of the world contentment tho' there is a temptation to call it that, or resignation tho' that seemed nearer. There is of course no word because there is no word to define the mental attitude of the foetus in utero, which is precisely what we want to describe—safely inside the abdomen, safely inside the uterus, safely inside the amnion, its little eyes tight shut, its little lungs nicely packed away and preserved

* Now at the London Clinic of Psycho-Analysis.

from the horrid tides of life of that dear ductus arteriosus, drawing its existence through an absceme string *secondhand*—secondhand oxygen much of it—Oh, for a breath of air, or that the cord would get round its neck. Rage overcomes me.... The fancy may strike you and give you something to play with for a minute or two. The ductus arteriosus is philanthropy, music, art, dress, philosophy, what they call service, patriotism, afternoon tea, all the fiddling, ogling sentimental womanly woman and manly man bunkum—in fact the whole repertoire of Punch and Judyism with which we manage to short-circuit the real thing. . . . If I could mix the metaphor worse I would do it—to such a pitch have I worked myself up. What must Nietzsche have felt with his dazzling vision of the Will to Power and the Will to Death—I wonder that he managed not to go off with an actual physical detonation."

What we profoundly agreed about was that the organising of life in a community would never be satisfactory until it was based on a full knowledge of the biological, including psychological, motivation of man; and in this conviction we have neither of us ever wavered. But impatient youth always grossly underestimates the complexity of any social problem. I have never shared Trotter's later pessimism, but I have learned that to build up an adequate knowledge of psychology, for example, quite apart from making a sensible use of it on a social scale, will be a matter of generations or centuries rather than the decades allotted to a isngle life. Trotter once grandiloquently assigned to me the task of "putting psychology on a sound basis in England". Well, I have laboured faithfully for forty years, and what is the pitiful outcome? In a lethal war, in which psychological factors played a central part, the only "psychologists" engaged by our government to advise them were advertising agents, while I accepted the post of salvage officer to my village!

Our campaign was to begin with a book containing nothing less than a detailed, and no doubt scathing, indictment of the maladies of civilisation, but ending with a signal that should show the way in which the most promising remedies were to be found. I still retain some moving passages in Trotter's most inspired style of this expression of youthful optimism. The final sentence of such books is often written early: I remember it ran: "False hopes may be cheating us; the courage that used to resist illusion may be breaking; but surely in the long-watched east the darkness is no longer impenetrably black."

Some ten years later, when Trotter had moved into the serene life of a great surgeon and teacher, I made an allusion to our book. He sternly denied any memory of such a book, and his tone of voice made it plain that he would discountenance any further reference to our youthful ebulliences.

In a letter, in 1907, he wrote: "Those 'names in our ears of all the lost adventurers our peers' are never quite absent from my mind, and I think they still go on teaching that we must, *must* have certainty. 'Such a one was strong and such was bold and such was fortunate', but was there one who was inexhaustibly patient? Well, I think there are two. The immensity of the task, the appalling immensity of it leaves me quite cool and collected; my cowardice, which inflicts upon me every day fifty unnecessary pangs, I can bear with philosophically, but the thing which really shakes me, which leaves me sweating and atremble is the fear that I may be becoming impatient. As you know I have had a bad attack of this lately, but have come out of it I hope tougher and cooler but—and I am almost sure of this—in no way weakened or less determined that what I want done must somehow and somewhen get itself finally and irrevocably done."

As he said, we were only two, but he pictured there being five leaders; perhaps it was from this number that I, years later, made the committee of five as Freud's bodyguard. In his more megalomanic moments the five great cities of the world would be renamed after them, much as Petrograd became changed to Leningrad. And by free association it occurs to me that there must have been something in common between our attitude to society and Karl Marx's, without of course his hate and obscurity. I am relieved to think that our illusions did not survive as his did, and so have not inflicted on the world any of his harm.

Naturally, the world-old problem of "good" and "evil" lay athwart our path. Years before we had both independently been struck by Huxley's essay on *The Evolution of Ethics*, in which he bravely acknowledged his defeat when faced with the paradox of human and cosmic ethics. It was Karl Pearson who had found the way round the paradox by pointing out the racial survival value of altruism, and I think this must have been the source of Trotter's conception of the "herd instinct", for which his name is now famous. He expressed his views in two essays published in the *Sociological Review* (1908–9), which he later, in 1916, expanded into his well-known book *Instincts of the Herd in Peace and War*. He regarded these social instincts as biologically fundamental, though in later years he came to agree with Freud's derivation of them from the still more deeply based sexual instincts. When Bertrand Russell announced in 1914 that he proposed to dispense with his social instincts for the duration of the war, Trotter sardonically commented: "He might as well talk of dispensing with the nitrogen in his bones." His dream was that some day these powerful instincts would get harnessed to the aim of rational thinking.

Trotter's pessimistic views about mankind, and the desperate need he saw to lift it out of its muddle, were so strong that he naturally, like Nietzsche, toyed with the idea of breeding a better race, though not the same kind of superman, and this tallied with my own interest in problems of heredity. The natural selection that now goes on is of doubtful value, being chiefly against infectious diseases that could be dealt with otherwise. We have in the past ten thousand years acquired a slight degree of immunity against tuberculosis as compared with South Sea Islanders, but at what a frightful and literally immeasurable cost! How many thousand times over have we lost a John Keats in this way, not to speak of the holocaust of suffering? How much more sensible to concentrate on exterminating tubercle bacilli. But to know what qualities to breed for is another matter, the unsolved question for all eugenists. Trotter speculated with the thought of "sensitiveness to reason", a very interesting idea. He said one day, only half seriously but wistfully, that in the future people would be so sensitive ("conditioned" would be the word used nowadays) that they would develop a nervous breakdown if they heard such an irrational word as "sunset".

Meanwhile, however, more mundane problems were pressing on the new *ménage*. Although my father was good enough to forgo any rent for the house, still there were considerable ground rents, rates and taxes, and the general upkeep of an establishment in Harley Street. Trotter, who had a modest fixed income from Sir Victor Horsley, whose private assistant he was for some years, was expected to pay a certain sum towards it, but he was also supporting an out-of-work brother and in any case always had a rather lordly attitude towards mere money, as a nuisance to which other people should attend without troubling him too much. The main responsibility thus fell on me, or rather on my poor sister, Elizabeth, who had nobly undertaken to keep house for us. I have known several women break down or at least need periodical recuperation, from the strain of running a house in Harley Street, and for an inexperienced girl of twenty-four to take on such a task on behalf of two impecunious young men needed great courage and a cool head. Both these qualities, however, my sister possessed in a very high degree, and she succeeded admirably in the face of great difficulties. How she did so I shall never understand, nor how she kept our creditors at bay. With her quiet charm, and her willingness to assume all responsibility unaided, the house ran on the smoothest wheels so far as we were concerned. Trotter and she must have made a quiet note of each other's attributes, for they seldom exchanged much conversation; so it was not altogether surprising when, two years after the establishment was broken up, he took the first opportunity, on her return from Canada, to marry her.

Her firm morale, perhaps her most striking characteristic, was very evident at a time when Trotter performed an operation on her thyroid. Mine was less so, and when I made a startled remark when some instrument fell down I was reproved: "No one assisting at an operation should strike the note of a defeatist general."

My younger sister Sybil also lived with us part of the time, and then went to America to pursue studies there.

It must have been this move to Harley Street that broke up my engagement with Maude Hill (one of the well-known Birmingham Hill family). Years older than myself, she was naturally eager to get married as soon as possible, and kept pressing me to settle in some country practice. Apart from my being unfitted for such work, I could not surrender my still ambitious hopes of a higher career, and—even more—of making some original contributions to medical science. Her unsuitability for the position of a consultant's wife became evident when I discovered she had surreptitiously visited my old chief Dr. Bradford and begged him to procure a hospital post for me.

I had hurriedly to apologise to him for this unwelcome petticoat influence. Soon after that we parted, but thirty years later she called on me and I was glad to hear she had made a happy and successful marriage.

It was useless to expect much consulting practice at my age, though in fact there was more of it than I had thought likely; Dr. Bradford told me at that time he didn't know of any London physician who earned more than his tobacco before he was forty. Still, the novelist's picture of the young physician having nothing to do but gnaw his nails behind closed doors is extremely remote from the truth. If he has some private income he is fully engaged in conducting original research and in working at a hospital or perhaps at several; if not, he has to take up a deal of his time, as I had to, in earning a livelihood by otherwise unprofitable activities. I have seen the character of too many irresponsible youths deteriorate under the influence of an inherited fortune ever to think it particularly desirable, but a couple of hundred a year in one's own right often makes the difference between freedom and slavery at a time of life when the most should be being made of one's talents. I have been happy to be able to provide for my children this modicum which I lacked in my own youth.

My first need was to habilitate myself, despite the handicap of my youthfulness, in justification of my new pretensions; and I shall never forget the drudgery and humiliations that the endeavour to do so entailed. There was at the moment a vacancy on the staff of a teaching hospital, Charing Cross, and I ventured to apply for it; the committee appointed Dr. David Forsyth, an able man and a model of respectability, who was thus avenged for having come second to me at the M.D. examination. Undaunted, I applied for a similar position at the West End Hospital for Nervous Diseases, but unfortunately another candidate was Dr. (later Sir James) Purves Stewart, a very senior neurologist of high standing; he partly compensated for defeating me, for he enabled me to earn some guineas by attending to his private practice during his summer holidays. He did some good work by injecting nerves to control that terrible disease trigeminal neuralgia, of which I had seen enough with Horsley; it attacked me when I reached the age of seventy-six, but fortunately not severely.

And so it went on, until I found myself reduced to applying, but still in vain, for admission to the staff of various second- or third-rate hospitals for children or for nervous diseases. A vicious spiral was at work. Every failure was registered and added to the previous ones. Every application refused meant that I became more and more widely known as a person who was in some way undesirable, and thus to be avoided. This could be felt in the increasing coldness with which I was received as time went on. The technique of application in those days was this. It was not merely a matter of obtaining testimonials, preferably fresh ones, to append to one's statement of special qualifications for the post, and having them printed and circulated. To begin with, one called on one's supporters, such as former chiefs, and asked them whom they knew personally at the hospital where the vacancy was so that they could write to him, or interview him, on one's behalf. Then one made a personal call on every member of the staff, of whom there might be twenty or thirty, from the senior physician to the dentist. How familiar I became with the waiting-rooms of Harley Street and its purlieus, especially the latter, from the grandest to the dingiest! And what a closed corporation, like an expensive club, the consulting world of those days was, where everyone gossiped with the other and looked askance at anyone who was not quite the thing! And many of them were intellectually very inferior people, a fact that did nothing to mollify the rage in my heart.

At last some minor successes appeared. I was accepted on the staff of the Faringdon Dispensary, one of those curious City institutions that had survived in seclusion the original need for them. It still catered, nevertheless, for the class of people intermediate between hospital and private practice. It provided me, not only with further experience, but also with cases of special psychological interest that I could investigate at more leisure at home.

At the end of that year I was also appointed assistant physician to the Dreadnought Seamen's Hospital at Greenwich, which opened a new field—that of tropical diseases. Sir Patrick Manson, the doyen in that field, had objected when I applied that I was too young, but he gave me a friendly smile when I promised to remedy the defect in time. The hospital had recently established a post-graduate school, called the

London School of Clinical Medicine, in which I was given the position of Lecturer in Neurology. Two or three journeys a week to Greenwich meant adding to my labours, but my energy has never been easily exhausted. Backed by this position, I obtained another a year or two later as pathologist and medical registrar to the West End Hospital for Nervous Diseases, where I might then reasonably hope to be promoted to the permanent staff. It would be a second-rate position compared with what I had expected to achieve, but I might perhaps hope to compensate for this by the good work I was determined to do. At all events, it was the only remaining chance of becoming a consulting neurologist in London, and fate willed it that I was to lose even that.

I had already completed and published in *Brain* the task Sir William Gowers had set me on "The Onset of Hemiplegia", the conclusions of which it was gratifying to see incorporated in medical text-books. Dr. Henry Head took his editorial work very conscientiously and several times got me round to his house to improve my composition. In these ten years I made a number of neurological contributions, clinical and pathological, a few of which—e.g. the isolating of tactile aphasia—were perhaps of more than temporary value, and I was even beginning to acquire a reputation as a budding neurologist. I had also written for foreign periodicals, and I can recall being very pleased on getting a request for a reprint from the distinguished Pick, Professor of Psychiatry in Prague. Trotter's comment was: "Your idea of bliss is for the Almighty to despatch the Archangel Gabriel for one of your reprints."

In the meantime Trotter had himself embarked on a more concentrated piece of research. Henry Head, one of the most famous neurologists of his time, had had the enterprise to sever a small nerve in his arm so as to study the recuperative processes. On this he had built a far-reaching theory: namely, that there were two fundamental processes in the sensorial world, which he entitled the "epicritic" and "protopathic" respectively. He believed that the former dominated and regulated the latter, and much later on even attempted on this basis to give a physiological explanation to Freud's theory of repression. I do not know what aroused Trotter's scepticism in the matter, but he decided to make an extensive examination of the problems.

Knowing how completely occupied I was, he enlisted the co-operation of Hugh Morriston Davies. Davies, a young surgeon who soon after was appointed to the staff of University College Hospital, was one of the pioneers of thoracic surgery, but a few years later a disabling condition, contracted in his work, compelled him to exchange the surgical for the medical aspects. Trotter severed six, or perhaps seven, nerves in Davies's arms, and they made the most minute investigation of the healing processes. In this Trotter certainly could not complain of lacking in patience; I recall the occasion when they tore up the results of half a million tests because of a possible flaw. The upshot was that they showed conclusively that Head's theory had been based on a fundamental fallacy in his isolated experiment.

I was at the time also engaged on some research in the sensory system, which will be presently described—the most original I ever did outside the field of psycho-analysis—and Trotter predicted we should both some day be given the F.R.S. for what we were doing. His work in the psychophysiological field met with its due reward, but my more purely psychological work, in spite of two applications by kind supporters, will for long appear too remote for the more orthodox circles of science.

I had already acted for some time as clinical assistant to Dr. Harry Campbell, who comes into this story at more than one point. We got on to visiting terms, and he used to amuse Trotter and myself with the earnestness of his various faddy beliefs. Horsley used to refer to him as "that scoundrel Harry Campbell", which Trotter told him was an outrageous way to refer to a perfectly respectable citizen. We certainly never saw any sign that could warrant such a description, but Campbell did prove himself to be a weak man.

I had also to address myself to the task of earning a livelihood, and my friends used to be amused, not at my success in this respect, for I only just managed to pay my way, but at the multiplicity of the devices I contrived for the purpose. There was, of course, as a basis, the salary for my school work. A little money came from fees for administering anaesthetics when friends who had entered general practice ventured to perform some minor operation. It was work I had been fond of, and I had had the experience in hospital of administering over a thousand.

Then I somehow became for some years the invigilator at all the medical examinations of the university, and a hood and gown could be hired at less than the guinea a session which was the regular fee. It was amusing to discuss with the examiners the ambiguities in their questions and then to clarify them to the toiling candidates. I also made a number of interesting observations on the frequency of the various gestures, mannerisms, and tics which these unhappy creatures unconsciously used for relieving their state of mental tension.

The next job came through Harry Campbell. He was the editor of the *Medical Press Circular*, and I was increasing my experience by devilling for him, naturally unpaid, in this capacity. I had by then joined various societies, the Neurological, Pathological, Clinical, Ophthalmological, etc.—this being before the time when they were brought together under the mantle of the Royal Society of Medicine—and Campbell invited me to report their proceedings for his journal, at the fee of a guinea an evening. The present excellent system, in which the various speakers write down subsequently in their best English what they had intended to say, and post it on to the editors, did not then obtain. The accredited reporters of the three medical periodicals sat below the president, with a good view of the audience and speakers, and decided themselves which remarks were worthy of being preserved in print. My two colleagues, much senior to me, were *blasé* after years of this work, and would often lazily allow their zealous junior to make full shorthand notes, out of which they would make suitable abstracts. Now it commonly happened that a speaker would be concerned about how he would be reported, and therefore would anxiously explain to us after the meeting what he had really meant and why it was important. This was one of the ways in which I got to know who was who in the consulting world of that period. After a couple of years there could have been hardly a consultant in London I did not know by sight, and not many with whom I did not have some acquaintance.

The most tedious way of earning money was by giving evening lectures for the London County Council. People of all ages attended them and, I suppose, it was good practice in keeping contact with a varying audience. The subjects were mostly hygiene and first aid. There were also special lectures for the police in the latter subject, with drill in ambulance work; I was struck by their greater nervousness, particularly when it came to the examinations which it was also part of my duties to carry out. These evening classes were mostly held in quite remote suburbs, such as Lewisham, Tottenham, Ealing, and so on, which in horse-omnibus days took a considerable time to reach. My school work was similarly widely distributed, as were of course the infirmaries where I was carrying out my private researches. Between one thing and another, I acquired a knowledge of the topography of London that was almost as extensive and peculiar as Sam Weller's.

The most remunerative activity was coaching. I now got Weymouth to extend his business into the field of personal coaching, and this turned out a success for all concerned. Classes were formed wherever possible, being more remunerative to us and cheaper for the candidates than individual tuition. The greater part of this work came to me, and for some years I must have had easily the most extensive coaching practice in London. R.A.M.C. Captains, for instance, had to pass an examination before being granted their Majority, and there was usually a group of them waiting for me in Harley Street. In this connection I recall a remark of Trotter's which will illustrate at the same time his capacity for paying fulsome compliments and his propensity for Biblical quotations. He had passed a group of the officers on their way out, and on entering my room murmured: "The officers answered, 'Never man spake like this man.' "

I made a number of friends among these candidates. The closest of them was M. D. Eder, although he was one of the very few I was unable to get through his examination. He had plenty of knowledge, and wrote excellent papers, but some vein of defiance or obstinacy always possessed him at the oral examinations, with disastrous results; a degree, therefore, remained permanently beyond his reach. He ran a queer little practice in Soho among foreign waiters and to the undiscerning might have been taken for one of the down-and-outs of the profession, but very little acquaintance with him was needed to discover that he was a man of exceptional parts. His merits may not, it is true, have been the professionally conventional and generally approved ones, but he had a heart of gold and a serious concern for the future of socialism, so that I was doubly drawn to him. I frequented his home, during the time of both his first wife and his second, and was always likely to meet there some interesting personality or oddity. I shall say something about them in a later chapter.

It was Eder who introduced me to the Fabian Society. Although I never joined it, I attended their lectures and some discussions for many years, and so became familiar with the leading figures there—Bernard Shaw, H. G. Wells, Sidney Olivier, Sidney Webb, etc. To some extent it replaced my earlier attendance at the Sociological Society, where one came across such men as Frederic Harrison, the successor of Comte, and Lord Avebury, the creator of "St. Lubbock's Bank Holiday" and one of the founders of British archaeology. From Cardiff days onwards I had been familiar with the doctrines of the better-known "revolutionaries" of all kinds. It is a field where every actively-minded young man seeks for inspiration and direction. But, like all true physicians, I have a deep aversion to anything at all resembling quackery, and prefer the certainties of knowledge to the certitudes of enthusiasm. Envy of the more fortunate was never in my nature, but hatred of oppression, impatience with conservatism, and a wish for a happier society are stimuli that are bound to affect any sensitive person. They move one to endeavour, but then comes the crucial question of how most profitably to bend one's efforts. One thing became plain to me: that the complex interrelationships of human society were such that no political or social revolution ever brought about the results expected by the agents of it; the results might be better or worse, but they were always different. Another thing was also evident enough: that the more intensely fanatical the reformer the more likely was he to concentrate on one remedy, or nostrum, and on one facet of what was usually a complex situation. Short views and quick results made no appeal to me; it was sure results, and therefore long views, that I needed. And I have never found among revolutionaries—in spite of the incredible labour that many of them, notably Michelet and Marx, were prepared to devote—the preliminary scepticism and open-mindedness necessary for any scientific investigation of their problems. Ardour and science can very well be combined, as I know from personal experience, but it is the latter that is the most trustworthy guide: the former is quite capable of degenerating into mere emotional relief. I yield to no one in the passionate desire for a happier world, but I see no prospect of our reaching it except on the basis of greater advance in biology, anthropology, sociology, and above all psychology. I have devoted my life to the last of these, and among the driving motives in so doing the meliorist ones were among the chief.

This thesis may be illustrated by an example. It was all very well for Marx to announce as a great discovery that most of human misery was due to man's unkindness to man, and that the victims of ill-treatment tended to rebel against it when they could. His personal experience, or even his own treatment of Engels, could have taught him that the formation of groups was far from being indispensable for this state of affairs. To remedy it by forcibly forbidding the existence of groups, e.g. by abolishing class and national distinctions (if this were possible!), argues a fanatical optimism. A schoolmaster can prevent any given variety of bullying, but that does not alter the nature of boys or remove the endless possibilities they have of expressing it. One would like to know far more about the cruel, aggressive, exploiting tendencies in man, their nature, their origin, the agencies stimulating them, the relation between them and other sources of human misery, and so on, before one could build an Utopia on the basis of abolishing them. By all means restrain cruelty and oppression as far as possible, but a true revolutionary wishing to bring about a radical change in human society should be more ambitious than that.

It was through Eder that I came to know one of the most remarkable personalities one could meet: a young Dutch-Jewish lady, whom I propose to call by her first name, Loe. We became acquainted after she brought a protégée of hers to consult me, on Eder's recommendation. For seven years our lives were closely linked and my story can only be enriched by a description of her extraordinary qualities and even more extraordinary doings. Her peculiar kind of psychoneurotic constitution manifested itself mainly by developing various character traits in a much higher, and also finer, degree than is to be met with among the so-called normal. Some of them were distressing, such as an exquisite sensibility to suffering, but most were ennobling, such as an indomitable courage, an invincible will, and a devotion to all that is fine and good in life. Perhaps her most prominent character trait was an extraordinary passion for complete thoroughness in everything she undertook from the smallest to the biggest, a trait which did not make life easy for those near her.

She had a great fondness for London, and having some independent means decided to make her home there. She had not been happy with her family, which was not surprising with her peculiarly defiant character. I remember an early photograph illustrating this where she stands with her foot on a hat-box, the occasion of a successful legal action which as a young girl she had brought against the milliner. I got into the habit of sharing her flat; among those we entertained there comes to my mind a deputation from the Russian Duma, then visiting London, who made a disappointingly unrevolutionary impression. But neither of us had any thought of marriage. Loe suffered from renal calculi, and her kidneys had already been operated on more than once. Trotter gave her ten years to live at the outside, but she was present at his funeral, thirty-three years after. For the pain she took morphia twice a day and this developed into a heavy drug addiction. In those days the sale of such drugs to the public was quite unrestricted.

She took my name, and we would frequently visit our respective families as a married pair. There were also occasional trips abroad together. Those were the days when such abominations as passports, permits, identity cards, ration books, and police inspection of hotel registers had not yet been invented, the individual's relationship to the government being confined to paying his income-tax.

My school French I had kept up by reading extensively, in both medical and other literature. I had acquired a working knowledge of Italian grammar in early boyhood, as was mentioned earlier. These, together with Latin, were adequate for the Romance languages, at least for the present purpose. I was learning some Dutch from Loe and from visits to her family in Holland, where I spent a number of short holidays. German was the glaring hiatus. Before I was twenty-five I knew hardly a word of it, sharing the common English prejudice against its supposed ugliness. However, it was high time to remedy the lack, and Trotter was in a like case; so we engaged a tutor to come two or three times a week to get us forward. He was a typical Berliner, and my Viennese friends used later to rally me on my Prussian accent, but when I met him again by chance in the First World War he replied to my question of how he escaped internment by stating firmly that he was Swiss. I let it go at that, and indeed he had, I think, got so far as marrying a Swiss wife. But he was a good fellow.

Neither Trotter nor I were specially apt pupils, but perhaps I showed the more perseverance. Trotter learned to read scientific periodicals in German, as in French, but not to speak either language. His insularity went with an intensive study of the English background, whereas I was always more internationally minded. I can recall only three occasions when he went abroad, each time under strong persuasion. On the first he accompanied Barker, his chief, to a surgical congress in Berlin, and I reproduce here a characteristic letter from that city of ill omen.

(*April* 7, 1907)

"This is merely to convey to you my address . . . but I could not let so characteristic a product of this great country leave me without a word of comment. This sheet of paper represents Berlin with admirable exactitude—it is the expression of the determination that being successful it is now necessary to be beautiful. This is what the Germans have done and God forgive them; they are tackling the problem of how to be beautiful in their . . . serious way as a matter no doubt in some respects *schwer* but in essence simple. It has been revealed to them that decoration is beauty, hence this placard which is called note paper and this cake shop which is called a city. This is but one of the less amusing aspects under which this hobbledehoy Empire has already presented itself to my eyes, so that you will perhaps understand that in spite of the physical terrors of 13 hours in a German train and the amusing sense of personal inadequacy my clumsiness with the language produces, I have spent my time so far in a rapture of ironic contemplation.

"The crossing was perfect. . . . We stayed on deck all night . . . and at 4.30 with the moon sliding down in the West and the lights of a fishing fleet under her, Europe revealed herself coming to meet me hanging beneath a dawn of dusky red. It was, I think I may say, *reizend.*

"*Also sprach Zarathustra*—This country is no longer virgin but is she pregnant? The tempting answer is an ironic affirmative. I don't know whether this cryptic utterance has any meaning for you. It compasses for me my impressions but probably my sense of its significance is illusory."

Three months later I sent him off, for the good of his soul, on a short trip to Switzerland, and I quote some passages from letters written at Ouchy:

"It is curious how difficult it is even when one is quite idle to find time to write letters. But I have just managed with great skill to miss the boat to Geneva so I am going to take advantage of the $1\frac{1}{2}$ hr. thus saved.

"I wish I could describe the journey down the lake last night between 7 and 8. It was one of those rare and absolutely flawless enchantments the sunset works for the delectation of the initiated. It was particularly interesting as it broke in upon me when I was in a mood of disgust at this Pleasure Province and its beauty. I was badly wanting something real—but I mustn't start guide-booking.

"The people here seem to me to be quite indistinguishable from the rest of their funny species. I discovered yesterday rather to my disappointment that I have become too charitable for satirical description of them, so that any chance of being able to write interesting letters has gone from me."

"The wandering Scholar to his Sage at home sends greeting (health and knowledge, fame with peace)—I rather fancy I have quoted that in a letter to you before—anyhow it is appropriate enough to be repeated."

The work for Nettleship meant long hours in the British Museum or the Royal College of Surgeons library, where already I was spending for my own researches every hour I could snatch. I was very interested in the art of accurate bibliographical work, and used to conceive of vast schemes whereby scientific literature could be codified and abstracted. This was to be done, as it were, on a tri-circular plan: there were to be fairly extensive abstracts for the use of those working in the same field, shorter ones for those working in cognate fields, and very succinct ones for those working in distant ones. Perhaps an American millionaire will some day put it into action; no government would be intelligent enough to.

Scientific knowledge concerning heredity is of the utmost importance for the founding of any stable social organisation. It is a necessary presupposition for an adequate discussion of any social problem whatever. And yet it is extremely hard to come by—for many other reasons than the two I mentioned above. In the absence of exact knowledge we have more advocates than workers (who themselves are often biased too): those who, from motives of justice, sympathy, and the like, lay stress on the environmental factors, and those who, like so many eugenists, wish to simplify problems by making out the hereditary factors to be all-determining ones. It was only through the rediscovery of Mendel's work—which took place just before the time I am writing of, and by which I was at once greatly excited—that one began to have some idea concerning what exactly was inherited, some idea of the units of inheritance. And even yet, in spite of Spearman's work, I am very dubious whether we know much about the mental units, which is the field in which I have been principally interested.

There are few things I would rather discover more about than the nature of the inherited elements of the mind, and I cherish hopes that further work in the psycho-analytic investigation of the unconscious mind may bring us nearer this desired goal; it assuredly gets closer to the root impulses of the mind than any other work does. At that time hopes were principally built on intensive mathematical study of various data, and obviously mathematical instruments will always be essential for such studies, once we have the data clarified, and that is the point I am making. Karl Pearson, then Professor of Mathematics at University College, London, a truly great man for whom both Trotter and I had the utmost respect because of the work he had done in clarifying the philosophic basis of science, was the leading authority on such studies, and I conceived the plan of working under him to see if I could acquire the necessary knowledge of higher mathematics to apply his special and highly technical methods to the investigation of mental heredity. I had, it is true, begun to follow Nettleship by collecting similar material in the neurological field—work that had to be abandoned later—but my real interest was in the sociological, and therefore psychological, field. I went to see Karl Pearson, and put my ideas before him. He assured me, however, that his mathematical methods were so devised as to swamp all fallacies of observation, and even to make superfluous any more exact knowledge about the inherited elements (it is well known that

Mendelism took him by surprise and vitiated much of his work). He even shocked me by maintaining that the current social standards of worldly success were valid measurements of permanent human values, and would not listen when I questioned whether the qualities making for such success in a mercantile age were necessarily the same as those operative in a different order of civilisation, e.g. a priestly or military one. In short, neither convinced the other, and I withdrew politely. When I told Trotter of the interview he dryly remarked that it was probably the only one Pearson had ever had with a medical man where the greater scepticism lay with the latter.

I had thought in my student and hospital days that I knew what hard work meant, and what it was to be fully occupied, but in the Harley Street days I was to learn that I had only been a novice. Were anyone to take the trouble of setting forth all the activities I have mentioned above he might well ask how a man could manage to get through them in a day of only twenty-four hours. And I have hardly alluded to the scientific papers I contributed in those few years, of which there was a considerable number. Yet there seemed to be occasionally times for relaxation. We even attended the theatre now and then, particularly for a play by Ibsen or Shaw. And we had season tickets for the Promenade Concerts. The Queen's Hall was only three or four minutes away, and we became adepts at timing the programmes so that we could stroll over to hear a particular piece.

Nevertheless I was getting into the unfortunate habit, of which I have never been able to rid myself, of taking on more tasks than I could perform to my entire satisfaction. At first this was dictated by eagerness or ambition, in later years by a sense of duty; in either case there always seemed to be some irrefutable reason why the next task had to be accepted. Well, as if I hadn't enough else to do, I felt I must not waste the opportunity the school work provided of carrying out another piece of research that lay in my path. Earlier on there was talk of the importance of speech in connection with the great body-mind problem, and it was now becoming associated in my mind with the search for the mental units of heredity. The illustrious Hughlings Jackson, most philosophically minded of neurologists, had told me he had reached an impasse over the matter of aphasia, and he recommended me, if I were ever to work at the subject, to forget all that hitherto had been written about it and start entirely afresh. So I resolved, instead of studying the speech-brain-mind complex through its most enticing problem, that of aphasia, to begin at the very beginning and gain a thorough knowledge of the mechanism of speech itself. Phonetics, despite Sweet's brilliant work, was then essentially a branch of physiology; it was long before the days when Scripture and Daniel Jones were to revolutionise it by the aid of electrical recording. My work was thus to begin with a detailed study of the articulatory process, its variations and deviations. The development of the articulatory function in children seemed a promising theme, and I got permission to carry out investigations among both normal and mentally defective children. In a couple of years I had records of some two million tests, which then demanded a very lengthy and detailed statistical treatment. I never had the opportunity to complete this latter task, but a few findings of interest emerged in the four or five papers in which some of the results were incorporated. One, for instance, was that girls use lip reading in learning to talk much more than boys, who rely almost entirely on hearing.

It was in connection with this research that I underwent the most disagreeable experience of my life. One morning, early in 1906, Dr. Kerr, the head of the department, sent me an unusual summons, to meet him at a certain school for mental defectives. I was puzzled to know what he wanted, and should have been more than perturbed had I known. To my amazement and horror I was confronted, on arriving there, with a teacher who said that two small children in her class maintained I had behaved indecently during the speech test I had carried out with them: what was worse, she appeared to believe them. (For the tests the children were seen singly in a teacher's room for four or five minutes each.) Dr. Kerr, although he himself wished to dismiss the matter, felt obliged, in the face of the teacher's attitude, to report it to the Education Committee. They were naturally rather at a loss, and after a delay of a couple of weeks made the panicky decision of placing the matter in the hands of the police. Presumably the fear of the public weighed more with them than any duty of protecting their servants from risks in their work. I was privately informed that they had done so, and that I could expect to be arrested at any moment.

I shuddered at the thought of the publicity, and of the pain it would cause my poor parents. It was as unexpected a blow as my rejection at the National Hospital, but bringing with it distress of a very different nature. There was one moment of light relief. On the following morning the parlour-maid announced that a policeman wished to see me. I steeled myself for the ordeal, and found that he wanted to sell me a ticket for a police charity! After lunch, however, two higher officials presented themselves, and the senior of the two opened with the absurd declaration: "Doctor, there are two ways out of this room, the door and the window; I hope you will choose the door." This theatrical behaviour, as I learned later, expressed their persuasion of my guilt and their fear lest I should endeavour to escape them in some Wild Western fashion. I calmed them and obtained permission to explain to my dumbfounded sister what was happening, and to telephone home to get my father to come up to London. They also granted my request to be allowed to take something to read, and showed curiosity at my literary choice, which was, I remember, Nietzsche's *Thus spake Zarathustra.*

So, till the next morning, a young Harley Street physician, with top-hat and frock-coat complete, was alone in a cell furnished only with a stone bench, a book serving as a pillow at night; outside, the evening papers made the most of the sensation on their placards. It was a very different experience from my two former amusing ones in a police cell. The next morning the case was remanded and I was, of course, bailed out. When filing through the crowd I overheard a workman say to a companion: "He can cut his bloody throat, he can." It was not comforting to observe that the police were not alone in their suspicions of me.

In the meantime the services of Mr. (afterwards Sir Archibald) Bodkin were procured. It was just like me to try to argue with him about the conduct of the case, although legal etiquette allowed me to address him only through the medium of my solicitor. My view was that the children had really been concerned in some sexual scene, and that I was being made the scapegoat for their sense of guilt; I wanted him to direct his endeavours to discovering the origin of the whole thing. Bodkin, on the other hand, insisted on being free of all preconceptions and on dealing empirically with whatever turned up. In the event he was right.

I was now to learn the meaning of the law's delays, and the apparently interminable circumlocutions in a matter I was burning to bring to a head. There were several remands of the case, each time for a fortnight. The police told me they expected the magistrate to commit me to a criminal court, though even they did not think I should be convicted there. To the evening headlines were now added supposed likenesses of myself as conceived by the amateur draftsmanship of reporters. For two dreadful months I lived on the edge of an abyss. If the police were right in their surmise of my being committed for trial, then a subsequent declaration of not guilty would still leave me with an ineffaceable stain; it was bad enough as it was. As time went on, with all my professional activities suspended, I made the curious observation that I was developing a sort of shamefacedness, as if I were in some way to blame for the whole thing; no doubt unconscious sources of guilt of my own, probably of sexual origin, were gradually being stirred. It made me understand how it was that Hans Cross's promising experiments in detecting criminal acts by means of association tests foundered on the general frequency of guilt reactions, even when the person was innocent of a particular crime.

At last the magistrate decided to dismiss the case, and he afterwards took the unusual step of sending me a friendly and sympathetic letter. The medical press then broke the silence they had had to maintain while the case was *sub judice*, and trounced the London County Council for not protecting their servants from dangers incurred when carrying out their duties. The staff of my old hospital got up a subscription to cover my legal expenses, which had been considerable, and this was formally presented to me at a meeting held at Sir Victor Horsley's house. The cloud under which I had lived for nearly two months was lifted, and I resumed my usual professional life. But I was under no illusion that life would henceforth be just the same for me as before. It had already come to my ears that some colleagues had been inclined to lend credence to the accusation, under the doubtfully flattering pretext that clever people were apt to be queer. Personal respectability would not be enough in the future; only the most rigid medical orthodoxy would save me. But I was already embarking on lines of thought in psychology, of which I have not yet spoken, which could only bring me into sharp conflict with the medical profession. How ill nature could combine with opposition in science I knew, and I was to experience it to the full in later life. No, such affairs do not quickly "blow over"; one's enemies see to that. Disagreeable echoes of that episode, in increasingly distorted forms, reached me for very many years after.

The next two years passed quietly enough. They were filled with the activities I have related above, and with those which I shall describe separately in the next chapter. My acquaintance with Continental life was gradually extending. It became a frequent habit in the summer to leave London on Saturday evening by the half-past eight train for Newhaven, returning by seven on the Monday morning. It was remarkable how much one could see in that day. Studies of the time-table disclosed that one could dispose of no fewer than twenty hours in Rouen, fourteen in Paris, or a satisfactory number in many other places. By other routes a day could be spent in Brussels, Ghent, The Hague, or other delectable places, and even two hours in Cologne—though I never took this extreme step. The museums, churches, picture galleries, and—last but not least—the café life of these and many other towns became increasingly familiar. My sisters spent one summer in Dresden and another on the lower Seine, professedly for linguistic purposes, and I paid them short visits. Brief holidays were also spent in the more remote parts of Normandy, Brittany, and Holland. I was beginning, in a very small way, to be a traveller, but the thrill of putting foot on foreign soil never lessened. Memories of sights seen and incidents enjoyed in those days crowd in on me, but they do not deserve individual mention here.

Nor was the theatre forgotten, thanks to the foreign institution of Sunday matinées. Coquelin, Sarah Bernhardt, and Mme Réjane were at the height of their fame, and I missed no opportunity of seeing them. Then there was always the Comédie Française with its repertory of French classics. More than once I was lucky enough to get a ticket to private performances given by Yvette Guilbert, where she sang with deep psychological penetration ditties that would not bear the light of outer day. More than thirty years later I told her of my experience and mentioned two of the songs, whereupon she graciously repeated the performance for the sake of bygone times.

There was one specially enjoyable excursion which I owed to the kindness of the late Dr. Leonard Williams, physician to the French hospital in London. There was in Paris a society of balneo-therapists who naturally worked hand-in-hand with the doctors and local authorities of the various French spas. Periodically they toured a number of spas and held conferences at them, and this was such an occasion. One spa, Plombières, offered to pay the expenses of a London physician to take part in the tour, and Leonard Williams was commissioned to select one. It was enormous fun. At Paris a special train was put at our disposal, with porters attached to it who took our luggage from the train to the bedroom. It was an example of how "they do these things better in France". Every spa we visited was beflagged and illuminated, and we were given free entry everywhere. Every day there was a banquet at which a mayor in evening-dress would expand in finest oratory. Each spa had of course an ambition to eclipse its rivals in displaying its attractions and setting forth its virtues. The Paris specialists had the duty of giving numerous lectures expounding the more or less mythical value of the local waters and climate, and each lecture was an exercise in oratory that far transcended as a work of art anything I had ever heard from English physicians. You may be sure I came back entranced with the charm and *savoir faire* of the French—as I was intended to—if unimpressed by their scientific scepticism, of which there were very few traces indeed.

When I was twenty-eight I encountered my most lasting and obstreperous bodily enemy, "rheumatoid arthritis" with its accompanying neuritis. The fifty years of suffering from it, with seldom a minute's intermission, make too dreary a story to embark on. Its onset was so severe that I was given morphine, the only effect of which was, unfortunately, collapse. I mention it because of an unexpected feat on Trotter's part. Without a pause he carried me through four rooms and up four steep flights of stairs. Since he usually counted as a rather frail person it must have been a remarkable example of will-power.

At the beginning of 1908 there occurred another painful

episode, which hastened the transition in my career from neurologist to psychiatrist, but which proved to be the last item in the run of ill luck that has been narrated in this chapter. As I shall presently describe, I had already for a couple of years been interested in psycho-analysis and learning to practise it. Naturally I had also discussed it with various friends and colleagues and encountered astonishment at the then novel idea of young children possessing any sexual life. Harry Campbell was particularly intrigued—as one says nowadays—at this notion. Well, it happened that at the West End Hospital for Nervous Diseases, where I was still acting as his assistant as well as being medical registrar to the hospital, there was a girl of ten with an hysterical paralysis of the left arm, and Campbell challenged me to see if I could discover any sexual basis for the symptom, as according to Freud's theory of hysteria there should be. Having been made chary of interviewing children alone, I demurred, but—to my undoing, as it turned out—I allowed him to over-persuade me. The patient was one of Dr. Savill's. This gentleman, having written a banal book on "neurasthenia", was regarded as an authority on the psychoneuroses in general, and, although I had the free run of the wards, I should have been wiser to obtain his express permission to examine the case. Still, it seemed safe enough to talk to the child in the operating theatre with the door open and nurses moving in and out. The case certainly proved an interesting one, and I was able to ascertain that the symptom had made its first appearance in a sexual scene. The girl had been in the habit of going early to school to have a few minutes "play" with a slightly older boy, and one day he tried to seduce her. She turned on one side and warded him off with the opposite arm, but at the critical moment this went numb and weak and remained paralysed. It was a pretty example of a "compromise-formation" between the conflicting impulses working on the child. Savill soon after published a more orthodox account of the case, where it was explained as one of imperfect blood supply to one side of the brain. He told me he did not know enough German to make a study of Freud's work, but Trotter opined that there were more than linguistic obstacles in his way.

Shortly after I saw the girl, she boasted to other children in the ward that the doctor had been talking to her about sexual topics, and this got to the ears of one of their parents. The incensed father complained to the hospital committee, who at once interviewed me. The atmosphere was charged with suspicious antagonism, and I well remember one elderly clergyman who was very worked up. I was told later that he got a hospital rule passed to the effect that no sexual topic was ever to be broached with children. The inevitably antagonistic matron was also present, and deposed that I spent too much time mapping out the anaesthesias of hysterical out-patients, giving her much trouble in providing chaperone nurses. Campbell was too weak, or frightened, to stand by me, and the upshot was that I was called upon to resign.

This meant that all hope vanished of ever getting on to the staff of any neurological hospital in London, and the prospect of styling myself a freelance neurologist, besides being distasteful, was in those days simply not feasible; one would have been regarded as little better than a charlatan. So I had to do some hard thinking. There came to my mind Bradford's telling me once that his life had been guided by two mottoes: "On and on, and no regrets," and "Never explain and never complain."

Dr. C. K. Clarke, Professor of Psychiatry in the University of Toronto and Dean of the Medical Faculty there, had just been touring all the European psychiatric clinics and intended to found one, for which he had obtained the sanction of the Ontario Government. I chanced to hear of this and, furthermore, that he was on the look-out for a younger man to be the director of this new Institute. It was already plain to me that I was going to be associated with psycho-analysis, and I confess my heart sank at the prospect of having to sow its ideas on the peculiarly arid soil provided by the medical profession of London. I was therefore attracted by the opportunity of starting afresh in some other English-speaking country, keeping open the undefined possibility, if things went well, of one day returning to England. Parenthetically, this latter reflection, in the circumstances I have just described, shows that it takes a great deal to deflect me altogether from a set course.

Sir William Osler, whom I had met through Bradford and who had recently been made Regius Professor of Medicine in Oxford, was a Canadian. Hoping that he could give me the information I wanted, I called on him; incidentally, he was a most learned and cultured man, and his private library was undoubtedly the most beautiful I have ever come across. He was very kind to me, told me about the new plans in Toronto, and offered to write to Dr. Clarke on my behalf. My qualifications and testimonials secured me the appointment, but I stipulated that I should not take up my duties till the autumn; it was then March, and I wanted to seize the rare chance of spending six months pursuing studies and carrying out research on the Continent. Thus it was I came to leave London, but the feeling in my bones that I should one day return proved to be well founded.

Chapter Eight

Approach to Psycho-Analysis

IT is a tenet of psycho-analysis that man is throughout a social creature, and that the attempted distinction between individual and social psychology is inherently fictitious. By this is meant that his mind develops entirely out of interactions between him and other human beings, and that an individual not so built up is unthinkable. If the earliest interactions are well integrated and harmoniously co-ordinated, the later ones are of less importance and the person achieves a high degree of independence, but even then—and even with a misanthropic hermit—an analysis of the mind will show that it was built up as I have just indicated: from social relationships.

I mention this consideration here because, on looking back, I observe that my interest in psychology did not begin, as it so often does, from concern about some personal individual problem so much as from a wide interest in general social problems. It is true that this in its turn could only have arisen from what I have termed a "socialising" of some personal set of problems, but that merely illustrates the point I am making—that the social and individual are not to be separated. It is plain, for example, that my preoccupation during my teens with first religion and then philosophy, with all its intellectualising and generalising, ultimately proceeded from concern about the salvation of my soul, i.e. atonement with the Father. Fortunately it was not very long before more pleasant and lasting solutions of this momentous problem were found, once the unreal elements were abolished with the supernatural beings and their imagery of another world.

It was thus the injustices, stupidities, and irrationalities of our social organisation, which move every thinking youth as he looks around, that impelled me to learn something about that curious thing responsible for it all: human nature. It did not take long to perceive that little was to be learned concerning it from text-books on logic, and possibly less still from those on academic psychology. The artists, notably poets, dramatists, and musicians, were evidently concerned with it as their subject-matter: it was the will, the emotions, and the impulses of man that they observed, felt, and expressed. With their sensitive perceptions and with their genius for divining the essential and the characteristic, they had much, very much, to teach one. But it had its self-imposed limitations. The necessity they were under to transmute their perceptions into aesthetic terms brought with it an unavoidable and stringent selection. Their interest was concentrated on the technique of expression in these terms rather than on the intellectual understanding through correlation that is the hall-mark of scientific knowledge. After all, they did not in essence proceed beyond observation, which is only the first of the three stages in full knowledge. So they opened one's eyes, showed one things, provided material for thought and study, but accompanied one no farther in the search.

One other great lesson the artists—using the designation in its properly wide sense—taught us both; by us I mean Trotter and myself, since to begin with our thoughts were working in much the same direction. That was that the secrets of the human soul were to be apprehended and understood only in connection with suffering: through being able to suffer oneself and thus entering into contact with the suffering of others. It is a road shut for ever to those, the majority of mankind, who flinch from being deeply moved.

This principle is of fundamental importance. One may well divide people into two broad groups on the basis of it. Trotter used to call them the "sensitive" and the "insensitive" respectively, but these are tentative expressions valid only for a first approach. Better descriptive terms are "psychologically minded" and "unpsychologically minded", though they tell us nothing about the significance of the distinction. The principle annuls at once all the nonsense that has been talked about "abnormal psychology" and the inapplicability to the "normal" of conclusions derived from the study of it. The so-called "normal" are simply those who have dealt in other ways—by various inner defences such as deadening, inhibiting, and so on—with the deep disharmonies that lie at the centre of human nature. I cannot say now when it dawned on me—such insight was probably gradual—that the unhappinesses of the afflicted are nearer to these disharmonies than are the more complicated distortions of the "normal" mind, and that they present, so to speak, a magnifying lens through which it is possible to get a more direct vision of the mysterious unknown that would yield understanding of that curious thing called human nature. Some such intuition, however, was already impelling me in that direction.

In the meantime such matters lay directly in my professional path. What were called "functional disorders", i.e. psychoneuroses, constituted one of the most puzzling sets of phenomena in the purview of the neurologist, and they at once riveted my attention. In those days the medical outlook was even more one-sidedly materialistic than it is now. The body was thought to be able to influence the mind, but not the mind the body. The mind,* if it existed at all—which it was hardly allowed to—was but an emanation from the brain; it was but a function of an organ; so it followed logically that if it showed perturbation the only proper way of dealing with it was to track the organ that was allowing it, or causing it, to do so. This attitude was reinforced by the fact that the most vividly striking, and therefore better known, manifestations of the psychoneuroses were the bodily symptoms of hysteria. These symptoms—such as paralyses, anaesthesias of parts of the body, epileptiform convulsions, all of which were much more frequent forty years ago than they are today—bore a superficial resemblance to disorders that do actually proceed from affections of the brain, and these resemblances were naturally put in the foreground. The brain had therefore to be treated. Since there was no hint, however, of any particular method of treatment, one could only fall back on generalities. The brain should be rested: good, put the patient to bed, regardless of the observation so easily made that the mind is apt to suffer more when less distracted by the outer world. Improve the condition and nourishment of the brain: administer milk or tonics. The central nervous system happens

* To guard against possible misinterpretations I would here disclaim belief in any metaphysical entity named "the mind", a word which to me is merely a convenient shorthand expression for the many and well-known phenomena commonly called mental processes. Although the intrinsic nature of these is quite unknown, they represent realities of the highest significance to human beings, and it is against the discounting of this significance that I am here protesting.

to contain a minute proportion more phosphorus than other parts of the body. The bodies of fish similarly contain slightly more phosphorus than do those of mammals. Therefore feed such patients on fish. I will not stop to enumerate the canons of logic this syllogism violates.

Thus simply did the doctors resolve the age-old riddle of the relationship between mind and matter—perhaps the most baffling one in all philosophic thought, and assuredly the one in respect to which least advance in knowledge is manifest. The most celebrated neurophysiologist of our age, Sir Charles Sherrington, stated that all our knowledge of the universe could ultimately be expressed in terms of the categories, energy and mind, but that he could see no prospect of correlating the two or of bringing the relationship between them any nearer to our understanding. Now, it has taken science some three centuries to come to close quarters with the concept of energy; how many will it take to do the same with the more difficult concept of the mind?

As a young man I was impatient with the attitude I have just described. I used to ask neurologists why mental processes were to be excluded from their field of daily work and from nowhere else in their lives. The same man who would attempt to change an obsessional idea, or fear, by acting on the brain would think anyone crazed who should propose to teach his child a foreign language or a standard behaviour by a similar procedure. I claimed liberty of investigation in both spheres. Let the neurologist by all means try to find the physical "substratum" of various mental processes, those underlying the obsessive idea, the use of French, the love of truth, and so on. I was not much drawn in that direction myself, for I could perceive no promising opening: the speech one I mentioned earlier could fructify, if at all, only after generations of research. On the other hand, openings presented themselves right and left in the mental sphere itself by means of which one might reasonably hope to reach some understanding of the distressing symptoms one was constantly encountering. I could not see why anyone should frown on this line of investigation: I know better now why they do!

In spite of being a professional surgeon, Trotter was really always more interested, and I should say remained so, in mind than in matter, and so he encouraged me in my predilection. We started from the same sociological motives and cherished the same biological goal—that is, of comprehending psychology in terms of biology. We began with the writings of William James, Frederic Myers, and Milne Bramwell, which we thoroughly dissected together, and ranged out in all directions radiating from that simple basis. We were especially interested in what is now called medical psychology, to which the French had contributed by far the major part; I soon acquired a practically complete library of their writings on the subject in the eighteenth and nineteenth centuries, and—what is more—read them assiduously.

The cases of multiple personality, and the beautiful experimental work carried out on patients in a state of deep hypnosis, seemed to furnish convincing proof that the mind was not co-extensive with consciousness, and that complicated mental processes could be going on without the subject being in the least aware of them. The conception of an unconscious mind was therefore perfectly familiar to us, though we knew nothing about what it contained.

In 1905 I had the good fortune to come across a case of exceptional interest which I studied very fully. The patient, a very intelligent man called Tom Ellen, was a post office railway sorter, whose symptoms dated from a train collision. When I saw him he was stone-blind, being unable to distinguish the strongest light from darkness, had lost the sense of taste and smell, had extensive memory disturbances, and suffered from severe pain and various mental attacks. Most striking of all was the remarkable symptom of feeling that his body was folded over on itself, so that he consisted only of one side, a condition called allochiria; for practical purposes one could say that he was paralysed on the other side. I saw the patient regularly for two or three years, and at one time intended to write a book on his case—which it richly deserved. It furnished very definite contributions to both psychology and clinical neurology, which formed the basis of a number of papers in scientific periodicals. The patient provided, however, an interest which was not only theoretical, but also personal and dramatic. It was thrilling, for instance, after some months of patient work, to restore his vision completely: first in a blurred fashion, then clearly except for faces, all of which looked like plain white paper; then for faces as well, with the sole exception of his wife's!

Once he showed me a large healing bruise where a cartwheel had gone over his anaesthetic foot; he had never felt anything of it. In hypnosis he released the suppressed sensations, and in half an hour groaned his way through the various pains that normally would have occupied a month, from the original crush to the final stiffness. He was a museum of material, where one found oneself in a new and unexplored world.

It took me also a year or two before I detected the fallacies that had misled a famous worker. The subject of allochiria was a very recondite one, though it opened the way to the study of how the mind receives its various impressions of bodily feeling; of many experiences of research it was perhaps the one I enjoyed most. With one exception, all the explanations that had been given of the condition I was investigating had been of a physiological nature, whereas the evidence in Ellen's case, and in a couple of others I managed to encounter, made it plain that it was purely psychological. The exception had been proffered by Pierre Janet, the most distinguished worker we had yet seen on the experimental aspects of medical psychology, and a man I therefore held in the highest esteem. He had offered an explanation which he called psychological, and I followed closely his train of thought and experiment. After a deal of cogitation, however, I discovered that his explanation was simply an ingenious trick, that really his thought had proceeded on physiological lines and had then been clothed in a psychological terminology. It was very revealing to observe just where he had burked the problem and what sort of timidity had made him flinch. What I learned then of his disposition was borne out more than once in later personal encounters with him. I continued to admire his ingenuity and skill, also his beautiful command of language in both lecturing and writing, but my respect for his scientific integrity had gone for good.

This experience had a very considerable significance for me. It doubtless repeated a reaction in early life on discovering that my father was not omniscient, a reaction compounded of triumph at the thought that I could know better than he did and of resentment—ostensibly against him but really against myself—at having been credulously misled. Never again did this happen to me. It did not need to, for I was achieving a truer independence. I was to differ from the three men for whom I had the highest respect—Rose Bradford, Trotter, and Freud himself—but my only feeling on those occasions was one of simple regret.

By this time I was getting to know who was who in the world of medical psychology and gradually to meet them personally. So far as I could see, for the sun of Freud had not yet risen above my horizon, there were only three: Janet in France, Boris Sidis and Morton Prince in America. With the last of these I was already in regular correspondence, which came about from my having been an early contributor to his new *Journal of Abnormal Psychology*. Psychotherapists, of course, there were, but they seemed to have little interest in the psychology of the conditions they treated. I watched Bérillon at work in his clinic in Paris a few times, and even in England there was Lloyd Tuckey and others. Paul Sollier of Paris I think I met first on the spa tour, and then often after; he was very friendly to me. He told me once, and I did not properly appreciate it till much later, that scientific writing was a habit like any other and one not easy to resume if one allowed it to be interrupted for long. Déjérine of Paris, Dubois of Berne, and then Bernheim of Nancy, all of whom I met at Congresses, were mere practitioners; it was Liebault, who I think died before my time, that was the thinker of the famous Nancy school.

So if I surveyed the scene there was really only Janet who had broken new ground, and I felt I had measured his limitations. My father had evidently been right: there is always room at the top. With my genuine enthusiasm, fresh sceptical outlook, and some mental discipline from my strict medical training, it looked as if I might be somewhat of a pioneer.

Then came Freud, and I soon found I had to go to school again. It was Trotter who first mentioned his name to me. Mitchell Clarke had published in *Brain* in 1898 a review of his *Studies in Hysteria*, and Havelock Ellis had also alluded to him. The first of his writings I came across was the Dora analysis, published in the *Monatsschrift für Psychiatrie*. My German was not good enough to follow it closely, but I came away with a deep impression of there being a man in Vienna who actually listened with attention to every word his patients said to him.

I was trying to do so myself, but I had never heard of anyone else doing so. I had better explain this, since the importance of the observation may nowadays not be evident. And yet it was to me perhaps the most significant thing about Freud. It meant that he was that *rara avis*, a true psychologist. It meant that, whereas men had often taken a moral or political interest in mental processes, here for the first time was a man who took a scientific interest in them. Hitherto scientific interest had been confined to what Sherrington calls the world of energy, the "material" world. Now at last it was being applied to the equally valid world of mind. For Freud the most casual remarks of his patients were really facts, data to be seriously examined and pondered over with the same intentness as that given by the geologist, the biologist, the chemist, to the data provided in their respective fields of work. What a revolutionary difference from the attitude of previous physicians who would hear, without listening, their patients' remarks, discounting, forgetting, or even pooh-poohing them while their own thoughts were elsewhere, concerned perhaps with the patients' welfare but from a totally different angle.

So here was a man who was seriously interested in investigating the mind. I must get to know more about his work, and so I was spurred on to make progress with my German. I sometimes say I learned German from reading Freud's *Traumdeutung* and Heine's *Reisebilder*, and for some time my vocabulary showed amusing traces of its compound restricted origin. Perhaps not so much as that of a friend, Hanns Sachs, who learned English by reading *The Tempest*, *The Tale of a Tub*, and Kipling's Soldier Stories, and whose style displayed an astonishing medley derived from three separate centuries.

I may pause here, at the introduction to psycho-analysis, and reflect on how well or how badly I was prepared to receive it. As I remarked earlier, Trotter and I fully realised that the secrets we wished to discover were in a region of the mind outside consciousness—it was Freud who drove home the conception of an unconscious mind and its biological nature, just as Darwin had that of evolution, however much both ideas may have been "in the air"—but we were at a loss for a suitable means of exploring it. I had extensively used direct inquiry in hypnosis, but, though this could restore forgotten memories and yield interesting hints of subsconscious happenings, it had definite limitations. As with most pioneers in science, Freud's discoveries came about through an advance in method, and it may well be said that his invention of what he called the "free association" method of investigation was his most original achievement: it was where he most showed his genius. The device was of course entirely new to us, and yet the idea of flawless continuity behind it at once appealed to us as an intelligible example of law and order in an apparent chaos; it made sense. That apparently disconnected remarks should from the mere fact of their contiguity prove to be bound together by often invisible (i.e. unconscious) links was a brilliant illustration of determinism reigning in the sphere where it was most often denied: it was a most impressive extension of scientific law. This discovery of Freud's is a striking example of the qualitative difference between genius and mere talent. I do not doubt that I should have gone far in the fields of medical and social psychology had Freud never lived, but I see no reason at all for supposing I should ever have hit on the key that opened the way to the exploration of the deep unconscious layers of the mind; and without this one would have had to rely too much on hypotheses instead of facts.

As to sexuality, we were unusually free of any conscious prejudices—unconscious ones were to be encountered only later —and as I remarked in the first chapter, I had the best of reasons for having no doubts about the sexual life of children. This side of Freud's work, which so shocked his contemporaries, raised not a qualm in us. Even the incest motif, which plays such an important part in it, was by no means unfamiliar to us. We had recognised the contents of the Golden Bough as gigantic ramifications of the father-murder theme. Frazer himself must have been near to this at the inception of his work, but repression impelled him farther and farther away from it—to be replaced by the more harmless one of vegetation and crops. When Freud sent him a copy of his terrific book *Totem and Taboo*, based on Frazer's writings, he did not venture even to acknowledge it.

The third of Freud's fundamental conceptions, that of repression, was one on which we had much discussion. The fact itself, the tendency to put or keep disturbing thoughts "out of one's mind", was obvious enough, but the nature of the forces at work was less so. That it was due to some inner conflict of a starkly dynamic nature was evident to anyone who had pondered on religious writings, with their stress on the fight against sin and the devil. No one could have put the matter more forcibly than did St. Paul: "But I see another law in my members, warring against the law of my mind." Such considerations made Janet's explanation of his *désagrégation psychologique* as due to instability of associations simply puerile.

What, however, was the real nature of the incompatibility of the repressed ideas with the conscious mind? Freud for long contented himself with general expressions such as horror, disgust, moral aversion, but we felt—as indeed proved to be the case—that there was a need for a more precise formulation in biological terms. Trotter thought he could get far with special kinds of sensitiveness derived from his favourite herd instinct, but that too did not satisfy me. It is a problem which even yet is not completely solved, although Freud and others have made important advances in it. As for the matter of symbolism, which was the focal point of opposition with so many people, it gave us no serious trouble. We were already very familiar with the great variety of sexual symbolism to be found in anthropological data, in the phallic religions of the East, and so on, subjects in which we were pretty well read.

I was therefore in the unusual position, thanks to previous preparation, of being unaware of any conscious "resistance" or prejudice against Freud's principal tenets. They simply carried me along in the very direction I wished to pursue. When it came to considering the details of the published analyses, I do remember feeling rather dubious that things could be as simple as all that. Most people seem to complain that psycho-analysis makes the mind out to be unnecessarily complicated, but for some reason I had quite the opposite impression. It was not altogether unjustified, being in large part due to my desire to be more satisfied about the dynamic agencies responsible for these plays of association. At all events it was the only form of "resistance" I was aware of. I began practising his method at the end of 1906 and well I remember my first patient, the sister of a colleague.

* * * * * *

So far I have said nothing at all about the subject of insanity, and to do so will enable me to resume the chronology of my story. The subject was in those days at an incredibly low ebb in England, disgracefully so when compared with the advances already being made on the Continent or in America. Alienists were held in great contempt—mostly with justification, though of course not always so—by the rest of the profession, and were largely recruited from those who wished for a life of complete mental stagnation. The education of medical students in the subject certainly supported this estimate; I will not inquire how much it has changed since then—it might prove invidious. We were supposed to attend six lectures, and I was one of the few who actually did. They were quite the most dismal and unenlightening I have ever heard. In addition there were six visits to an asylum. Sometimes this was entered on in the same spirit as the fashionable visits to the Salpêtrière in the days of the *ancien régime*, in the hopes of seeing something diverting; in the worst case there was always the chance of playing cricket with the "looneys". But more often one did not go at all and got someone else to "sign up" for one, as with the lectures.

Naturally I felt that an embryo neurologist should have some knowledge of insanity, so I took the matter more seriously. After qualification my friend Ward joined the L.C.C. Asylum Service, and I used to make a practice of spending as many Sundays as I could with him, making ourselves familiar with the various symptoms and problems of diagnosis exhibited by the patients. Through him I met other young alienists, and after his death I continued to some extent my studies with them. As time went on I became increasingly dissatisfied with the possibilities of acquiring any serious knowledge in this way, and managed to get a month away from my work in November 1907 to attend a special post-graduate course in psychiatry at Kraepelin's Clinic in Munich, my German having got on far enough to make this possible.

The course was organised with superb German thoroughness and efficiency. Some of the foremost authorities in the world presented their subjects in special courses: Alzheimer on cerebral histology, Plaut on sero-diagnostics, and the great Kraepelin himself on clinical diagnosis. There were many others: forensic psychiatry was taught by von Gudden, the son of the psychiatrist who had been drowned struggling with the mad King Ludwig, which gave an occasion for brushing up one's history of this interesting dynasty. We began punctually at eight o'clock, the dark and cold of the Bavarian winter being no deterrent, and were kept hard at work all through the day. At the end of the month we really had seen and learned something.

The experience was highly interesting in other ways too. It gave me my first glimpse of daily life in Germany—for the view one thus got of it was very different from a tourist's—and I shall presently say something about my impressions. Then it was my first opportunity to make foreign friends, students having assembled from many countries in Europe. The chief friendships I made were with Gustav Modena of Ancona, later the director of the Asylum there, Otto Maas of Berlin, and W. Peters of Vienna. I was to meet the latter two again in very changed circumstances, for on the same day some thirty years later one turned up to lunch at my house in London, the other to dinner; both had become distinguished professors, the former of neurology, the latter of experimental psychology, but both were refugees from the Nazi régime.

On my way back to England I made a detour to visit Jung at Zurich. I had met him three months before at the International Congress of Neurology in Amsterdam, where we both read papers. He appeared to have been struck by my scepticism in various matters, such as the role of heredity in mental disorders, and warmly offered me his friendship. He was the first psycho-analyst I had met; he was surprised to hear that knowledge of psycho-analysis had reached England. He was then at the Burghölzli Asylum, the director of which was Professor Bleuler, and I spent several days watching and discussing their work. With his cousin Riklin he had already established a Zurich Psycho-Analytical Society, and I was present at one of its first meetings. It was well attended, and even von Monakow, the distinguished Professor of Neurology at the University of Zurich, had climbed the mountain on a winter's evening to participate eagerly in a discussion on the symbolism of dreams. They were amused when I remarked that if only his respectable colleagues knew about it they would say he might as well climb the Brocken to attend a Witches' Sabbath. It was then that I met Brill, a young and eager psychiatrist from New York, for the first time; Abraham had just resigned a post there the week before, and was on his way to settle in Berlin.

Jung was already a man of international fame in psychiatry. Two years before he had published his great *Studies in Association*, perhaps his most original contribution to science, which had provided confirmation from the side of experimental psychology of the theory underlying Freud's empirical "free association method", and in the present year his book on the *Psychology of Dementia Praecox* had just appeared. Nothing that he wrote later ranked, in my opinion, with these, and in three or four years he was to begin his descent into a pseudo-philosophy out of which he has never emerged. At that time I could best describe Jung as a breezy personality. He had a restlessly active and quick brain, was forceful or even domineering in temperament, and exuded vitality and laughter; he was certainly a very attractive person. He cherished the notion, rightly or wrongly, that his descent owed something to one of Goethe's love affairs, and I feel sure his career was influenced by a medley of scientific, literary, and philosophical pretensions in which he tried to emulate his great ancestor. With all his intelligence and learning, however, Jung lacked both clarity and stability in his thinking; I was not surprised when, not very long ago, someone who was in school with him recollected as a prominent feature that he had a confused mind. My first observation of this was his attempt to combine his important discoveries in the psychology of dementia praecox with the pathological findings in that condition by postulating a "psychical toxin" whereby the mind poisoned the brain. His grasp of philosophical principles was so insecure that it was little wonder that they later degenerated into mystical obscurantism.

In the following February, 1908, came the trouble I have described at the West End Hospital, after which I decided to spend six months on the Continent before proceeding to Canada. The first half was to be spent in Germany, the second in France, partly for linguistic purposes. I first visited Jung, with whom I had been in regular correspondence, and discussed with him our plans for organising the first Psycho-Analytical Congress. I remember vainly protesting against his wish to call it a Congress for Freudian Psychology, a term which offended my ideas of objectivity in scientific work. Jung, Brill, and I then went on to Salzburg, where the Congress was to take place on April 26, 1908, and there I first met Freud.

My first impression of Freud was that of an unaffected and unassuming man. He bowed and said: "Freud, Wien," at which I smiled, for where else did I think he came from? This German custom of announcing one's name and town on being introduced, which by the way is a very sensible one, was still novel to me. His first remark was to say that from my appearance I couldn't be English; was I not Welsh? This greatly surprised me—only one other foreigner, Otto Gross, ever made a similar remark—since I was getting accustomed to the total ignorance of my native land on the Continent, where, if known at all, it was regarded as one of the counties of England with perhaps a dialect of its own that could be distinguished from Cockney. We then had a long talk together, of how I had come across psycho-analysis and the like, and later on in the evening, so I heard, he told Jung he found me "very clever"; so our first impression of each other, like all subsequent ones, had been favourable.

But it was the next day that I was to get the tremendous impression of his intellectual powers. His paper was the first on the programme and dealt with the analysis of a classical case—well known later as "the man with the rats". Delivered without any notes, it began at eight o'clock and at eleven he offered to bring it to a close. We had all been so enthralled, however, at his fascinating exposition that we begged him to go on, and he did so for another hour. I had never before been so oblivious of the passage of time. As is well known, Freud was no orator and all arts of rhetoric were alien to him. He spoke as in a conversation, but then his ordinary conversation was so distinctive as to be worthy of a literary recording. His ease of expression, his masterly ordering of complex material, his perspicuous lucidity, and his intense earnestness made a lecture by him—and I was to hear many—both an intellectual and an artistic feast.

The Congress itself, even apart from Freud, was full of interest. In the same hotel Aldren Turner, a Queen's Square neurologist, was spending a holiday, and perhaps wondered what the bustle was about. He could not have known that a new era was beginning which would, among many other things, radically change most of his field of work. Jung had told me in

Zurich what a pity it was that Freud had no followers of any weight in Vienna, and that he was surrounded there by a "degenerate and Bohemian crowd" who did him little credit, so I was curious to see them. I soon found that Jung's description was a highly coloured one, to put it mildly. None of the painters and poets he had imagined existed, and the members of the Vienna Psycho-Analytical Society, which had been formed the year before, were much what one might have expected them to be. I was obliged to ask myself whether his account had proceeded from anything more than simple anti-Semitism, for it is true that they were all Jews; so for many years were all European psycho-analysts except those in Switzerland and England. They were all practising physicians, for the most part very sober ones, and if their cloaks were more flowing and their hats broader than what one saw in Zurich, London, or Berlin, well, as I was to find, that was a general Viennese characteristic. They were decidedly middle-class, and lacked the social manners and distinction I had been accustomed to in London. On the other hand they were more cultivated and better educated; the theatre, opera, and concert hall meant much to them, and they were at home in both German and classical literature.

The membership and transactions of the Congress have been recorded elsewhere, and of the personalities I shall have occasion to speak later. My own paper was the only one not in German, but it seemed to be generally understood. Trotter turned up on the first evening, but significantly he did not attend the meeting when Freud spoke; he gave his poor German as an excuse, but one might have supposed that curiosity about a great man would have transcended this obstacle. After a couple of days in what was evidently an atmosphere uncongenial to him, he abruptly left for home, and so ended one of his two or three brief visits to the Continent. He was to meet Freud next in London, more than thirty years later; they were to die soon after within three months of each other and to rest in the same place.

Trotter's conduct in Salzburg was characteristic of him. An outstanding difference between us was that, whereas I could be happy in any strange assembly, whether I was playing a personal part or simply enjoying myself as an onlooker, Trotter was at ease only on his own ground and on his own conditions.

Like so many Englishmen, for instance, he could not bear to use a foreign language unless he could speak it well—which in consequence he never could. His discomfort in unfamiliar surroundings was illustrated at the banquet held by the Congress when a youth next to him—it was Wittels—tried to entertain him with jejunely facetious remarks about the hysteria of some Greek goddess; turning to me he muttered revealingly: "I console myself with the thought that I can cut a leg off, and no one else here can."

From Salzburg Brill and I travelled to Vienna. This first visit to Vienna, and my last one, were the only occasions on which I stayed at an hotel other than the one dedicated to psycho-analysts, the Regina; the first time because I did not yet know of the rendezvous, the last because it had been commandeered by Hitler's soldiers. I did not see much of Vienna itself, however, our stay being but a brief one. I remember one amusing and instructive episode. At a party Dr. Max Steiner gave for us, I observed a man straddling a chair and pouring out with an air of gusto a flow of conversation to—I had almost written "into"—a young lady whose demeanour was particularly receptive. When the hostess brought a tray of liqueurs, as was the custom, this confident youth brushed her aside with a superb gesture and waving his hand towards his rapt partner asked: "Do I need a liqueur?" The symbolic significance of alcohol as a substitute for a more personal essence could hardly have been more illuminatingly displayed.

We made the acquaintance of Freud's family—it was to ripen later into a close friendship with all its members—and of course had long talks with Freud. He was naturally interested in the spread of psycho-analytical work to America, whither we were both about to proceed, and gave Brill the right to translate his writings. Freud was fifty-one years old, at the height of his powers and full of energy. He was most genial and friendly to us, and was in a specially happy mood because of the dawning recognition of his work, as evidenced by a Congress specially convened to discuss it. His revolutionary discoveries had all been made in the past ten years, and now that he was emerging from the years of isolation and ostracism he was full of plans both for extending them further and for disseminating the knowledge of them. He spoke English to us. He had an excellent, rather literary command of it, and we discussed the best translation to use for various technical terms; it was he who thought of "repression" for "*Verdrängung*". His voice I found unmusical and rather rough; perhaps that was why he always spoke quietly, even in lecturing, for a louder tone might have brought out some harshness in it. His manner was gracious, and at times hearty, especially in a handclasp. His eyes constantly twinkled with perception and often with humour, of which he had a highly developed sense.

We were privileged to see something of the birth of the famous Vienna Psycho-Analytical Society. At that time it was simply an informal group, which met every Wednesday at Freud's flat; it had not yet been constituted into a regular society with rules and officers. Freud took the chair and did not speak until the discussion was finished, when he would bring together the salient points and add his own comments. I remember there Friedjung, a paediatrist, Steiner, an urologist, Adler, Hitschmann, Sadger and Stekel, general practitioners, Wittels, the *enfant terrible* of the group, and a few others; Federn had recently joined, but not yet Jekels, Rank, or Sachs.

Adler had not yet acquired the patronising benevolence of his later years. He struck me as sulky and pathetically eager for recognition. I remember his writing to me not long afterwards thanking me for quoting him in an article. Hitschmann, already dry, witty, and somewhat cynical, was doing good work on a book which I got translated soon afterwards; it still contains the best exposition of the obsessional neurosis. Sadger was active at that time, and had not yet developed the curious reaction of mutism he displayed for some years before disappearing from the circle. He was a morose, pathetic figure, very like a specially uncouth bear. One of his social gaffes was so terrific that it deserves recording. Seated at a Congress banquet next to a distinguished literary lady, he fumbled his way through the dinner, and finally ventured to address her. His ever-memorable remark to this stranger was: "Have you occupied yourself with masturbation?" one which in its German guise was even more ambiguous than in English. The egregious Stekel we shall encounter later.

The reader may perhaps gather that I was not highly impressed with the assembly. It seemed an unworthy accompaniment to Freud's genius, but in the Vienna of those days, so full of prejudice against him, it was hard to secure a pupil with a reputation to lose, so he had to take what he could get. Many of the assembly had at least one shining merit above their neighbours: they knew how to appreciate the significance of Freud. To their credit that must never be forgotten.

We then went on to Budapest, at Ferenczi's invitation. Since we had only two days to spare—Brill had to catch a ship and I was eager to resume my work—Ferenczi had with true Hungarian hospitality arranged with his friends to make themselves free for a few hours in turn and escort us around the various sights of the city. How we enjoyed it, and how different was this reception from the harshness I had left behind me in London! Such experiences of being welcome, and I was to have many of them, endeared the Continent to me more than ever. I was rapidly becoming a good European.

From Budapest I journeyed to Munich, where I proposed to spend the first half of my recess. I went first of all to interview Professor Kraepelin, then and for years the leading psychiatrist in the world. Freud's opinion of him was that he was "a coarse fellow", to quote the words he used in English. He certainly had a somewhat gruff manner and showed no sensitiveness or sympathetic insight whatever into his patients, something indeed of the rough lack of consideration I often found with German doctors. I was surprised to hear that in later years he developed a genuine capacity for writing poetry. He received me friendlily enough, gave me the complete run of his famous clinic where I quickly found myself at home, and told me I might carry out whatever research work I liked. I chose to work on cortical histology under Alzheimer and experimental psychology under Lipps, these being the two branches of my work in which I was most deficient.

On my previous visit I had stayed at the Bayrischer Hof, just above the beer cellar later associated with Hitler, in the Promenaden Platz, where historic events were to happen later. This time I took lodgings and began to feel still less of a visitor. Munich itself I greatly liked: its imposing buildings, its opera and music, its glorious collection of picture galleries and museums, its cleanness, neatness, and quiet air of being well ordered, and, not least, its geographical position. The last point would, of course, appeal to my topographical sense. How wonderful, I thought, it must be to live in a town, half-way between Paris and Vienna and also between Berlin and Rome. One respect in which I am very English is that it seems to me reasonable to ask of any place, "where can you get to from here?" a question which greatly amuses more stay-at-home Parisians and Viennese. The question finds a ready answer with Munich, for it lies not far from the foothills of the Bavarian Alps, and a very few miles brings one to the enchanting country of Upper Bavaria with its fantastic castles, romantic lakes and woods and mountains. It was spring-time and I made full use of my opportunities. My Sunday excursions stretched into longer and longer week-ends, mostly in good company. After walking through those woods at night from one beautiful lake to another still more beautiful and returning at dawn, I began to understand why Germany was the land of youth, of romanticism, of wine, women, and song. It is my considered opinion that the characteristic appeal of Germany is to youth, that of France to cultured and sophisticated maturity. For the only time in my life, work was subordinated to enjoyment.

My spirits were again rising after the dour time I had been through in London those last three years. I was bound for a New World, charged with new ideas. There might still be a future worth having. It was fortunate that I saw Germany in this very mood, the right one to match her, since it enabled me to catch glimpses of her bright self—now, alas, so long overlaid by brutality and intolerance. When in later days I have been forced to judge this other side of her hardly, and when I meet people who see and know no other side, my mind goes back to stimulating talk and song in the cafés of Munich, to the village dances in the uplands of Bavaria, above all to the circumambience of spring and youth in both town and country, and I say to myself that such things cannot vanish for ever, that all nightmares pass away.

Of course there were even then disturbing moments. Once, after I had crossed—as one would in London—a huge lawn in the Englischer Garten and was about to leave it by stepping over a six-inch-high railing, a policeman stepped up and insisted that, since I had no right on the grass, I should retrace my steps for a quarter of a mile and leave by the way I had entered. I pointed out that if there was any sense in such a rule it could only be because walking on the grass might harm it, so what he proposed was that I should do immensely more harm than if I went my way. It was staggering, and rather terrifying, to come up against an authority who surrendered all reason in favour of blind deference to a fixed rule, and it made me wonder what was the basis of life in such a country. It is true the man relented on perceiving that I was a mere Englishman who had never had the advantages of German discipline, and it is also true that later I came to experience far more baneful examples of the bureaucratic mind in other countries. Furthermore, the Prussian spirit had only penetrated the rest of Germany, it had not yet overwhelmed it. Bavaria, for example, was still at least as proud of being Bavaria as of being part of the German Empire. It was the year of Agadir and I recollect a cartoon in the Bavarian satirical paper *Simplicissimus* depicting a Prussian soldier saluting at the door of an Alpine chalet where a Bavarian peasant was stolidly standing. The caption ran: "To arms! Your interests in Morocco are threatened." And yet, fifteen years from that date, a more sinister form of Imperialism was founded in Bavaria than was ever dreamed of in Prussia. Such is the plasticity of the human spirit.

Leonard Seif, a local physician who was interested in psycho-analysis, though he later recoiled together with Jung, had a villa near Partenkirchen to which he used to invite me. From him I learned what depths of resentment the inferiority feelings of Germans could cherish against France and England. As he talked, the devastations of the Thirty Years' War and the arrogant tyranny of Napoleon's soldiers became matters of yesterday that still needed to be bloodily avenged. I heard of "the final reckoning with France", which Hitler so dramatically achieved thirty years later. Such themes were naturally disquieting and seemed above all highly unnecessary. Were there not much pleasanter and more fruitful occupations in life than indulging such savage emotions?

For someone like myself who readily strikes up acquaintances, it is sometimes hard to recollect how and where one first met such and such a person. I found a large circle in Munich, but it would not be easy to say how. No doubt the nucleus was the considerable group of co-workers at the university. But I also belonged to a Bohemian set of artists whom I probably got to know at the Café Passage, then the equivalent of London's Café Royal. I have a vivid memory there of Ludwig Klages, since an original and famous philosopher. He was a handsome fellow of fresh countenance and expansive personality; he had a magnificent command of German, but not a word of any other tongue. One evening he coined the phrase: *nüchterne Phantasie* (calculating imaginativeness) to describe the English mentality, one which I found very trenchant. He was already engaged in the graphological studies where he was to make a serious contribution to knowledge, and one evening I showed him a letter written in English. He made a comprehensive, objective, and very accurate dissection of the writer's character, and then added: "Between ourselves, I find her very attractive," to which I replied: "Between ourselves, she is my sweetheart." At this he exploded into a diatribe against the self-control of the cold English which so misled innocent Germans. How often has that happened since then in the sphere of politics! It was Klages also who remarked one evening that Schwabing (a district of Munich that connoted much what Bloomsbury or Chelsea does in London) "is not a district of a town, but a conception."

In the same café I came across my first experience of what is called transvestitism. This was an English artist, of manly enough appearance, but whenever we accompanied him back to his rooms to continue some discussion or other he would apologetically explain how uncomfortable he felt dressed as he was, and would forthwith change into woman's clothes—to his manifest relief.

First and foremost, however, in the circle was Otto Gross, the son of the eminent anthropologist of Graz, Hans Gross. He was the nearest approach to the romantic ideal of a genius I have ever met, and he also illustrated the supposed resemblance of genius to madness, for he was suffering from an unmistakable form of insanity that before my very eyes culminated in murder, asylum, and suicide. He was my first instructor in the technique of psycho-analysis. It was in many ways an unorthodox demonstration. The analytic treatments were all carried out at a table in the Café Passage, where Gross spent most of the twenty-four hours—the café had no closing time. But such penetrative power of divining the inner thoughts of others I was never to see again, nor is it a matter that lends itself to description. Shortly afterwards he was in Burghölzli asylum, where Jung did his best to help him. Jung had the laudable ambition of being the first to analyse a case of dementia praecox, and he laboured hard at the task; he told me that one day he worked unceasingly with Gross for twelve hours, until they were almost reduced to the condition of nodding automata. Gross, however, escaped from the institution and sent the following letter to Jung, which must be unique of its kind:

"Dear Jung,

"I climbed over the asylum wall and am now in the Hotel X. This is a begging letter. Please send me money for the hotel expenses and also the train fare to Munich.

"Yours sincerely."

The only flaws in my enjoyment of Munich were the disquietening glimpses I have mentioned of the aspects of Germany that were to become so horribly prominent in years to come, and the deplorable sartorial efforts of the women. It was a time when German women in general had a reputation for dowdiness, but the Bavarian ones certainly excelled the rest. I never was in a town with such unattractive females, though fortunately there were a few foreigners there; with one, a lady from Styria, I left a little volume of poems after my stay in Munich, appropriately inscribed: "And May and June." It seems strange now to think that, greatly as I liked Munich, I have never revisited it except for business purposes. I had found it so "continental" after London that Peters mystified me by calling it a dull hole and constantly bemoaning his exile from the only possible place to live—Vienna. Poor fellow, he never got back to his beloved Vienna. It was not long before I came to share his taste, however, when Vienna won an unforgettable place in my heart.

At the end of June in that eventful year of 1908, I found myself in Paris. But, much as I admired Paris and later came to love it, my affections did not rapidly change. My heart was still in Bavaria, I frequented Austrian and German society in Paris, and I once even made a trip from it to Speyer on the Rhine to meet a friend from Munich. That naturally delayed my appreciation of what Paris had to offer, though in time I responded warmly enough. It was, of course, by no means new to me; I had already tasted its charm. I took rooms off the "Boul Mich", though the glory of the Quartier Latin now belonged to its past; the art world was already moving to Montmartre, since displaced in its turn by Montparnasse. Nevertheless the Bal Bullier was still full of liveliness, the street-dancing on the "quatorze" was as animated in the Quartier as anywhere in Paris, and the local cafés retained enough of their character to enable one to get back in imagination to the days of Maupassant and Verlaine. I savoured in general the sights, ways, and features of Parisian life, but cannot pretend to have anything to say about them that has not been well said by so many others.

I did more work in Paris than in Munich. I had greatly hoped to be able to work under Janet at the Salpêtrière, but although he received me kindly he explained that he always worked alone and had no student assistants. So I decided to continue my neurological researches on hemiplegia and tongue deviations, for which purposes Professor Pierre Marie was good enough to place his ample material in the Bicêtre Hospital at my disposal.

The time soon passed, and at the end of September, after paying a hurried visit to my family, I sailed for Canada in the *Empress of Britain*. It was the last time I was to see my mother.

Chapter Nine

Life in Canada

THERE was the opportunity now of a fresh start in life, alone in a new and unknown world. It was the time for a self-critical stock-taking, and the voyage served well for the purpose. The ups and downs of the past few years had left deep impressions on me. Many illusions, as well as hopes, lay shattered. Life was not such an easy affair as I had once thought. One had less power to mould and determine it than had seemed. More depended on the chance of circumstance, and on relations with other people, than I had liked to think. It would be wiser to expect less and be glad of anything good that came. I had by now got into the habit of taking other people far more into account, and had revived a capacity for tact which in school-days had softened roughness, but which had subsequently lain dormant. This went on developing, and many years later Freud was to say laughingly that my diplomatic abilities might lead to my being taken over by the League of Nations.

The first impression of the American continent showed me startlingly that I was in a New World, far from the easy suavities of the old one. I naturally planned to break my journey for a couple of days at Quebec and Montreal to visit those towns, or I should say cities. On disembarking early one morning at Quebec I found one could hire a cab; so far so good. We drove to the Château Frontenac, an imposing hotel with a famous reputation. I expected a bowing manager to emerge and to give orders about the luggage, but no one appeared. Not being familiar with the financial arrangements of Canadian cabmen, I advanced to the desk—there being no porter—and asked the clerk that the suitable amount be paid and put on my bill, and I still remember his stare of surprise at this evidently extraordinary request. My next hope was at least to be shown to a room, but it was dashed by the curt remark that if I cared to

Wilfrid Trotter

Ernest Jones in 1936

Katharine Jones in 1936

come back that afternoon (!) they would see if they had one. If, however, I wished to register my name in the hotel book no objection would be raised. The last hotels I had stayed at had been in Vienna and Budapest, where you became "highly well born" merely by your deigning to patronise them, and I found the change from East to West distinctly abrupt.

That I was far from Europe came home to me again a couple of weeks later when I asked which days the mails left for England and received the disconcerting, though perfectly obvious, reply: "It depends on the sailing dates." I felt as if I were marooned on an island where one waved a suitable garment to attract the attention of a passing ship.

These little anecdotes alone show that, however enterprising I might be intellectually, I was not intended for a pioneer's life in a new country, and so it proved. Timber-cutting in a virgin forest, or camping out in the wilds where one would shoot game while digging the ground for a livelihood, was not in my nature, much as I might approve of it in others. I yearned for a cultured life with an historical background, and the need for this grew stronger instead of less as time went on.

In the meanwhile I had to establish myself in Toronto. I had letters of introduction to the leading physicians and surgeons, and they received me with true colonial hospitality. I must have been something of a novelty, for Canada was now populated by Canadians—no longer by settlers. I remember one old lady at a party asking me where I came from: I innocently answered, "From London," whereupon—thinking I must have meant London in Ontario—she encouragingly remarked: "It must be pleasant to come to a big city after living in such a quiet little place."

I soon found out, however, that Englishmen were not particularly popular. The legend "no English need apply" was really placarded at factories. They were known as "broncos" because of their habit of "kicking", i.e. of criticising their new environment. So I fell back on my Welsh origin and, since most of the people who counted appeared to be of Scottish descent, this went down better. I resolved at all events not to be a "bronco", for sensitiveness to criticism was plainly a national characteristic. It was evident to Canadians that the inhabitants of North America were there because they had discarded the inferior ways of an effete Old World and, since respect for the law was undoubtedly more manifest in Canada than in the United States, then the question of which was the most superior race in the world settled itself. This, however, was a view I accepted with private reservations.

My future chief, Dr. C. K. Clarke, Professor of Psychiatry at the University and Superintendent of the Government Insane Hospital, was a man of parts, an excellent Canadian type. He was a very kind and humane person. He could rough it in the wilds with anyone, and was fond of doing so; a missing forefinger was a souvenir of an adventure "up north". Like King Otto's physician, he had had a madman jump into the lake with him, but he showed more presence of mind than the Bavarian psychiatrist by knocking him on the head and swimming ashore with him on his back. It was the sort of thing that was all in the day's work with him. He possessed little scientific knowledge, but his heart was set right in this respect and his ambition was to develop it in his sphere to the best of his abilities. His ambitions, however, unfortunately ran beyond the means at his disposal. He wanted to establish psychiatric teaching and research in Canada on a level approximating to that obtaining in Germany and the United States, and to found a proper Psychiatric Clinic; but he had to contend with authorities whose only view of the insane was that they were a costly nuisance, and who would calmly hang a murderer however mad he was. In the circumstances we were not able to do very much. Clarke instituted daily consultations among the staff in the approved fashion, and insisted on regular methods of note-taking. I became the Lord High Everything Else. It was my duty to conduct the pathological examinations in a little laboratory we started, to carry out psychological research, to act as director of the new out-patient clinic, to edit the new *Hospital Bulletin*, and so on. Finding me a willing horse, Clarke soon got me to give all his lectures at the university, hold the demonstrations, and carry out the annual examinations of students.

Holding two government appointments, of pathologist to the hospital and director of the clinic, I was advised to pay my respects to the Home Secretary—to kiss hands, so to speak. So, duly armed with a top-hat that caused a stir in the street, I proceeded to do so. He bore the somewhat humourless title of Provincial Secretary, and his behaviour was in keeping with it. He received me in his shirt-sleeves—it was now November—and during the audience did not take his feet off the table. However, he was affable enough and, I believe, a very capable man: by name, W. J. Hanna.

The president of the university, Sir Robert Falconer, had the good idea of increasing my income by making me a demonstrator in both medicine and pathology, as well as an Associate in Psychiatry. A year or two later I pointed out that I was performing all the duties that pertained to the Chair, so I was raised to an Associate Professorship. Falconer was a great figure, who did well by the university, and his biography is well worth reading.

All this teaching work came well my way, since I was fresh from my coaching exploits in London; in fact, I continued all my correspondence coaching for another fifteen years, both from Canada and afterwards. I found the students more boyish and unruly than English ones, but easy enough to get on with; they seemed genuinely interested in some of the psychological parts of the course, and it was good practice for me learning to introduce it to them. What I never got over, however, was the appalling illiteracy of their written papers; few of them appeared to know how to compose a grammatical sentence, and often they wrote in a fashion one would associate in England with the servant class. Many of the students, of course, came from country districts where schooling was fitful and not very accessible, so I suppose that was the explanation. On the other hand, one could only admire the sturdy efforts many students made to obtain a university training, efforts entailing sacrifices that transcended those we have been told of in Scottish stories; the American custom of earning enough money as waiters or farm hands during the long—very long—summer vacation to pay for their fees and keep for the rest of the year was common enough.

My teaching duties at the General Hospital naturally brought me into relation with the visiting staff, to most of whom I had brought letters of introduction. I especially remember Mr. Phedran, the genial and canny Professor of Medicine, Bruce, a dashing surgeon, and Primrose, a more cautious one and, incidentally, a good friend. There were, of course, many younger men, Hutchison and others, and with one of them, G. W. Ross, I carried out some interesting pathological work on the spinal fluid. There came out of it a new chemical test which, to our gratification, was named after us.

Before beginning to practise, it was necessary to secure a medical qualification, for in those days British and Canadian ones were not interchangeable. That meant passing all the examinations over again, including the earlier subjects of anatomy and physiology. There was a curious law that no one might act as examiner for the State in any subject he taught, and in practice examiners seemed to be chosen from remote country districts. In the oral examinations my English speech betrayed me, and it came out that I had London degrees, which were regarded with reverential respect. The examiners at once ceased to question me and began to consult me on moot points; it was the only examination in which I got 100 per cent.

Practice turned out better than I dared to expect. Somehow or other I was getting known in various quarters, and patients were sent to me from Montreal, Winnipeg, etc., and the United States; actually I had more patients from "across the border" than from Canada. This did not, of course, all happen at once; but in a year or two, together with my salaries, it was possible to lead a very comfortable existence. My only extravagance was with books, of which I formed a collection of some five thousand that overflowed into every room in the house. It meant a weekly visit to the Customs House, for duty had to be paid on all English and French books except very old ones, so that all incoming books had to be inspected. There was also a strict censorship, but my medical position eluded that. It was fortunate, since some of the books I acquired, such as Fuchs's *Sittengeschichte*, would assuredly have come off badly before a Canadian magistrate. I recollect the case of one poor bookseller who was sent to prison for selling Boccaccio's *Decameron*, the magistrate remarking severely that he would not allow the modern writings of any French degenerate to be sold if he could prevent it!

On arriving in Toronto I had rented a small house to await the arrival from England of Loe and my elder sister, who were to share the housekeeping responsibilities. Soon afterwards we went house-hunting and selected another in Brunswick Avenue, which at that time was on the outskirts of the city. We could stroll out of an evening towards the country, which, however, was too infested with odd shacks to be very inviting. One episode in those outskirts I well remember. A savage dog, which the post-mortem examination proved to have been suffering from rabies, dashed at my little terrier, which I picked up in my arms. He bit us, and his method of salivation made me suspicious enough to take the trouble of telephoning to Philadelphia for the materials for the Pasteur treatment. I had recently seen a veterinary surgeon die of hydrophobia in the Toronto General Hospital, and one such sight is enough for a lifetime.

Six months after my coming to Canada I received a cable saying that my mother was dying of cerebral haemorrhage at the untimely age of fifty-four. The news caused me a normal grief, but was not deeply distressing. All her children were on the American side of the Atlantic, and my father begged that one of my sisters should come home to him. There was no competition for the duty, since it would probably mean being indefinitely immured in an unattractive country village. In the end it was decided that my younger sister should go. She was at the time in Boston, Massachusetts, rather lightheartedly oscillating between medical studies and artistic ambitions, both of which she soon surrendered. We met in Montreal, and I broke the news to her. She dutifully returned and two years later got married. My sister Elizabeth stayed with me a year or two longer, and then expressed the wish to spend a holiday at home. She had been corresponding with an eligible suitor, and I imagined that she intended to inspect him more closely. The outcome was more dramatic, since Trotter, who had wind of her movements, intercepted her on the way and made a proposal of marriage on the railway platform. I doubt if they had ever been alone together; they had certainly never written to each other, and the only intimate passage between them had been an operation he had performed on her thyroid gland. But during the years in Harley Street they had silently taken each other's measure, so that when the appropriate moment arrived there was no hesitation. Theirs was as successful a marriage as I have known.

I saw Trotter every year on my visits to Europe, but our

correspondence was sparse and became increasingly so. He was always an erratic and reluctant letter-writer. Indeed, writing altogether was for him a painful labour, as was evidenced by a certain turgidity of style that contrasted vividly with his fluency of speech both in public and in private. It is sad to think that such a wide and profound thinker should have produced, apart from his technical contributions to surgery, only one book—the famous Herd Instinct one. His son, it is true, has partly remedied this by issuing a posthumous volume of masterly addresses, which is not yet so widely known as it deserves to be.

From a small collection of his letters I have preserved I propose to quote a number of characteristic passages, and will begin with some that illustrate his attitude towards the art of writing.

(*November* 1907)

"I was never so disgusted with my incapacity to express myself in a letter as I am now; I am absolutely lost when I cannot watch the effect of what I say, cannot hastily slip in a parenthetic qualification, or eke out with histrionics a particularly thin bit of thought. All of which you know well enough, so that you won't expect anything— Still there have been times when I have seemed able to do something and you will remember that though the words are dry and fumbling —this is the same voice."

(*November* 1908)

"Do you understand how this letter business tells against me? I can't exaggerate how difficult it is to me—it's like talking a foreign language—you have to let the conversation be regulated by what you can say and quite give up any idea of following consecutively what you want to be saying. The harshness and falsity of it vex me continually. To drop from a highly developed specially organised means of communication to this monkey jabber seems to me quite frightful, and is not remedied by my very clear consciousness of the ironic recommendation to practise, which the complaint must arouse in you."

Even with his published writings he constantly expressed great dissatisfaction, a feature common enough among notable authors. Thus when his two essays, which later formed the basis of his Herd Instinct book, appeared in the *Sociological Review*, he wrote:

"I am sending the second Sociological reprint—they kept the thing over till the Jan. no.—with the effect of completing my disenchantment with the miserable thing. It seems to me the most shockingly jejune piffle. It really is too bad conducting Reviews on this principle of the Resurrectionist—The thing ought to have been born and buried long ago, instead of popping up in this untimely way to shock its maker. You will let me know who ought to have reprints unless you think we should not interfere with the natural process of decay."

Trotter's inviolately calm exterior gave no hint of any anxious temperament, yet I know he had secretly often enough to wrestle with the demon of fear. I sent him once a description of an interesting nightmare I had experienced, which incidentally was the occasion of my later writing a book on the subject, and he replied:

(*November* 1907)

"I think I have felt something of what you describe—always as a consequence of the most intensely personal feeling, some frightful stroke to myself which like a near flash of lightning left one not only crouching and trembling from its ferocity, but as it were by a kind of ghastly by-product, appalled by the nightmare landscape it had revealed."

At one time he hit on the diary type of letter, with which he evidently felt less constrained.

(19 *March*, 1909)

"*Days and days later.* I hope you will not much mind this diary kind of letter (and not make puns about diarrhoea)—it seems better suited to my straggly mind than the formal composition—and I enjoy so much when I come in of an evening and can sit down and chat to you for a bit—You will remember how we always seemed best to get into communication when we were doing up our boots of a morning. Opening the mind is still so much a matter of the spell and the 'Open Sesame!' that it seems some element of the casual must still be left—This I find the diary form just supplies enough of. I feel so much more *comfortable* than if I were writing a regular letter. And you—if that were of any importance—get so much more of the truth.

"Not that I can always make this a substitute for talking to you. When I really must talk *with* you. I have taken lately to reading Nietzsche—and I find more and more in him and get flashes when I seem to catch exactly the extent and feeling of his greatness. Not I think however more satisfaction because of his insubstantiality—the obvious incommunicability of his fiery illumination to any other living soul. Aren't there three modes of approach to the truth about man?—the classico-aesthetico-moral (N.), the morbid (F.), and the biological (E.J. and his school). The first two have to me that element of the insubstantial. The first is like algebra—it is so difficult to be sure that your disciples know what x and y and z are representative of—so it comes that all Europe jabbers about Nietzsche—quite grammatically (algebraically, that is) without understanding a single word. It seems to me much the same with the one swell I could ever discover in antiquity—Plato. Everybody is ready to jabber about the Republic but not a soul knows what the poor man meant. The morbid method seems to me too much like histology—depends too much on magnification."

We used to subscribe to a large number of scientific periodicals, between fifty and a hundred, so when I went to Canada a precise division of them had to be made. They were supplied by the excellent firm of I. Nutt & Co., of which the head was at that time the late Alfred Nutt. He was much more interested in folk-lore and mythology, in which fields he made a considerable name for himself, than in the administrative details of bookselling, and his unconcern had maddening effects on our arrangements. Here are two references to the state of affairs.

"As I am in the complaining mood I naturally glide into the topic of the unspeakable Nutt. Such grotesque fantasias as he has played upon the distribution of journals would shock even your pessimism. I have been constrained to write to him no less than twice, so you may imagine the state of affairs. He is steadying down a bit now. I was much consoled by the thought of surgical journals hurtling across the Atlantic. By the way, I don't remember what we decided about the Grenzgebiet-Central-blatt—I am now going on with it—apparently thro' a caprice of Nutt's so it may not last. But I believe the earlier numbers are amongst your furniture."

"Levity first—I celebrated the New Year by sending our old friend Nutt a long and embittered explanatory letter. He replied admitting there had been troubles and explaining with sanctimonious particularity how they had arisen—referring throughout to our late domicile as 35 Harley St., and finally by way of demonstrating how his coolness and presence of mind had made everything clear he addressed the envelope to Dr. Wilfred Jones! I really *yelled* when I got it."

The extracts that follow are in a similarly light vein.

"Introspection is the art of looking thro' one's own mind into someone else's. The introspector's mind is a lens and not a back plate so he cannot focus on it. It is easy enough to know what other people feel, what is hard is to know how strongly they feel it—the first needs moderately strong eyesight, the second an extraordinarily strong stomach.—The startling irrelevance of this latter Einfall makes it quite clear that I must go to bed at once."

"I suppose the chief item of news about me is that I had my appendix out last week. . . . It wants a certain amount of faith in the rational method I find to make up your mind in the middle of work to go in for an experience at any rate unpleasant which is not obviously necessary *at that particular moment*; and I suppose every surgeon when he is operated on feels the pathos of the fact that for *him* the best skill can never be available—but of course all the circumstances are full of delightful openings for irony and the more astringent varieties of humour."

"Bradford becomes more eminent every day and I believe now sits quite continuously upon Commissions and things, including I suppose his fellow commissioners."

As would be expected, the serious part of our correspondence concerned the burning question of psycho-analysis, which was becoming increasingly significant to me. Not only was it in my direct path as a neurologist and psychiatrist, and so could in no case be avoided, but from early on I perceived something of the importance it was to yield for the biological study of man's nature in general. Trotter had to concede the first point, but was very reluctant to admit the second. As others have done, he likened psycho-analysis to morbid histology, highly useful or instructive in its place, but with very restricted consequences. Six months after the Salzburg Congress he wrote to me in Canada as follows:

"As to Freud. I think you write greatly about this business and I have read and reread your letter with much joy.

"In the early part where you deal with what our attitude is and should be towards the new stuff—you will remember your vertigino-genie metaphor of the bottles and the wine—I get as I have often got before in our talks about F. a certain sense that you are letting me down easily, a so to say 'therapeutic' flavour which gives me an uneasy feeling that the distance between us has a quality of the indefinite and certain ominous hints that it is large."

"As regards the facts, as far as I know them, I do not think I am resistive. Thus ignorance may of course be partly the cause of the trouble, and no doubt is, but not all. The actual state of affairs is, isn't it, that I do not get the sense of illumination, the sense of splendour that you do. Essentially surely it is a matter of 'significance' in our old technical sense. That seems to me to bring in deeper and more difficult things than ignorance, jealousy and the like superficial and easily recognisable (by us) shades of feeling: and things that you are technically much more capable of dealing with than I am. You talk very good stuff I think about our temperamental differences—one point you don't mention tho' you probably know—You say suppose we came to a parting of the ways and you chose what you 'knew' to be the upper path, you would have no pang of doubt lest you were wrong but would feel lonely—the point is that at the same time things with me would be *ungekehrt*. I should I think not be lonely in quite the same way but I should feel full of doubts that I was wrong—(the first part is put in chiefly I think for symmetry, but it is true enough about the doubts).

"Well, illumination is a difficult subject and altogether above me—I incline to the heresy that it is very satisfactory as long as the 'illuminator' doesn't share it. This *custodiet custodes*—Shaw, Nietzsche, Freud, all seem to me 'illuminate' and therefore having something of opaqueness in them."

Wit could of course not be kept out of such a tempting field. He once jestingly remarked that he could not imagine a more agreeable way of earning money than by telling people what you really thought about them, though we agreed it was rather a question of having to listen to what people really think of the analyst!

Trotter made one prediction and gave me one piece of advice: both were sound, though I was not in a position to follow the latter. The former was that, whatever he or anyone else might say, I should come into the open as a supporter of the new doctrines and risk any odium attaching to them or any danger to my remaining chances of academic success and "respectability". The advice was that I should retain as much independence as possible, else I should surely have to associate with, and become identified with, inferiors. I had too little pride—or perhaps too much—to be greatly impressed by such a consideration, but in any event there was no choice. The few men, such as Adolf Meyer, Paul Schilder, and others, who later on took up a benevolently aloof position did so at the price of never truly assimilating the new realm of knowledge. A bowing acquaintance with the unconscious mind is a very different matter from a direct apprehension of its workings, which could only mean a whole-hearted co-operation with whoever was bent on the same aim. That science mostly transcends its votaries I was to learn in many different fields, not only in that of psycho-analysis.

Naturally one of the first things I did on arriving in Toronto was to inform colleagues in the United States, to whom I was already known by correspondence or otherwise, and I accepted with alacrity an invitation Morton Prince sent me in December to stay with him in Boston. I was to meet a circle of physicians who were interested in the newer aspects of clinical psychology. The only people who at that time seemed to me to matter at all in that sphere, apart from Freud and his group, were Janet, Morton Prince, and Boris Sidis. Janet I knew; now I was to form an opinion of the others.

Morton Prince was a handsome man with great gusto for life, shown by his hearty boyish laugh. He was well born and well circumstanced, a prominent yachtsman, a popular clubman, an active local politician who had been mayor of Boston: in short, a many-sided man of the world, a member of what Jung would call the extraverted type. He had some scientific curiosity, was even to some extent reflective, but had no great depth of mind or patience for difficult problems. In my opinion his greatest effort of thought was a thesis written as a young man on the then interesting philosophical theme of "mind stuff". He was now known chiefly for his attempt to interest American neurologists in the problems of psychopathology, particularly of hysteria—a very uphill task. He had written a rather sensational book on a case of multiple personality; Trotter wounded him by calling it a "shilling shocker". He had achieved some therapeutic success by suppressing the most troublesome personality by the aid of hypnotic suggestion, but he had thrown no light on the genesis or the dynamics of such conditions. His work had, however, convinced him of the reality of what he called "co-conscious" states, and my common ground with him was this admission that the mind was wider than consciousness. We became good friends, and I acted as assistant editor of his newly-founded *Journal of Abnormal Psychology*—a term he insisted on in spite of my protest that workers in that field would not be very willing to call themselves "abnormal psychologists". He failed to develop any understanding for psycho-analysis, and he felt some pique that his pioneering work was not much recognised by analysts. As the years passed this difference naturally came between us, for, although he was most generous in opening his *Journal* freely to psycho-analysts at a time when other periodicals fought shy of them, he came later to make attacks that we felt contained unfair misrepresentations. Though our friendship cooled somewhat, it continued to exist, and he called on me in London on his last visit there in the 'twenties.

Boris Sidis, a clever Russian refugee, had devised some original and interesting experiments in the hypnotic investigation of hysteria, but he was a conceited and self-sufficing person who was not open to ideas from outside. Although he was a young man at that time, he made little subsequent progress, and his work has, perhaps unjustly, lapsed into oblivion.

There were a number of others present at that first meeting in Morton Prince's house: Waterman, who was to be his successor, but who never became more than a fashionable practitioner; Coriat, a loyal and painstaking, but uninspired psychotherapist; Hugo Münsterberg, the Professor of Psychology at Harvard University; Taylor, who later succeeded Putnam as Professor of Neurology at Harvard; and Putnam himself. Of these the only two who came to adopt a positive attitude to psycho-analysis were Coriat and Putnam; Sidis and Münsterberg became active opponents. I have summarised my general estimate of Putnam in a biographical sketch written for the volume of his *Addresses on Psycho-Analysis* which I edited after his death in 1918, so that here I may confine myself to a few personal memories.

When I was introduced to him—he was then sixty-two and I

only twenty-nine—he behaved with a deference quite absurd in the circumstances, and then, with his characteristic frankness, said he was disappointed in my appearance since he had expected to meet a tall man with a grey beard. At this point Prince jovially slapped him on the back and said: "Come, Jimmy my boy, we are not so old as all that; we'll have a jolly good time for another ten years." As it happened, Putnam was to live for another ten years, but his notion of spending his allotted time was different from Prince's; he used it to support psycho-analysis in America with all his strength and to try to bring about a union of science with philosophy, which he deemed essential for the good of humanity. He adhered to a particular brand of philosophy which I never fully grasped; and felt it incumbent on him to convert all psycho-analysts to the same belief. It was a pain to him that he could secure nothing more than polite attention from them: as Freud put it, "Putnam's philosophy is like a beautiful table centre; everyone admires it but nobody touches it."

But Putnam was much more than his philosophy. For one thing, he was the only man I have ever known, in a vast experience of scientific discussions, to admit publicly that he had been mistaken. He had a superb integrity of soul, and no personal interest ever even weighed with him in the balance against his devotion to his ideals. In those meetings at Prince's house—there were more than one—questions and criticisms were fired at me, but the only ones put with the serious desire to know more about the subject were Putnam's. We became excellent friends, and maintained a constant correspondence. In the following May he came to New Haven, Connecticut, to support me at the American Therapeutic Congress when I opened the campaign for psycho-analysis; it was the first time a paper had been read anywhere on the subject at a medical congress. I well remember the shiver that went through the audience when I said that Freud had sometimes treated a patient daily for as long as three years, though a member admitted to me afterwards that he knew of neurotics he would be proud to be able to cure in that time. Altogether the time factor in psychoanalytic treatment was a reason for strong criticism in America, where speedy results are at a special premium. Putnam also rendered me a similar service two years later by taking the trouble to travel to Toronto, where I was to read a paper before the Canadian Medical Association. We had heard that two American neurologists had decided to attend the meeting so as to discredit me in my home town; I had treated the wife of one of them, and it had resulted in her summoning courage to leave him because of his cruelty. Their attack was certainly virulent enough, but it did not disconcert me and I felt that Putnam and I got the better of them.

Incidentally, it comes to my mind that Harvey Cushing, the American Victor Horsley, was my guest during that meeting. In the evenings he would discuss a distressing neurotic symptom that afflicted him before each of his great brain operations. He wished me to analyse him for it, but that never proved feasible. I told Freud of it afterwards, and rather to my surprise he said he would not have advised treatment in such a case: it might prove that the surgeon's superb achievements were so closely bound up with the neurotic symptom—in a sense conditioned by it—that to disturb the one might disturb the other. My own opinion is that such an eventuality could only be temporary.

The late summer of that year, 1909, saw Freud's one and only visit to America. He and Jung were to deliver a short course of lectures at Clark University, Massachusetts, on the occasion of its centenary, and were to receive honorary degrees there. Ferenczi, of Budapest, had also travelled with them. I met them in New York and, together with Brill, took an overnight boat from there to New Haven, then the train to Worcester. They had just visited Niagara, and Freud had already received an unfavourable impression of the United States, which was to prejudice him strongly, and I think unfairly, for the rest of his life. It is hard to say what was the real reason for this. He said the food didn't suit him and gave him indigestion, but he had a healthy digestion and it is just as likely that his dislike of the food was simply an expression of other aversions. He had difficulties with the language and described to me his relief at hearing an English guide speaking on the Canadian side of Niagara; I heard him remark once to Jung that the people seemed not to be able to understand their own language when they talked together! He was plainly disgruntled. I imagine that the aversion had something to do with a feeling that commercial success dominated the scale of values in the United States, and that scholarship, research, and profound reflection—all the things he stood for—were lightly esteemed. At all events, he came later to take the rather cynical view that it was a country whose only function was to provide money to support European culture, an attitude that was to create many difficulties for me in my role of mediating between America and Europe. He grudgingly admitted American achievements, but coined the epigram: "Yes, America is gigantic, but a gigantic mistake."

The invitation to Clark University doubtless came from Stanley Hall, its president, whom I was to see much of in the future. He had a great reputation in American psychology, having been the first man to establish there a laboratory in experimental psychology and having written a number of pioneering works particularly concerned with childhood and adolescence; I had been very struck by a monograph of his on phobias in which he had tried, manfully if not very successfully, to connect each variety with some ancestral experience of the race. He greatly admired Freud's works, ranked himself as a psychiatrist, and was a foundation member of our societies; in later years, however, he became an adherent of Adler.

Among the company was the great William James, whose name I had long revered. He had an intuitive perception of the importance of the unconscious mind, and the case of dual personality he had himself investigated had convinced him of its reality. One day, with his arm across my shoulders, he made the weighty remark: "Yours is the psychology of the future." Had he been a younger man, I feel sure he would have espoused psycho-analysis. But he was near the end of his days. During a stroll with Freud he suddenly said: "Please walk on ahead," and lay down under a tree. Freud perceived he was in the throes of a heart attack, a condition that not long afterwards proved fatal, and that he wanted to go through it alone.

The first day I ever met Freud he had remarked: "What we most need is a book on dreams in English; won't you write one?" Since nothing of his work had then been translated, I was a little surprised that he should want to be known abroad by his theory of dreams. But I learned later that he thought very highly of it, much more so than of his conclusions about infantile sexuality, which, as he said, were or should be "obvious". On reviewing his life work I should myself be inclined to regard his theory of dreams as his most valuable contribution to science, one singularly complete in itself and opening out so many avenues of research.

On the present occasion he told me he had wanted to devote his course of lectures to the subject of dreams, but had refrained on the ground that it might not make a good impression with the practical-minded Americans. He recollected this the following year, when I told him of an experience I had had on reading a paper on dreams before the American Psychological Association, only three months after his visit to Clark. A lady rose during the discussion and in tones of heated indignation assured me that while repressed ideas might have something to do with the dreams of Europeans they certainly didn't in her country, since Americans had no repressed ideas.

As is well known, Freud gave an introductory course on psycho-analysis in general. It was listened to with great attention. After the third lecture a disappointed lady came and asked me to intercede with Freud to talk about sexuality, a topic he had not mentioned. I passed on the suggestion to him and he replied in a decided tone: "*Ich lasse mich in Bezug auf die Sexualität weder zu- noch ab-bringen.*" ("I do not let myself be moved either to or away from the theme of sexuality.") Then came the ceremony of conferring degrees, in which Freud made a touching speech expressing his gratitude for this first official recognition of his labours ("*die erste offizielle Anerkennung unserer Bemühungen*").

During all the odd moments of that inspiring week we five psycho-analysts held animated conversations on the problems that concerned us. Of an important practical plan we decided on I will say something in the next chapter.

The four years I spent in Canada were the most prolific of my life in respect of literary output. My monographs on the Nightmare and on Hamlet, as well as a host of other contributions, were written then. There were several reasons for this. I was unhappy in my personal life, so that work was a welcome refuge. Then there was the inspiration of the new ideas, of whose truth I was now fully convinced from my increasing practical experience, and which it was a pleasure as well as a duty to promulgate, expound, and add to. Also, I had more leisure than in previous years, with two excellent libraries to

Ernest and Katharine Jones in 1957

The Plat, Elsted

explore—my own and that of Toronto University, to which I had the fullest access.

My writings had procured me membership of the American Neurological Association, the American Psychological Association, the *Gesellschaft für experimentelle Psychologie*, and the *Gesellschaft deutscher Nervenärzte*. Every summer I crossed over to Europe to read papers before some international Congress. Then I must have given some twenty papers or addresses before various American societies in that time. My sister used to refer to these numerous visits to the United States as "raids over the border". It was certainly a happy idea of Americans to use the word "border" instead of "frontier", and it will be a happy day when Europeans treat their frontiers in the same way. These visits took me mostly to Washington (three times), Baltimore (four times), and the relatively near range of Chicago, Boston, New York, etc. One of these was a specially notable occasion—the opening of the Phipps Psychiatric Clinic in Johns Hopkins University, Baltimore. Adolf Meyer, who incidentally was also a friend who once stayed with me at Toronto, was to be the new Director, moving there from Ward's Island, New York, where I had first known him; he was very sympathetic to psychoanalytical ideas, but was too narcissistic a personality to risk investigating them himself. Americans know how to make the most of such ceremonies. Bleuler and a number of other distinguished European psychiatrists participated, with whom it was interesting to renew my acquaintance on foreign soil.

There being no neurologists in Canada, I joined the Detroit Neurological Society. To attend their monthly meetings meant an eight-hour journey each way, which, I think, showed unusual zeal on the part of a physician. But such contacts with American colleagues brought not only scientific benefit; it enabled one to get to know in a personal way the attitudes of mind, outlook on life, and daily customs of one's colleagues in another country. I liked the Americans from the start, and the numerous friendships I made in those years have ripened well with the passage of time.

Life in Toronto was in many ways very pleasant. Curiously enough, one partook of cultural activities more than in London. There, where so many were always available, one had to make an effort to find the necessary free time. In Toronto there was only one serious centre, the Massey Hall, and everything that came there did so only for a week. So it became always a weekly habit to attend, and it was very rewarding, since the most celebrated artists of the musical and theatrical world always included Toronto in their American tours. Any gap would be filled by the Montreal Opera Company, which was very good indeed. Then there were regular visits from the magnificent American orchestras, with their famous conductors, all on a level which London has never reached.

I made many friends apart from the medical ones. One was the eccentric Professor Mavor, an Englishman well acclimatised in Canada. He had been a friend of Tolstoi, of Goldwin Smith and other famous settlers who had died before my time there, and of many other people of note. He had the most extensive private library I have ever seen; in fact, most of his large house was given up to books, and domestic life must have been confined to an attic. Not only were all the walls in the various rooms lined, but there would be two rows of stands or bookshelves in the middle as well, and one had to pick one's way among books piled all over the floor. Mavor himself sat huddled in a small chair in a corner, from which of course he had to displace books whenever he wanted to use it. Another English friend was Brodie, the distinguished physiologist, who had just been appointed to the Chair at Toronto. His sophistication was a change from the naïveté of so many Canadian acquaintances, but in the last resort he was a conventional Englishman and prone to discount any enthusiasms.

Daily life I found in many ways much easier and simpler than in London. It made me realise how ineradicably complicated English civilisation is, and how every effort to bring about the simplest and most desirable change is hampered by the likelihood of its dislocating some set or other of interwoven hidebound interests. When I went to live in Harley Street, for example, I was overawed by the elaborate legal formalities that had to be slowly, very slowly, gone through before one could acquire even the lease of a house, and then I was introduced to the maze of obligations like ground rent, house tax, water rate, etc., etc. Even after that one had to submit one's *curriculum vitae* to Lord Howard de Walden, with testimonials to justify asking his permission to attach a brass plate to one's front door! What a contrast it was when I bought a house in Toronto! Buying a house was a complete act in itself, there being no such thing as a ninety-nine years' lease or still less a nine hundred and ninety-nine years' lease. Let me describe what happened when I sold it. A stranger, who had heard I was leaving, telephoned one day and asked at what price I was willing to sell it. When I told him he said that would suit him and asked at what time would it be convenient to meet me at the City Hall. There we informed the clerk of the transaction, and he promptly looked up the address in his register of property, erased my name and inserted the stranger's. There was not even a fee for the performance, and of course not the slightest need for lawyers, agents, "inspection of deeds", or any of the paraphernalia considered indispensable in England. A minute ago the house was mine; now it was another's.

Banking matters were equally simple. No need to work out one's balance. A cheque-book, so neat and tiny that it was kept in a waistcoat pocket, was so arranged that every time one drew a cheque or paid money into one's account the corresponding change in one's balance was entered in the stub at the same moment. Best of all was the income-tax form. No pages of Schedule D, etc., which defy all but the bravest to fill up without expert and highly paid assistance. Simply three spaces: amount of income, rate of tax, resulting amount of tax due; this last being often only a matter of shifting a decimal point. Yes, one needs to visit other countries to see how unnecessarily we complicate our lives here.

I greatly regret that I never had the opportunity to go West, where the grand scenery is, in North America; the scenery I saw in the East did not impress me over much. I really saw very little of Canada itself, apart from various tours in Ontario where I was invited to give addresses, and of course the inevitable Niagara. The academic session was almost continuous except for the long vacation, and then I always went to Europe. Dr. Clarke, *en route* for his beloved camping in the North, told me he was going away from civilisation, to which I tartly replied: "And I'm going back to it." It was, I hope, the only lapse in Canada from my newly-won tactfulness. But I was not making a good Canadian. Nor did I feel like accepting the several invitations I received to settle in the United States. I did not want to leave my bones so far from Europe, and it was not seemly to settle down in New York or Boston or Chicago unless one was prepared to become a good American.

There was no denying the home-sickness for Europe, especially for the Continent. It showed itself not only in my dashing there whenever I could get off, but even in the absurd form of my joining the German Club in Toronto, much to the surprise of the other members. I recall being present there at a festival on the occasion of the Kaiser's fiftieth birthday, and singing "*Er lebe hoch*" with the best of them; altogether it was the communal sing-songs that most drew me there. He was being praised as the only European monarch who had had an entirely peaceful reign, and only four years later came the outbreak of the Huns! More sensible was the forming of a dinner club with a group of exiles like myself: we called ourselves the Horatians. It consisted of Bell, the first to leave us when he returned to join his father's well-known publishing house in London; Brett, the Professor of Philosophy, and the only member who never got away from Canada; Jan Hambourg, the famous violinist, who with his brother Boris was then assisting his father at a Conservatory he had established; L. C. Martin, now Professor of English at Liverpool, who left first for the Sorbonne and then Sweden; H. V. Routh, Professor of Latin, who used the pretext of the war to get back to Europe, and then remained.

After all, I had only two complaints to make of Canada, though, I must admit, they were serious ones. The lesser one concerned the climate, with its changes from 10 degrees below zero to 105 degrees in the shade. To anyone like myself, who tolerates both extremes of temperature badly, it was very trying to have to expend so much energy and thought on the mere problem of keeping warm or cool as the case might be. There was really only one tolerable month, September, for the spring lasted hardly a week. I came to appreciate the old saying that a man can work out of doors in England on more days of the year than he can in any other country. More serious, however, was my attitude to the intellectual atmosphere. It was not merely that I found myself back in the Biblical and Victorian atmosphere of my boyhood—that would have been bad enough to someone bent on emancipation—but it was the dead uniformity that I found so tedious: one knew beforehand everyone's opinion on every subject, so there was a complete absence of mental stimulation or exchange of thought. I should much like to revisit Toronto now and observe the great change which, I understand, has taken place in this as well as in other respects.

Most serious of all was the state of Loe's health. In addition to a worsening of a dangerous physical condition, her neurosis had also greatly worsened, and since my sister's departure she had seldom left her bed. Both conditions urgently needed treatment that was not to be obtained in America. So in 1912 she decided to go to Vienna and place herself in Professor Freud's hands. I may add that as a result of his treatment we decided to part, after which we both married happily.

In June of that year we once more transported our belongings, including my now vast library, across the Atlantic. My intention at the time was to spend part of each year in England and part in Canada, since the university work itself could easily be got through in four or five months. But this proved unworkable in practice, and a year later, after one more return to Toronto, I resigned my position there.

We installed ourselves in a little flat in Vienna, where I stayed for a few weeks. I spent the time exploring the art treasures and the social life of that entrancing city, and made many good friends there. Two or three evenings a week would be spent *tête-à-tête* with Freud. He had taken a liking to me, and seemed to wish to open his heart to someone not of his own milieu. He was a magnificent talker, and we ranged over all sorts of topics in philosophy, sociology, and above all psychology. More than once I had to reproach myself for allowing him to continue till three in the morning when I knew his first patient was due at eight o'clock. Those were days when I got to know Freud well—his fearlessness of thought, his absolute integrity of mind and character, and his personal lovableness.

On returning in September 1912 from his holiday, Freud expressed the opinion that I had better not remain in Vienna during Loe's analysis. I did not need to go back to Toronto before the middle of January, and I decided to spend the time till then in Italy. What I had seen of Italian art in Paris, Munich, and the Low Countries, as well as in London and now again in Vienna, made me wishful to become really familiar with it in its home, and also to make some study of its architectural aspects. But why give a reason for spending some months in Italy? What good European would forgo any opportunity of doing so?

Most of the time was spent in Venice, Florence, and Rome, but I also visited Bologna, Padua, Pavia, Pisa, Siena, Verona—and other smaller places. Putting aside for the time being all other preoccupations, I threw myself into the study of this aesthetic world with my customary intensity. Every evening was spent reading Vasari, Ruskin, Berenson, and many other writers on either the principles of aesthetics or the history of Italian painting. Then, armed with a modern critical guide-book, Hutton or some other, I would start off early to be ready when the various museums or churches were open. My topographical sense helped me to arrange the tour of the day so as to waste little time in unnecessary journeys, with the result that I really saw an immense amount in the time. What is better is that I remembered what I saw. I have, to my regret, never been to Venice since, but not long ago I took my wife to Florence and Rome and was able from memory to make a good selection of the choice treasures for her to see. I saw so much in 1912 because I had no companion to distract me, for, although an old friend, Jack Evans, joined me for a time in Rome, he was too much occupied in getting over an unhappy love episode to be able to give his mind to sightseeing.

My aesthetic taste is of the acquired variety, not of the natural, but I have always been very susceptible to beauty in sight or sound, and the overwhelming beauty of what Italy has to show made a powerful and ineffaceable impression on me. Those months count as among the richest in my life, which they have permanently widened and deepened. From that time Italy and France completely displaced my fondness for Germany, and nothing their political leaders may do can alienate my affections for them and their people, as has long since happened with Germany. Perhaps, after all, that is another way of saying that I was becoming mature.

My psychological interests were by no means in abeyance during this stay, and two of my essays—on Andrea del Sarto and the Madonna respectively—were direct products, each derived from intent absorption in a particular picture.

All good things come to an end, and in January 1913 I was

back in Toronto, for the last time. When I returned to Vienna in May, I was planning to set up again in practice in London, but as the result of a talk with Freud I decided to make use of the opportunity of not being tied by time and to undertake a didactic analysis with Ferenczi in Budapest. I was the first psycho-analyst to do this. At the time it was a revolutionary idea, but it has since become part of the normal procedure for studying the subject. My analysis, like the rest of my life, was intensive. I spent an hour twice a day on it during that summer and autumn, and derived very great benefit from it. It led to a much greater inner harmony with myself, and gave me an irreplaceable insight of the most direct kind into the ways of the unconscious mind which it was highly instructive to compare with the more intellectual knowledge of them I had previously had.

The sparkling city of Budapest itself was a source of great delight, but I renounced the effort to learn more than a few words of Hungarian. Ferenczi was good enough to let me see something of the domestic life of his friends, both in town and in the country, so that I acquired a certain knowledge of yet another nation. In the autumn I went to London and set up, outside the proper area of medical consultants, in a flat in Great Portland Street.

This would be the place to say something about Ferenczi himself. He had an altogether delightful personality which retained a good deal of the simplicity and a still greater amount of the imagination of the child; I have never known anyone better able to conjure up, in speech and gesture, the point of view of a young child. These were invaluable qualities for psycho-analytic work, but he possessed others equally so. He had a very keen and direct intuitive perception, one that went well with the highest possible measure of native honesty. He instantly saw into people, but with a very sympathetic and tolerant gaze. Then he had an exceptionally original and creative mind. His ideas were far too numerous for more than a small proportion of them to be committed to writing, so this quality could be fully appreciated only from repeated conversations with him. As is often the way, however, with people who throw out masses of ideas like sparks, their quality was very uneven, since judgment—objective and critical judgment

—was the one gift denied to Ferenczi, and when that is feebly developed it shows, not only in the subsequent appreciation of the ideas, but also in the kind that emerge. This defect of his became more manifest in his later life, but I could not but be aware of its presence earlier.

The picture I have in mind of Ferenczi is therefore of a boyishly lovable person, rich in vitality and zest of living, simple, direct, and honest to the core, scintillating with interesting ideas that were mostly tossed off for the moment, and with a keen perception of other people's thoughts and motives. This is what he was when I first had to do with him, before the unhappy deterioration that set in some twenty years later. He had, it is true, other less praiseworthy characteristics. He had a great notion of male superiority, and was often unchivalrous in his attitude to women except when he, so to speak, pulled himself together and remembered how he should behave. He had also rather masterful, and even dictatorial, tendencies, which seem to have led to a good deal of trouble with his colleagues in Budapest; they either adored him or resented him. For myself I never took these tendencies very seriously; they were so evidently boyish and were so very easy to cope with; a joke, and his attitude would alter.

As is well known, some very deep layer of mental disturbance began to give trouble a few years before he died, largely in conjunction with the organic disease from which he suffered, and his character changed in many respects. He lost most of his old cheerfulness and vitality, became heavy, depressed, and ungracious, withdrew from his old friends, and—most serious of all—allowed his scientific judgment to be gravely deflected. It was a very sad end to a precious and rare personality.

Chapter Ten

The Psycho-Analytical "Movement"

SINCE I played a prominent part, from start to finish, in what has been called the psycho-analytical movement, it is well to single it out for special consideration. It has been by far the most important thing in my life—without it this book would have had no justification—and, so I think, it will also have a not insignificant place in the history of science.

Before I can set out to describe the features of this remarkable episode—from an historical point of view it can be called that, although it extended over some thirty years—I have, to get a proper perspective, to consider it in relation to a more general topic, namely, the attitude towards scientific discoveries. Ideally speaking, such a discovery presents new facts and connections that can be confirmed by further observation—or better still, if the opportunity offers, by experiment—in such a way that it ceases to belong to an individual and is brought on to an objective impersonal plane. Those to whom it is presented are interested in the promise of an enrichment in knowledge and understanding, but appraise the evidence critically and impartially—free from the enthusiasm of the discoverer—before they gratefully decide to accept it. We know, however, that this is not what actually happens. Apart from the deep apprehensiveness about the new, which is a long story in itself, the content of the discovery becomes immediately associated with various individual "complexes", from simple vanity and jealousy to the most subtle aspects of belief and prejudice, and the resulting attitude is never unbiased but always emotionally coloured, whether it takes the form of a blatant opposition or an excited approval. Nor is much help to be got from logic, in spite of desperate endeavours to find there an impartial touchstone. The most impeccable constructions, as with many of the scholastics, may turn out to be pure moonshine, while what seems to contradict all logic and common sense may nevertheless turn out to be well founded. The progress of scientific knowledge has therefore always been accompanied by animosities, prejudice, or even persecution, short-lived enthusiasms, and bitter personal quarrels. Although, as one might expect, these unfortunate features have been more pronounced when the discovery touched on emotionally significant themes, their universality can, like so many other matters, be tested by an appeal to mathematics, for in the cold and pure domain of mathematics they are no less prevalent than elsewhere. In short, there is no more fascinating problem for the philosopher or the psychologist than why, how, and when people regard a thesis as "proved".

If all this sad state of affairs holds good in physical science, where, after all, so many tangible criteria of observation and experiment are available, what can one expect when a discovery is concerned with the human mind, a sphere which most scientists and philosophers deny can belong to science at all? For the status of psychology as a branch of science is admitted only very grudgingly and only on the strict condition that it confines itself to matters of no import, and does not presume to interfere with the prerogative of the common man to have an expert opinion on all psychological problems that do matter.

A further consideration has to be borne in mind here. Although it is the first point of honour to a man of science to place truth before all things, and to use his best endeavours to retain an open mind or even to be prepared to find his most firmly held conclusions modified or overthrown by fresh data, still there is one situation in which it is quite peculiarly hard to uphold this grand ideal. This is when it has cost much to come to the conclusion in question, or, put in modern language, when one has overcome an emotional resistance that had stood in the way of perceiving the truth of the conclusions. Truths so painfully won are apt to be defended with great tenacity, and this may often interfere with the desirable readiness to modify them in the light of still more evidence. What began as a piece of insight hardens into a conviction and may at the end petrify into a prejudice; it did so with the great Lord Lister and his antiseptic spray. It is well known that after discoveries have been so accepted as to become familiar they acquire the quality of the obvious, and it is notoriously hard to imagine the efforts that their achievement originally cost. Harvey's great discovery of the circulation of the blood is as good an illustration of this as any.

The psychology of pioneers is therefore peculiarly difficult. They have to maintain, and often fight for, their hard-won convictions, and yet avoid allowing them to degenerate into dogmatic beliefs. Freud himself was an interesting example of this problem. He was quite immune to opposition or criticism from other people, but he remained always open to the pressure of new facts and constantly modified or even altered his conclusions in the light of them. They had, however, to be facts he himself observed; he did not easily take into account facts observed by other people, even by his co-workers and friends. He had a remarkably self-sufficing mind, and the great value of this doubtless overweighed any disadvantages it brought by way of detachment. So long as he was the main discoverer in the new field, and this was in fact so during most of his life, his attitude was successful, but plainly it could not permanently stay so when other explorers appeared. In that event there would be the danger, sooner or later, of the hardening into dogmatism which in fact he just avoided.

Another and crucial matter in the psychology of discoverers is that the perceiving of a truth to which the world had previously been blind is usually achieved by an inner revolutionary process of a special kind, and this then induces a particular attitude towards the resulting conviction. The problem in question becomes associated with some quite unconscious conflict, and when this has been overcome in a certain way it frees the person in respect of the conscious problem so that he is now able to "see" an answer previously invisible. The unconscious process of overcoming, however, is of a challenging or defying order—in the courage for this lies much of the pioneer's greatness. There is always a risk of a subsequent reaction of remorse or fear for what has been done. Then the discoverer has either to assert his painfully-won conviction with a tenacity or defiance that may border on dogmatism, or else deal with his sense of guilt in some other way. One may compare, for instance, the reactions of the two men who discovered the relation of Natural Selection to Evolution, which meant displacing God from His position as a detailed Creator specially concerned with mankind, and removing Him to an infinitely remote distance—at least in Natural Theology. One of them, Darwin, the one who stood in such awe of his own father, said it was "like committing murder" —as, indeed, it was unconsciously; in fact, parricide. He paid the penalty in a crippling and lifelong neurosis, and in an astonishing display of modesty, hesitancy, and dubiety concerning his work. The other, A. R. Wallace, compensated for the displacement of the supernatural by bringing it back in another sphere, by his quite naïve adherence to spiritistic beliefs. Copernicus, the only person whose discoveries rank in revotionary significance with theirs, took the precaution of dying before publishing them.

All these considerations are not so far from my story of the psycho-analytical movement as they may appear, and are necessary to understand the problems with which it was faced.

One of the central discoveries Freud made in investigating the unconscious was that of what he called the Oedipus complex: that every boy has the wish to sleep with his mother and kill his father, and that nothing is more important for the development of his later character than the way in which he deals with these wishes. Now this is a discovery about which one cannot well be indifferent. There are really only three possible responses to it. One can suppress all sense of its significance and calmly call it "very interesting". If one feels and realises its terrific significance, this leads either to a—usually vehement—repudiation of it, or else to an acceptance that has an overwhelming effect. What becomes of all our vaunted scientific impartiality and open-mindedness? That is the situation with which the first pioneers in psycho-analysis were faced, for Freud's immediate followers, necessarily identifying themselves to some extent with him, were in a similar position of responsibility to his own, even if on a minor plane.

Naturally his followers responded in various ways. A few of the weaker-minded, casting all responsibility on their leader, idolised him and regarded him as an infallible oracle. This attitude, absurd as it may appear, brought one nearer to the truth in the matters at issue than did one of crass opposition. Freud himself once said to me that the simplest way of learning psycho-analysis was to believe that all he wrote was true and then, after understanding it, one could criticise it in any way one wished;

I rejoined that credulity and denial were too near each other emotionally for the path to be a safe one. This response has been popularly supposed to be general, or even universal, on the part of psycho-analysts, but I may assert with assurance that it was not that of any psycho-analyst who achieved any serious standing by his work. There were others who tried to keep their independence of mind by petulant and petty quarrels with details of the work. Others again, after a first flush of enthusiastic acceptance, recoiled when they realised what they had done, and then tried to find a way of escape by reinterpreting the facts in some more harmless fashion. These became the seceders, who were so applauded by the world: Adler, Jung, and others. Finally, some of us were prepared to shoulder the responsibility ourselves, and to do all in our power to combine insight into the astonishing discoveries with the balance becoming to scientific investigators. Abraham, of Berlin, shared this attitude with me to the full; Ferenczi to a large extent, Putnam also in his special way.

It may have been noticed that I put one word of the title to this chapter in inverted commas—to pillory it, so to speak. It was one much favoured in Vienna, and they even for some years published a periodical with that title—to my considerable disapproval. The word "movement" is properly applied to activities, such as those of the Tractarian Movement, the Chartist Movement, and so many thousand others, characterised by the ardent desire to promulgate, or bring into force, beliefs that are accounted exceedingly precious; it is akin to what nowadays is called "propaganda".

It was this element that gave rise to the general criticism of our would-be scientific activities that they partook rather of the nature of a religious movement, and amusing parallels were drawn. Freud was of course the Pope of the new sect, if not a still higher Personage, to whom all owed obeisance; his writings were the sacred text, credence in which was obligatory on the supposed infallibilists who had undergone the necessary conversion, and there were not lacking the heretics who were expelled from the church. It was a pretty obvious caricature to make, but the minute element of truth in it was made to serve in place of the reality, which was far different.

The picture I saw, on the contrary, was one of active discussion and disagreement that often enough deteriorated into controversy; and, as for "orthodoxy", it would not be easy to find any psycho-analyst who did not hold a different opinion from Freud on some matter or other. Freud himself, it is true, was a man who disliked any form of fighting, and who deprecated so-called scientific controversy on the very good ground that nine-tenths of it is actuated by other motives than the search for truth, the only one he found interesting. Nevertheless, he was extremely patient and tolerant of divergent opinions so long as he thought the other person was sincere, and not merely impelled by some irrelevant emotion. Once, for instance, at a time when I was president of the International Psycho-Analytical Association, I read a paper before its Congress in which I differed radically from some views of whose truth I knew Freud was convinced, and offered another theory of the phenomena. Immediately afterwards we discussed the problem most amicably, failed to persuade each other, and agreed to look for more evidence that would throw more light on it. That is not, I imagine, in accord with the general idea of a Pope.

I have said that every pioneer has first to overcome personal inner "resistances" before he can tear aside the curtain that had hitherto obscured a particular aspect of truth: that, indeed, is the essence of his achievement. These resistances function in virtue of their indirect association with some unconscious thoughts and emotions. The most formidable of them—i.e. the greatest impediment to scientific progress—have always been those that had become connected with the idea of the Divinity, so that each step onward signified displacing this idea to a greater distance and to contemporaries could only appear in terms of blasphemy. The mid-nineteenth century saw greater boldness in this direction than any other period had.

Now, however, for the first time in human history it became a question not merely of circumventing the resistances induced by such indirect associations, but of actually seeing face to face, feeling, realising, and overcoming the final inner resistances in their naked form. That was Freud's unique achievement. We, his followers and colleagues, had to fight hard within ourselves in the endeavour to reach the same freedom of thought and to parry the subtle activities of still hidden resistances that sought to reimpose the previous blindness or at least to distort and obscure our vision. Some, as I shall presently relate, fell by the way. They found the light too hard to bear for long, and when they drew the curtain back again they had the satisfaction of receiving the plaudits of the world, which had been disturbed by the approach, however distant, of the new truth. At first all of us, including Freud himself, underestimated the strength, depth, persistence, and subtlety of the inner sources of opposition. We have learnt much in the thirty or forty years that have passed since then, but to this day I am of opinion that none of us has yet measured them in final fashion.

The counterpart to this internal resistance was, of course, the external opposition—or prejudice, to use a popular term—that was encountered from the first publication of Freud's works. I have no doubt that this opposition would have been more fierce, and perhaps overwhelming, than it actually was if the outer world could have realised the full import of the new doctrines. For inner psychological reasons, however, this was in the nature of things impossible, and the world had only to adapt itself by rearranging its defences, a process that took only ten or twenty years in one country after another. By means of the mechanisms of denial, of discounting, of accepting with lip service only, of reinterpretation in more innocent terms—by varying combinations of these and other attitudes—the disturbed outer world sooner or later came once more to a position of rest, feeling it had satisfactorily digested these new discoveries, but really reducing them in this fashion to harmlessness. While it lasted, however, the heat of the opposition was unpleasant enough, though it never became dangerous in the sense of seriously threatening to strangle the progress of our work. Freud has himself told the story of his own ostracism in the medical circles of Vienna, and after a few years it spread to Germany and elsewhere. I saw little myself of the opposition in Austria, for the simple reason that I hardly came into contact with any professional circles there apart from the psycho-analytical one. Of what I observed and encountered elsewhere I shall tell as I go along.

These, then, were the main factors of the heuristic situation in which the pioneers in psycho-analysis found themselves: an intense conviction of new truths, but one which could not fail to be emotionally tinged; some appreciation, however imperfect, of the difficulty of sustaining that insight; unmistakable opposition, often violating all the accepted canons of social behaviour, on the part of the outer world. What, now, was to be our response to it? There was a risk of erring in either direction. With rare exceptions, men of science feel it a social duty to communicate any new discoveries and conclusions to their professional colleagues—in this case the world of medicine and psychology—so that they may participate in whatever advantages may accrue from the advance in knowledge. This laudable attitude is hardly ever pure; mostly it is complicated by others such as vanity, desire for recognition, praise, or rewards, and all the allied manifestations of the instincts of self-assertion and power. These secondary motives are naturally stimulated if the reception of the communications is a hostile one. One may be altruistically disappointed at the potential benefits of the new work being wasted, or personally chagrined at the rebuff to one's intelligence. Commonly this leads to redoubled efforts to present the conclusions in a more persuasive fashion, to counter the criticisms brought forward, and there begins the slippery slope through argumentation to controversy and finally to personal abuse. The two main disadvantages of yielding to these temptations are the waste of emotion involved and the distraction of activity from fruitful work into directions that are always futile. Has one not performed one's social duty by simply publishing the work in question and thus giving one's colleagues the opportunity of making use of it? Is anything more demanded of one? Social consciences will of course differ individually, and only a cynic would shrug his shoulders with an indifferent "*tant pis pour les autres*". Again, what if the cold reception is not merely a blank one, but takes the form of emotional distortion? The work may, for example, be reviewed in a periodical or work with such unfairness that the reader gets a completely misleading account of its real content. How far is it desirable to rectify this by pointing out the distortions in the reviewer's account, the gross misrepresentations that may even make it out to be the very opposite of what it is?

The situation was still further complicated to some extent by the curious circumstance that, with the exception of the small Swiss group—who nearly all parted company after four or five years—and myself, all the early workers in psycho-analysis were Jews. I imagine the reasons for this were mainly local ones in Austria and Germany, since, except to some slight extent in the United States, it is a feature that has not been repeated in any other country; in England, for example, only two analysts have been Jews (apart from refugee immigrants). In Vienna it was obviously easier for Jewish doctors to share Freud's ostracism, which was only an exacerbation of the life they were accustomed to, and the same was true of Berlin and Budapest, where anti-Semitism was almost equally pronounced. The aptness of Jews for psychological intuition, and their ability to withstand public obloquy, may also have contributed to this state of affairs. It was one that had some influence on the form taken, especially at first, by the psycho-analytical "movement". It also had personal results for myself, since I found, to my surprise, that henceforth my life was to be lived mainly in Jewish company and that my best friends would for the greater part be Jews. This could not but be a matter of interest to me, and it makes it inevitable that I should say something about my attitude to this vexed and delicate topic.

Until this time I had had no friends among Jews, and had met very few of them. In childhood I remember my grandmother telling me that Jews were people who kept pawnshops, a fact with hardly any meaning to me, and that they were obstinate people who kept apart from the rest, even going to the length of having non-Christian synagogues of their own. So I suppose I started life with the usual vague prejudice against them. There were none in any school I went to, and only one or two in college or hospital; there was nothing, therefore, to arouse my interest in them. I doubt if I connected them much with the ancient Jews of the Old Testament, about whom I was of course fully informed. These lived far away and long ago, and had presumably disappeared, for the remarkable and incredible stories one read of their doings were hard to connect with any real everyday world.

The Jews I was now to get to know were of course all foreigners, from whom one must expect standards of all sorts and attitudes of mind different from English ones, so it was some time before I came to discriminate between them and other foreigners and to remark on their own distinguishing characteristics. As time went on, however, my position as the only Gentile sharing deeply their main preoccupation with, I think

I may say, my own unusual capacity for adaptation and sympathetic understanding, led to my being admitted to their intimacy on practically equal terms. They would almost forget my Gentile extraction, and would freely share with me their characteristic jokes, anecdotes, points of view, and outlook on life. After a quarter of a century's such experience I came to feel that I knew their characteristics with an intimacy that must have fallen to the lot of few Gentiles, and I have reflected much on them and the social problems that surround their lives. I am going to prove this to any Jewish readers of this book by an anecdote which I shall not attempt to translate to others. When the Nazis took possession of Vienna one of the urgent problems that arose was how to help the patients of the Psycho-Analytical Clinic there. The Nazis said we might for the moment continue to treat them, but that the Directorship of the Clinic must be in "Aryan" hands. On inquiring about Dr. Sterba, one of our colleagues who happened to be a Gentile, I was told he had left for Switzerland, whereupon, to the general amusement, I exclaimed: "*O weh, unser einziger Shabbes-Goy ist fort.*"

In one important respect, however, my knowledge on this topic is singularly deficient. It has never been my fortune to know a Jew possessing any religious belief, let alone an orthodox one. It may well be said that this quite disqualifies me from holding any opinion worth anything on any Jewish question, for to empty it of its religious kernel is surely to make it into a *Hamlet* without the Danish Prince. I should not myself agree, however. I fully admit that the greater part of what is called the Jewish problem emanates from their remarkable religious history, but I am sufficiently familiar with that history both from my first-hand experience in childhood and from extensive subsequent reading.

Well, after this preamble, all I am going to say here on a topic that might well fill an interesting book amounts to two personal expressions of opinion. The first is that the greater part of this bulky Jewish problem is related to a central characteristic of Jews that may very reasonably be derived from their peculiar belief of being God's Chosen People: namely, their intense, and practically universal, determination not merely to regard themselves as different from other people but also fundamentally to remain so despite any superficial compromise they may appear to make. Although every distinct community possesses something of this quality, no other seems to possess it in anything like the same degree, and no other maintains it when living as a minority amidst other communities.

My second observation is that, whatever other qualities Jews may possess, likable or the reverse, no one who knows them well can deny that they are personally interesting. By that I mean, specially alive, alert, quick at comprehending people or events and at making pungent or witty comments on them. My Celtic mind, a little impatient of Anglo-Saxon placidity, complacency, and slowness of imagination, responded gratefully to these qualities, and it was perhaps the chief reason why I enjoyed Jewish society. One might at times find the rather hothouse family atmosphere, with its intensities and frictions, somewhat trying, but one could be sure of never being bored. These are the qualities, together with the resulting swift facility in apprehension of knowledge, that go to support the Jewish belief, which they often impose on other people too, concerning the superiority of their intellectual powers. I have never been convinced of that myself, for one should not take one kind of intelligence for the whole of what the brain can do, and I greatly doubt if the first-class names in science, art, or literature are more often Jewish than their numbers or opportunities would lead one to expect.

These last considerations have a considerable bearing on the reactions of the psycho-analytical group when faced with their difficult internal and external situation. The opposition to psycho-analysis, inevitable in any event, was doubtless heightened by anti-Semitic prejudice, which, curiously enough, has often had a sexual accompaniment, just as the anti-"colour" prejudices of English and Americans have. A Jew was, so to speak, the wrong person to announce that the sexual instinct was a far more subtle and significant factor in mental life than had ever been supposed; and the fact that—in Central Europe at least, where anti-Semitism was so strong—only Jews could be found to support the new views confirmed the suspicions of outsiders. The Jews themselves, with their proneness, so often justified, to interpret any criticism or opposition as actuated by anti-Semitism, also tended to confuse the issue in the same way; and their natural eagerness to make converts conflicted with their innate tendency to retire behind ghetto walls with an outlook of suspicion and resentment.

I use the word "convert" advisedly, for approach to psycho-analysis cannot be effected by reason alone, however much it may speak the final word; it is necessarily an emotional process involving important inner mental changes of a more than coldly rational order. Every willingness to perceive new truth is of this nature. Hence it is always easy to arouse prejudice against pioneers of thought, even those in science and still more those in art, by comparing them to religious votaries, since religion is the final example we have of an emotional process which transcends reason. The pioneers themselves may fall into the trap by carelessness in their terminology, as psycho-analysts did by speaking of their "movement", or as Darwin did by writing to a friendly colleague the year after *The Origin of Species* was published: "If we can once make a compact set of believers we shall in time conquer!"

In the last quarter of a century of Freud's life the personal prejudice against him was greatly attenuated, and all the harsh things that were formerly said against him were now transferred to his followers, of whom nothing bad enough could be said. That is as it should be, even if some of us think it was carried at times to unjust extremes. It was helped by the circumstance that, in the complicated situation I have been adumbrating, Freud's personal reaction was certainly more balanced than that of the majority of his followers. It was marked by complete dignity throughout. Recognising the futility of "scientific" controversy—a contradiction in terms—he studiously refrained from entering into discussion with an opponent. Only once in his life, very early in his career, did he write a paper in answer to criticism, and that for the reason that the critic, Loewenfeld of Munich, was a personal friend. His masterly and objective reply on that occasion belied the reason he sometimes gave later for avoiding argumentative discussion: namely, that he was "not good at it". The truth was that he had a temperamental dislike of contention, buttressed by his opinion of its fruitlessness, particularly in scientific matters. Nevertheless, scattered through his writings occur many passages in which he gives a reasoned and impersonal reply to various criticisms of his work, so that he cannot be said to have neglected them.

On the question of "propaganda" Freud followed a middle course, and my own attitude always coincided with his on the matter. He was naturally desirous that his work should be as widely known as could be, and, if possible, accepted; but he would restrict activity in this direction to the publication of positive contributions alone and deprecated any that could be called solicitous or importunate. In fact, his attitude was the same as towards a prospective patient; he would place his services at the disposal of anyone who manifested a desire for them, but he would never think of pressing them on him. I do not think he entertained any undue expectation concerning the speed, or otherwise, with which his work would be accepted, nor much disappointment at its actual slow rate of progress.

Two things, however, caused him sadness. One was the early ostracism by his Viennese colleagues, a rebuff which I do not suppose he ever got over, and which affected his feelings about the medical profession in general. I should ascribe this to his being deeply surprised by their reaction, for it occurred at the outset of his career when he had insufficient experience of the unconscious mind to be prepared for it. His own mind was direct and in a sense curiously simple, so he was puzzled, and also chagrined, at the way his colleagues took what he considered his straightforward observations and conclusions. The other thing was the revolting abuse to which he was for years subjected by German physicians. Here again he was probably taken by surprise. He was by now prepared for any direct opposition or denial, but not for the scurrilous and highly personal calumnies emanating from neurologists and psychiatrists of high standing. That members of his profession could so debase themselves saddened him: for he was a great gentleman. He confessed to me his disappointment at this treatment, which he ascribed to "German unmannerliness". Before he died he was to find that this was a very mild understatement of how Germans could treat him.

Freud's attitude towards Gentile analysts was a somewhat mixed one. He evidently wished to expand beyond the confined atmosphere of his local adherents and extended a warm welcome to Jung, myself, and, later on, others from the outside world. On the other hand, he seemed to retain a certain mistrust of them, one which events did not justify, for of the five well-known analysts who later deserted him only one was a Gentile.

After this somewhat lengthy description of the psychological background of the psycho-analytical "movement", I now come to the events themselves. Those of us who were together at the Clark University celebrations in September 1909 decided that Jung, who had called together the Salzburg gathering in the previous year, should organise a Congress on a larger scale in 1910 and that this should then constitute itself the organ of a permanent International Psycho-Analytical Association (which from now on I shall abbreviate to I.P.A.). If I had to say which of us took the lead in planning the constitution of the new Association I should name Ferenczi, and it was he who moved the necessary resolutions when the time came for the meeting. We had to restrain two qualities in Ferenczi which led to over-excitement: his dictatorial tendency, which I mentioned earlier, and his strong Masonic feeling for brotherhood. It was essentially his influence that led in later years to the criticism, especially from American members, of the Association itself. He wanted, for example, to have a rule that no member of the Association be allowed to publish a paper before first submitting it to the president. There would be the strongest reasons against such a policy even with a small group, but the idea of imposing it on an international body was so absurd as to betoken a very unpractical mind.

The meeting was held at Nuremberg in April 1910, a time of year when I could not leave my duties in Canada. It was the only International Psycho-Analytical Congress I have ever missed. Freud was too mistrustful of the average mind to adopt the democratic attitude customary in scientific societies, so he wished there to be a prominent "leader" who should guide the doings of branch societies and their members; moreover he wanted the leader to be in a permanent position, like a monarch. In this, especially in the first half of it, I feel sure he was right, for one cannot understand anything about the development of psycho-analysis if one puts it on a level with old-established and relatively unemotional branches of science, with astronomy, geology, and so on. A strong steadying influence, with a balanced judgment and a sense of responsibility, was in the circumstances highly desirable.

Freud did not wish to play this part himself. In this again he was doubtless right, since, apart from his temperamental dislike of the rough-and-tumble such a position was sure to bring with it, it might have savoured a little of self-advertising publicity. At the time he only withdrew nominally; in fact he retained a tight hold on all matters of policy, and his influence was so powerful that the president could not deviate far from it. For reasons I have hinted at above, he wished an outsider to play this part, and Jung seemed admirably suited for it. His research work had made him a man of standing in both experimental psychology and psychiatry, where he had already won widespread recognition; he had an academic position and was expected at that time to succeed to the Chair of Psychiatry at the University of Zurich when it should next become vacant; he appeared to be enthusiastically devoted to the new science, and his hearty and confident personality inspired general esteem. He was young, about thirty-four at the time, forward-looking, and abounding in energy and ambition. Freud was evidently charmed with him, and was sure he had found the ideal leader for his purpose. All the auguries appeared fair, but nevertheless within three years the choice was proved to have been the most baneful one that could have been made. It was the first indication I had that Freud, despite his extraordinary genius in penetrating the deepest layers of the mind, was not a connoisseur of men.

This was one of his characteristics with which we became increasingly familiar as the years passed. He overestimated or underestimated people over and over again on the simple criterion of liking or disliking them on personal grounds. For myself, I was at the time disturbed. In private conversations both in Zurich and in Worcester, Jung had revealed himself to me as a man with deep mystical tendencies that prevented a clear vision of a scientific attitude in general or a psycho-analytical one in particular; the superstructure was brilliant and talented, but the foundation was insecure. The Viennese present at Nuremberg, who hardly knew Jung, raised objections to his being made president of the new association, but Freud rightly discounted these on the grounds of their jealousy at being passed over for a newcomer. As I said, I was not present at the meeting, but from what I was told afterwards I think the account given in Wittels' book of the scene that took place is substantially correct. So Freud and Ferenczi got their way: the Association with its officers was launched.

It was planned to hold a Congress every year, and the next one was held at Weimar in September 1911. It was in many ways the pleasantest and most successful of any. Enthusiastic interest in the new ideas was at its height. A new method of investigation had been put at our disposal, and each of us was using it, according to his capacity, to make one discovery after another in the unexplored field now made accessible. Jung was in excellent form and on good terms with everyone. Professor Putnam of Boston was present, and read us a homily on the need to unite psycho-analysis with philosophy. He was of course treated with the greatest respect, although there was no response to his views. Putnam wrote afterwards to Freud saying what a good impression he had received of the analysts he had met at the Congress, to which Freud replied admitting that: "*Sie haben gelernt ein Stück Realität zu ertragen*" ("They have learnt to tolerate a piece of reality"). Among others of note present were Professor Bleuler of Zurich, the psychiatrist who was to displace Kraepelin as the foremost of his time, van Renterghem of Amsterdam, one of the three or four best-known psychotherapists in Europe, and Frau Lou Andreas-Salome, who had the perception that made her a close friend of the greatest psychologists of the nineteenth and twentieth centuries respectively, Nietzsche and Freud.

Weimar itself, charged with memories of Goethe—though with no hint of its future as the birthplace of an ill-fated republic—provided a sympathetic environment. A few of us took the opportunity of paying our respects to Nietzsche's sister and biographer, who lived there, and she professed interest in various connections we had found between her famous brother's psychological insight and what psycho-analysts were now revealing in their daily work. Incidentally, this was peculiarly true also of Schopenhauer, so much so that Freud deliberately refrained from reading him. This was very characteristic of Freud; he was intent on seeing things through his own eyes and reflecting on them in his own way, undisturbed by any suggestions, even useful ones, from without.

Alarm at psycho-analytical doctrines was as yet not at all widespread. The local press, for instance, were innocently polite about the Congress, though evidently bewildered by the task of describing its doings. There was an amusing example of this. Ferenczi read a paper on the psychological causes of homosexuality, and Otto Rank read one on "the nudity motif in poetry and legend". The next day a local newspaper announced that the Congress had discussed homosexuality, nudity, and "other important current questions".

Next year no Congress was held. Jung, in spite of the rules, had postponed it on the ground of his being away in America on a lecturing tour. This was felt to be rather high-handed, for the Congress could of course have taken place in his absence. It was the summer I spent in Vienna. Freud was evidently beginning to be perturbed about Jung, who had written from America saying he had found there that by omitting to mention certain aspects of psycho-analytical theory he met with less opposition. Freud, who had a peculiar abhorrence of making any compromise or concession in scientific matters, had tartly replied that if he left out more the opposition would further dwindle, and that by not mentioning any of it he would find no opposition at all. Here was a pretty pass between a commander and his chief-of-staff. And worse was to follow. In the meantime, however, more urgent trouble had been brewing nearer home, among the Viennese themselves.

The first form this took was the disagreement with Adler. Now, Adler was a man with considerable gifts of psychological observation of a superficial order; he had little power of any deep penetration. Like many Jewish doctors in Vienna, he was a Socialist by political conviction, and moreover one of the type whose views were based rather on a sense of social inferiority, with consequent envy and resentment, than on more objective grounds. He came to psycho-analysis attracted by the stress it laid on suppression of personal wishes, and hoping to get from it some scientific support for his Socialistic strivings. He brought with him one or two good ideas. Taking up the old biological conception of compensation—i.e. the tendency of both the mind and the body to make up for deficiencies by developing, and often over-developing, compensations in some related field—he applied this to the influence of the body on the mind. He made some shrewd observations of patients who had some bodily defects from early life, and showed how they developed excessive compensations in mental attitudes symbolically associated with the parts of the body affected. He failed, however, to answer the question of why some people responded in this way and not others, nor did he attempt to analyse the special feeling of inferiority in such cases—or, to use the now popular term, "inferiority complex", one which Adler borrowed without acknowledgment from Marcinowski—which psycho-analysis had shown to proceed from unconscious guilt reaction to sexual impulses. He then went on to "compensate" for his omission to analyse the underlying sexual factor by blandly maintaining that it was always, in both sexes, of a feminine nature, and that the excessive reaction was a pretended masculinity. This over-simplification had little reference to the actual facts, except possibly in special cases, and it naturally evoked criticism. Whereupon Adler again altered his theory, this time for good, and asserted that the compensation represented the "striving for power" which he now put forward as the key to all human behaviour; even ordinary sexual desire was really a mask for this will to power, to use Nietzsche's phrase. Finding that this found still less support among his colleagues, he angrily resigned from the Vienna Society, and founded a school of his own which in later years had a temporary vogue, particularly in America.

I had known Adler fairly well in those early days, and we used to correspond when I was in Canada. My impression of him was of a dour and disgruntled personality, ambitious and narrow, but with a certain limited capability. I came across him again a couple of times in his successful period, and found him milder and mellowed, though more self-complacent.

When the Viennese analysts evinced so much opposition to Jung's leadership, Freud had tried to appease them by creating prominent positions for a couple of them. In accordance with his wish not to hold official positions himself, he had resigned the presidency of the Vienna Society and installed Adler in his stead, a solution which lasted only a couple of years. His other attempt met with no better success. At Salzburg it had been decided to found a *Jahrbuch* in which could be published extensive psycho-analytical contributions that could not easily be placed in the medical or psychological periodicals, and Bleuler and Jung—in practice the latter—were entrusted with the editorship, which again had not improved the temper of the

Viennese. So Freud determined to found a *Zentralblatt*, a more frequent periodical for which there was a real need, which would contain shorter contributions together with news of other psycho-analytical activities, book reviews, and so on; moreover, it was recognised at the Nuremberg Congress as the official organ of the I.P.A., the reports of whose proceedings it would publish. Stekel, a Viennese this time, was to be the editor.

Stekel, whatever his faults, was a much more entertaining person than Adler. He had come to Freud some six years previously as a patient. After a very dangerous condition had been remedied, however, he did not pursue his analysis further, so that much of his character remained unchanged. For a few years he retained a remarkable capacity for divining the unconscious counterpart of conscious mental processes, and he made, for example, real contributions to our knowledge of symbols. I use the word "divining", since he never went beyond guesswork. He had neither the patience nor the capacity to provide any evidential demonstration of his conclusions, and took up a lofty attitude when asked to prove any of them. "I discover things," he would say, "it is for ordinary people to provide the proof." This was all right so long as the guesses were correct, as they were at first, but his usefulness ceased when, as a result of personal lack of balance, they became simply wild and foolish. For of critical judgment he was destitute. He was an extraordinarily fluent writer, but with the inaccuracy and bad taste of the worst kind of journalist. I recollect his referring in one paper to Sancti di Sanctis, the famous Italian psychiatrist, simply as "Sancti", and when Freud remonstratingly asked him how he would like it as an author if he were referred to as "Wilhelm" he shrugged his shoulders.

A more disturbing quality was his irresponsible attitude towards the truth. So constantly did he comment on whatever topic came up at the weekly meetings of the Vienna Society with the words "only today a patient of this very kind consulted me" that "Stekel's Wednesday patient" became a standing joke. He made at one time the interesting observation that people's names often unconsciously influence their life and career to a remarkable extent, that they are often impelled to live up to them, so to speak, and he published a paper with an extraordinary number of examples from his practice to illustrate the point. Very astonished, Freud asked him how he managed to deal with the matter of medical discretion in publishing so many of his patients' names. "Oh, they are all made up," was the airy answer. Now it is one thing to publish a case under a fictitious name for reasons of discretion when the name is irrelevant to the topic, but when as here it was the essential point of the communication the matter is very different.

Once, when discussing with Freud his theory of the "ego ideal", that moral agency in us that urges us onward in ethical directions, I asked him his opinion about its universality. He turned to me with a puzzled air and asked: "Do you think Stekel has an ego ideal?" With his own high sense of integrity, he suffered a great deal from Stekel's vagaries. Another of this gentleman's unpleasing habits was to illustrate his contentions at Society meetings by quoting material from his personal life, especially his early childhood. It was mostly quite invented or else grossly falsified, and he would defiantly glare at Freud, who of course knew the real facts from his analysis, knowing full well he would not contradict him. This sort of thing must have been very irksome, and Freud unburdened his mind by telling me, as a foreigner, something about the actual analysis, but naturally I do not feel at liberty to repeat any of it. Incidentally, this circumstance of my coming from the outer world gave me a somewhat privileged position with Freud, who often used it to relieve his mind by discussing with me various troubles and difficulties which it would not have been expedient for him to discuss with members of his immediate circle.

All this was troublesome enough in the local life of the Viennese circle, but it became more serious when the editor of a scientific periodical took to writing things that were plainly nonsensical divergences from the standards of the work he was supposed to represent. Stekel would, for instance, develop fads of arbitrary interpretation. For some months every possible mental manifestation had to be given a "criminal" meaning. Then for some months everything bore a "religious" meaning, though I cannot imagine anyone more remote than Stekel from any comprehension of religion. And so on and so on. After a time Freud's cup was full, and he called on him to resign from his position. Stekel defiantly refused and the matter had to be referred to the owner of the *Zentralblatt*, a publishing firm in

Wiesbaden. Although Freud was the director, who according to German custom appointed the editor, the firm, with whom Stekel had got on personal terms, supported the latter.

In this quandary Freud called together a meeting of his chief supporters to help him deal with the matter, or, rather, requested Jung, as president of the I.P.A., to convene it. Munich was chosen as the most central meeting-place. Besides Freud and Jung, there were the latter's secretary from Zurich, his cousin Riklin, Abraham from Berlin, Ferenczi from Budapest, and myself. I was at the moment in Florence, and the date Jung put on his card to me was two days later than the actual one of the meeting. Luckily, Loe, who was at the time with Freud, notified me of the real date, otherwise I should have had a November journey from Florence to Munich in vain. When I turned up on time I thought I saw Jung start a little. In speaking to Freud about it afterwards I remarked that it was no doubt an unconscious slip; Freud retorted that a gentleman wouldn't have that sort of unconscious.

As regards the business in question, I was in favour of taking further steps to make Stekel vacate his position, for it seemed to me undignified that his chief should be the one pushed out. But Freud, ever averse to anything savouring of a fight, preferred to start a new periodical instead, the *Zeitschrift*, and of course we supported him, as did all but one or two of the previous collaborators of the *Zentralblatt*. Incidentally, the latter periodical, now managed by Stekel alone, survived only two years, whereas the *Zeitschrift* endured until 1941. Stekel, like Adler, had for many years a fairly successful career, especially in America. When the Nazis occupied Vienna he fled to England, where he committed suicide a couple of years later.

After disposing of this business we naturally used the occasion of coming together to discuss matters of common interest, and Freud took the opportunity of voicing his dissatisfaction with Jung and the rest of the Swiss group, who were showing evident signs of weakening in their convictions. They had been exposed to some angry abuse in their own country, including the local press in Zurich, an experience to which the Swiss are peculiarly sensitive. In this respect they struck me as being the opposite to the Jews. Whereas the latter do not mind quarrelling among themselves, but close their ranks the moment they are attacked from without, the Swiss are more impervious to external criticism but very sensitive about their internal unity. There is little doubt that these attacks at the hands of their fellow-countrymen had shaken the Swiss, and Freud instanced some of their recent presentations of psycho-analysis in which the new and disturbing elements in it were minimised and Freud's name not even mentioned. Riklin was defending himself in the matter when I heard a slight noise at my side and turned to see Freud collapse in a state of unconsciousness on the floor. Jung with his stalwart arms carried him from the room to an ante-chamber, where he soon recovered from what had turned out to be only a faint. His first words on coming round were: "How sweet dying must be," which surprised me very much. The incident must have been occasioned by an intuition that he would have to face parting with Jung, of whom he had been so fond. Later on he told me that the only other time in his life he had fainted had been years before in that very room, the dining-room of the Park Hotel, during a painful scene with a man who was perhaps his closest friend, Oscar Rie. The resemblance between the two situations was unmistakable, and they throw light on Freud's general avoidance of contention; his emotions, if allowed to be fully generated, were apt to be too much for him, hence the iron control in which he habitually kept himself.

In the same year, 1912, Freud founded another periodical, *Imago*, which was to be concerned only with the application of psycho-analysis to non-medical topics. For ten years or more Freud had clearly perceived the use to which his new methods and discoveries could be put in other fields, in general psychology (in relation to the problems of dreams, wit, determinism, sexuality, etc.), anthropology, aesthetics, pedagogy, folk-lore, sociology, etc., and he had been the pioneer throughout in applying them in those fields. They seemed to interest him more and more, mainly because of their vast intrinsic interest, partly because of his distaste for the contentious atmosphere in medicine. When he was only fifty-five he told me how he longed to retire from practice and devote himself to these other studies, and had it not been for the World War I think he might have done so. Before *Imago* he had begun editing a series of monographs with a cognate purpose, the *Schriften zur angewandten Seelenkunde*, in which some highly original contributions appeared. However, the publishers, Heller & Deuticke, although they were both personal acquaintances, gave him a deal of trouble in the conditions they imposed and by constant interference. That was why, with his pronounced love of independence, he welcomed the possibility after the war of establishing a publishing firm of his own.

The next Congress had been arranged to take place in Munich, in September 1913. When I arrived in Vienna in the spring of that year I could see that things were going from bad to worse as regards Jung's divergent tendencies. Much of the evidence for them stands recorded in his published writings of that time, so there is no need for me to describe it here. But I recollect vividly the moment when Freud told me that Jung had expressed his disbelief in the existence of childhood sexuality, one of the main factors of psycho-analytical theory. I was astounded and said: "How is that possible? Why, it is not long since he published an analytic study of his own child depicting as discerningly as possible the stages in the development of her infantile sexual life." At that time we had never had the experience of an analyst attaining clear insight into the buried regions of the mind, and then repudiating it. We were familiar with fluctuations of insight with our patients according to their emotional moods, but somehow this seemed different: one was under the illusion that analysts were above such things, that their knowledge rendered them immune to retrogression. This was the first, but very far from being the last, lesson demonstrating that it was not so, that analysts could be as fallible as other mortals. The same process must have been at work with Adler and Stekel, but we had not recognised it; Adler had never possessed the insight, and Stekel never the stability, for their behaviour to rank as a scientific apostasy. Now the fact had to be faced. Our chosen leader, the President of the Association, was failing us, and we looked forward to the approaching Congress with considerable perplexity.

Freud, I am persuaded, would have responded to the situation itself simply with a feeling of disappointment and regret, which in the circumstances would have been keen enough. But, after several unpleasant incidents, he recognised that the time was at hand when they could no longer work together with an adequate sense of co-operation in a common cause. He therefore looked forward to Jung's also recognising this and resigning his position as president of the I.P.A. After consultation with Ferenczi, he decided to recommend me—I was then thirty-four—as Jung's successor, and this was perhaps the reason why he advised me that spring to undergo a didactic analysis.

The Munich Congress was the least agreeable we have had. The atmosphere was tense, and the members were obviously grouping themselves in parties, although many were still ill-informed of the issues at stake. One Swiss member read a tedious statistical paper, on which Freud commented to me that there was one criticism of psycho-analysis he had never expected, namely, that it could be made boring. I read a paper myself which directly challenged one of Jung's recently expressed views and pointed out that the direction of them, if maintained, would diverge in essential respects from psycho-analysis as we understood it. At the business meeting nearly half the members abstained from voting when Jung's name came up for re-election, but he nevertheless accepted the position again. As he said good-bye he sneeringly remarked to me: "I thought you had ethical principles" (an expression he was fond of); my friends interpreted the word "ethical" here as meaning "Christian" and therefore as anti-Semitic. There was a general feeling that the breach between him and Freud was complete, and in a few months' time he sent in his resignation. For a time he still called himself a psycho-analyst, but he was gradually shamed out of doing so, his views undergoing a more and more radical change, and he then compromised by styling himself an "analytical psychologist"—a term perhaps verbally correct but open to ambiguity of a very misleading kind.

I had long learned the lesson that what man proposes is a very different thing from what happens. I have been president of the I.P.A. far longer than anyone else has been or ever will be again, but it came about in a quite different way from what Freud expected. At the time in question the Congresses were as a matter of course held in Austria or Germany, there being only a handful of members from non-German-speaking countries. So Freud, after Jung's retirement, asked Abraham of Berlin to make the arrangements for the next one, which was due to take place in Dresden in September 1914. When that date arrived, however, Abraham was at his post with the army in East Prussia, getting ready to attend the wounded at Tannenberg.

* * * * * *

Since I had many associations on the Continent besides those with psycho-analysts, I was in a position to hear at first hand the criticisms our "opponents", as we called them, made of Freud and his work. They mostly emanated from medical sources, and had little of the high moral flavour that characterised the theological denunciations of Darwin's doctrines. A nearer analogy would be with the venom and scurrility with which the theologists pursued Galileo. The Dominican Father Caccini earned promotion by his famous sermon—in which he proved that "geometry is of the devil"—from the text: "Ye men of Galilee, why stand ye gazing up into heaven?" and similarly wretched punning was resorted to in the campaign against psycho-analysis. Jests were bandied about linking Freud's name with the word *Freudenmädchen* (harlot) and I remember the president of an International Congress exhorting his audience not to let themselves be "soaped" (the German idiom for our slang phrase "being buttered") by the speaker, Dr. Seif (*Seife* is German for soap). The whole attack was on that vulgar and non-intellectual level: no scientific arguments were to be found. Since the libido theory played a central part in the psycho-analytical doctrine, the whole range of sexual bawdiness was opened up. One speaker at a meeting demanded whether, if Freud had his way, we should all have to go about with our respective erotogenic zones painted red, and any allusions to the theme of anal erotism brought us straight to the coloured behinds of the monkeys. What a loathsome atmosphere it all was! I was simply staggered to discover to what depths men of scientific standing could descend when once their unconscious minds were stirred by the new teachings. No wonder that Freud remarked to me once: "These people may deny the truth of psycho-analysis, but I am sure they dream of it."

I well remember an International Congress of Medical Psychology that was held at Zurich in September 1912, at which I read a paper on the sexual origin of morbid fears. In his autobiography Forel, the late Professor of Psychiatry at Zurich, wrote of it: "The Freudians with their usual vanity and presumption talked a lot of preposterous nonsense, but were sharply rebuked." He omitted to describe his idea of sharp rebuke, which consisted in his losing his temper and rushing about the hall in the midst of the discussion, violently shouting at us one after the other. Peace was to some extent restored in the evening when we assembled at beer tables. Bawdy jokes were the order of the day, and I pointed out that the symbols on which they were based, each of which was instantly recognised with hearty laughter, were identical with those I had been describing in my paper on Phobias. The chairman, Professor Vogt of Berlin, an eminent brain histologist, turned to me with an astonished air and said: "But this is not science; you must not mix the two things up." In other words, knowledge was to be permitted if laughed at, but not if taken seriously.

Even after the experience of his cold reception and subsequent ostracism at the hands of his Viennese colleagues, Freud was surprised by the vehemence of the abuse showered on him from Germany. It grieved him sorely and permanently influenced his opinion of the German character and culture. His dignity, as well as his sense of its futility, forbade him to enter the fray directly in a way that his followers could hardly avoid, but he never refrained from expressing freely his opinion of it all among his friends. Matters at one time became so bad that the possibility of officially forbidding the practice of psycho-analysis, thereby dealing it its death-blow, was seriously canvassed. The technical difficulties in the way, however, were almost insuperable, and Freud did not take the threat seriously. He received courteously enough those visitors, chiefly Americans, who were curious to interview the man who had promulgated such remarkable doctrines, and on one occasion even an avowed opponent found his curiosity too strong to contain and also paid him a visit. Fearing lest Freud would not receive him he gave a false name on the telephone: "This is Professor X from Frankfurt, who would like to call on you." Freud, knowing the names of all his German colleagues, was puzzled at the strange name, but politely assented. On making his appearance Professor X gave his true name and insisted that Freud must have misheard him on the telephone. The talk proceeded, and in a few minutes he referred to Freud's famous Dora analysis under the name of Anna. Freud leant forward intently and said: "If you please,

Herr Professor, we are not on the telephone now." He then seized the opportunity of pressing his theory of unconscious motivation in slips of the tongue and proceeded to question and analyse his victim, as he had now become. Freud could be severe at times, and he had much to make up for, so it is not surprising that the Herr Professor, when he finally left the house, bore a somewhat bewildered and dejected mien.

The polemics published against psycho-analysis in those pre-war years stand recorded in dusty archives, from which I have no inclination to disinter them. My only object here has been to convey something of the atmosphere of those days, and to show how inevitably psycho-analysts were, in the face of such opposition, drawn together in closer personal bonds of union than is customary among scientific workers.

I was myself responsible for one of these bonds, some mention of which will illustrate our situation. When we perceived, through the events narrated above concerning Adler, Stekel, and Jung, that danger could threaten the "movement" from within as well as from without, I conceived the romantic idea—derived, I think, from boyhood readings of Charlemagne and his paladins—of building a specially close inner group of trustworthy analysts who should stand to Freud somewhat in the relation of a bodyguard. The only pledge to be exacted was that if one of the group felt impelled to enunciate views definitely contradictory to recognised psycho-analytical teaching, he would undertake before publishing them to submit them to a private and full discussion with the rest of us, so that as much light as possible should be thrown on the meaning of the divergence. However romantically conceived, the idea bore useful fruit for many years. I mentioned it first to Ferenczi, and then asked Hanns Sachs to join us. Freud, whom we had naturally informed about the plan, suggested Karl Abraham, than whom there could be no more suitable colleague. Sachs and I then brought in Otto Rank, and I remember one very uncanny episode on that occasion. Rank, who for years was Freud's man of all work, was devoted to him. As for Ferenczi, he was the staunchest and most enthusiastic colleague anyone could ask for, and Freud would, I feel sure, have placed no one above him in his estimation. Well, when I introduced Rank to him as the latest recruit to our little group, Ferenczi eyed him keenly and put the question to him: "I suppose you will always be loyal to psycho-analysis?" I felt myself it was almost an insulting way to greet a new adherent, and Rank was distinctly embarrassed when he answered: "Assuredly." Now the uncanny thing about the episode, and as unpredictably improbable a thing as anything on earth, is that it was just Ferenczi and Rank who only a dozen years later proved to be the only members of the group who broke the promise that was to bind us together. Without discussing it with us, or even informing us about it, they wrote and published a book which, to the rest of us, revealed at once the seeds of serious divergent tendencies. We managed to draw Ferenczi back for a time, and he separated from Rank. But, alas, the end-result was much the same with both.

In the meantime, however, and for many years, the committee, as we called ourselves, functioned with admirable comradeship and with great practical value to the cause we had at heart —the furtherance and propagation of psycho-analytical knowledge. After the war we were joined by a further recruit, Max Eitingon of Berlin. We succeeded in keeping our existence a secret by the simple device of letting everyone know that we were close friends who naturally took every opportunity to come together; a visible sign of this was our custom of each addressing each as "Du". But really we acted as a sort of Privy Council to Freud, who mostly presided at our meetings, and we either made or influenced all the decisions concerning the doings of the Association, the periodicals, and many other affairs.

* * * * * *

So far I have been writing mainly about the years from 1908 to 1914, when the main psycho-analytical events were taking place on the Continent and for the most part in German-speaking countries. During the same period similar ones, though of course on a minor scale, were happening in Anglo-Saxon countries. Concerning England there is little to say in the pre-war time. I have mentioned my own work there in the years 1906 to 1908. After this I paid annual visits to London, and usually Wales, to see my family and friends. The only direct pupil I secured in that time was M. D. Eder, of whom I have already spoken. A year or two before the war an old acquaintance, Dr. David Forsyth, independently became interested in psycho-analysis to the extent of practising it. A general stir of interest was beginning, but there were no other practitioners. I had already published a couple of papers in English periodicals, and these were followed by three each by Eder and Forsyth —all before the war. The former had also addressed a British Medical Association meeting on the theme, no doubt to the astonishment of the audience.

I remember the first occasion when I spoke on it in public in England, at a meeting of the Psycho-Medical Society in January 1913. A discussion on Ferenczi's recent essay on the Nature of Suggestion was being held, under the able guidance of Dr. T. W. Mitchell, and what I had to say in exposition of the essay made it plain that something new was going on in the world of psychopathology outside of these islands. Mitchell himself, and Dr. Douglas Bryan, then the secretary of the society, were evidently impressed and before long could be counted as definite recruits. Mitchell was a cautious Scotsman with an informed historical knowledge and a very clear, level-headed brain, for which I conceived a high respect; I still regard his books as among those most worth while studying. Boldness, however, was not his most prominent chacracteristic, and a certain inhibiting tendency to reserve made him prefer a secluded life in the country, from which he would only occasionally emerge to deliver lucid and weighty addresses; he took little part in the rough-and-tumble of our life. Bryan, then a general practitioner at Leicester, was more enterprising and within a few years decided to move to London and concentrate on analytical work.

On settling again in England in the autumn of 1913, I naturally got into closer touch with those interested in psycho-analysis, and I decided the time had come to found a special society there, a branch of the International Association. It was a hardy venture, for the material then available soon proved to be of not the best quality. Of the fifteen original members only four got so far as the practice of psycho-analysis, the others contenting themselves with a more or less academic interest in it. Bryan was at first vice-president, then secretary, and later treasurer. He worked hard for us in those early days, though in later years he unmistakably fell behind in the continual scientific advances that were made. Of the early members a third lived outside Great Britain: two in India, one in Ireland, one in Canada, one in Syria. It was natural that, from the beginning as in later times, the Society in London should act as a mother to those elsewhere in the Empire.

These few remarks show that the frequently made statement that psycho-analysis was unknown in England before the war experiences of "shell-shock" is exaggerated. It became, it is true, far more widely known after the war, and it is likely that the general interest in psychotherapy was a good deal stimulated by the war neuroses, but on the other hand the background for the work had already been developed in the years before the war and the time was ripening for the more general recognition of it. There seemed to have been a psychological moment in every country when interest in the newness of psycho-analysis became acute. This naturally happened first in German-speaking countries, but it came about also in the United States before the war. I should date this "moment" in England to be within the first five years after the end of the war, some ten years before it happened in France and Italy.

I will therefore resume my story in America, where it was interrupted by my description of events in Europe; a little of it has already been told in the last chapter. Brill and I shared the pioneering task there, and we were in regular touch with each other in every stage of it. To work with him was a novel experience, for he was very unlike my former colleagues in Harley Street, suave, cultured, well-to-do people who for the most part had always led sheltered lives. Brill had emigrated *alone* to the United States from an eastern province of the Austro-Hungarian Empire at the tender age of fourteen, and had landed in New York with, I think, the sum of three dollars. He was the stuff of which so much of America has been made. He might have been called a rough diamond, but there was no doubt about the diamond. With unbreakable courage and self-assurance he fought his way through the hardships of a lonely immigrant and ultimately won to a position of high professional status. He told me once a pitiful story in illustration of his early fights. After having for years saved from his teaching earnings enough to enter on a medical curriculum, he found himself unable to pay the fee for his final examination. Appeal to the authorities for help or exemption was in vain; he had to stand on his own resources, and go back to his teaching for yet another year. He felt the hardship of it, but then said to himself: "You have no one to blame but yourself; no one asked you to take up medicine." And so he went bravely onward. He belonged to the school of rugged individualists that has made America what it is, to whom the idea of Socialism and "doles" is anathema. He possessed that curious and very characteristic Jewish quality of being at the same time very lonely and sensitive and yet, oddly enough, immune to the world's criticism, a quality of the utmost value to a pioneer who proposes to run counter to that world's conventional beliefs. And he had a heart of gold, as no one has better reason to know than myself.

With all this, however, his origins and early experiences left marks that called for a certain adaptation on my part. One of them was in the sphere of speech. He was endowed with the gift of easily acquiring the rudiments of many languages, from Arabic to Italian, that so often goes with an imperfect mastery of any one of them; and his pride in this gift prevented him from perceiving its drawbacks. It brought about the only major difference between us, and I claim some credit for preventing it, in spite of Brill's sensitiveness, from ever becoming a personal matter. On his first meeting with Freud he asked for the English translation rights of all his works, and Freud granted them without making any inquiry into his ability. For myself, being fully occupied, I was only too glad that someone else should undertake this huge task. It was only after the first set of translations appeared that I perceived what we had let ourselves in for.

As is well known, Freud had a reputation as a master of German prose so high that he was even awarded the Goethe Prize at Frankfurt for his literary merits. Well, the translations in question were not only seriously inaccurate, with misunderstandings of the German text and ambiguous renderings that greatly impaired their value for scientific purposes, but were also couched in an undignified and colloquial form that was unworthy of Freud's style and gave a misleading impression of his personality. I was horror-struck, and at once wrote Brill a letter sympathising with the difficulties of his task and offering to co-operate with him in it; I added that my name need not be mentioned. His pride, however, was at stake and he somewhat haughtily refused. I then approached Freud when I next saw him and remarked that the matter was too important to be subordinated to any individual's feelings. He answered: "Better to have a good friend than a good translator," to which I rather tartly replied that a really good friend would see to it that his translation was good. Unfortunately Freud conceived the notion, of which it took him years to be disabused, that I was jealous of Brill, and he dismissed the matter on that ground.

The incident shows that Freud was at times prone to very subjective judgments, since not only was he—almost ludicrously—wrong in this particular preconception, but he refrained from testing the matter objectively, which would have been a perfectly easy thing to do; he certainly knew English well enough to judge on the point of accuracy, and probably on that of style as well. I have not to this day been able to fathom his cavalier attitude in this matter of translations, which almost produces the impression of indifference concerning the promulgation of his work abroad. He was, of course, disdainful about America, but never about England. He had himself translated books, from both English and French, and could translate with consummate ease and skill. Perhaps, because of this, he found it hard to imagine that a translation could be deplorably bad. To Freud ideas were always more important than form, in every kind of art, and in writing his form evidently came from innate gifts rather than conscious striving or even attention; for, indeed, on close inspection one could not but observe ambiguities and even pieces of carelessness in his writing. So perhaps he took style for granted. Or was it that he was loth to admit his original mistake in entrusting his works so casually? I do not know at all. As it was, it took a steady stream of protests from both Americans and English before he unwillingly awoke to the situation, and by that time the relationship between him and Brill was naturally a delicate one on both sides.

On his return from working with Bleuler and Jung in Zurich in 1908, Brill at once gathered around him those whose interest in psycho-analysis had already been avowed; among them were several, such as Frederick Paterson, who had also studied at Zurich, or at least visited it. As in England, the chief opposition came from the neurologists, who doubtless felt their prerogative of treating "nervous" disorders (i.e. functional as well as organic) threatened. Charles Dana, Joseph Collins, and the rest fulminated against the new doctrines, while Bernard Sachs, who happened to have been a fellow-student of Freud's in Vienna, disseminated scurrilous and untrue stories about his youth. Brill, who had had no neurological training, was regarded as an outsider and an upstart, a judgment he waved aside with an amicable complacency; his convictions were immovable. There were, it is true, a few notable exceptions among the neurologists, Isidor Coriat of Boston and others. Chief among them was Smith Ely Jelliffe of New York, who later made some valuable contributions to our knowledge of the relationship between emotional phenomena and bodily disease. He was a genial companion, with a gift for racy speech. I asked him once how he came to speak German so fluently, and he answered: "I went over there and just made up my mind I would let my chin wag." Unconventional and unperturbed by opposition, he had a readiness in debate that often stood us in good stead.

There was, however, this important difference between England and America at that time. In the former country neurology, thanks to a surpassing array of talent, stood on an unique pinnacle; in no country, at any period, has any branch of the medical profession stood higher. Psychiatry, on the other hand, was almost non-existent; it was much below the level reached even in France and Italy. It was thus entirely subordinate to neurology, and took its cue from the latter. In America the reverse held. There the neurologists were a decidedly mediocre group, compared with most European countries, whereas American psychiatry was already beginning to match itself with that in Germany, the country where it had been most highly developed. Psychiatrists, therefore, were free to take an independent line, and they did so. The two leading ones at the time, both of Swiss origin, were Adolf Meyer, the weightiest, and August Hoch, the most gifted, of American psychiatrists, and they both came down definitely on the side of psycho-analysis, in fact joining our new societies. So did Macfie Campbell, a hard-working Scotsman who had settled in the United States and ultimately became Professor of Psychiatry at Harvard, and William A. White, a bosom friend of Jelliffe's, who was already Director of the Government Mental Hospital at Washington. White was a very friendly person, unfortunately with an inhibition about leaving his country, so that he was not well known in Europe, and he had two valuable gifts: one of inspiring and encouraging his staff at Washington in a remarkable degree, the other a capacity for fluent and lucid exposition that brought him a wide audience among all classes in the United States.

We received ecnouragement too from a few psychologists, notably Stanley Hall, the doyen of American psychologists at that time. His adherence did not last, however, and at the end of his life he joined Adler. Some of our chief opponents, however, were psychologists such as Hugo Münsterberg of Harvard, and British psychologists proved more friendly to psycho-analysis than did American ones. I do not know why; perhaps because they are less rigidly German in their methods and outlook, with more independence.

On the whole my centre was Boston, and Brill's New York, so we had fairly distinct territories. I used my influence there to found the American Psychopathological Association, the first meeting of which took place in Washington in May 1910. Three of the papers read were by Bostonians, the others being by Brill and myself. We of course made Morton Prince the first president, his assistant, Waterman, being secretary, and the committee, all supporters of psycho-analysis, consisted of Allen, Hoch, Meyer, Putnam, and myself. I have introduced all these except Allen.

He was a sympathetic young neurologist from Philadelphia, who once stayed for a few days with me in Toronto. An immortal phrase of his stays in my mind. He went to the railway station to book a ticket home, and explained his absence by saying he "had the intention of effecting a reservation of his transportation accommodation". Poor fellow, he lost his life in the First World War, the only psycho-analyst to do so. Prince's *Journal of Abnormal Psychology*, which I was helping him to edit, was made the official organ of the new Association, and both these institutions were freely open to psycho-analytical papers, largely because of Prince's generosity and broadmindedness. So we had a definite forum, with the added advantage of sharing it with other psychopathologists whom we might hope to influence. It was open to non-medical members, as is the similar body in England, the Medical Section of the British Psychological Society; Stanley Hall, for instance, took a prominent part in its activities from the outset.

Encouraged by this success, I began to think that the time was ripe for establishing a still closer group, one in which analysts could discuss their technical problems together without the time-wasting process of always arguing about the elements of their subject. Much criticism has been made of psycho-analysts for their supposed attitude of isolation, but I cannot perceive much justification for it. It has come mainly from those who take a very restricted view of the subject and who hope to be able to "pick up" its essentials casually and without labour. It seems to me preposterous to deny any special body of scientific workers the propriety of their meeting together to discuss their work and problems undeterred by outer wranglings; of internal wrangling there is always enough and to spare. How would a bacteriological society get on if half its audience took up time in denying the existence of germs and insisting on their being the product of imagination? The attitude I adopted myself, both in America and England, was that it was desirable to have such special societies, but that we should also freely participate in other societies, laying our conclusions before our medical colleagues there and discussing them openly. That, so it would seem to me, has the double advantage of being able to make technical progress and also to make our special knowledge freely available to any others who might be interested.

So Brill and I put our heads together and came to this agreement. He was to found a New York Psycho-Analytical Society, in which most of the workers could attend the monthly meetings, and I was to organise an American Psycho-Analytical Association, in which the other analysts scattered over the United States could unite once or twice a year for common discussion. As I write these lines the thought occurs to me for the first time what a sign it is of how much the world has changed since. There was I, a British subject, but there was nothing strange in organising such activities in what after all was legally a foreign country. But in those days one went in and out of the United States without let or hindrance, with no passport or visa or any questions asked, just as one passed from one country to another in Europe (except Russia). So free was life then. And how unnecessarily difficult and heartrending we have made it!

The inaugural meetings of these societies took place in 1911, the former in February, the latter in May in Washington. I got

Putnam to act as president of the latter, and I served myself as secretary for three years until I returned to England. The only other foundation members were Trigant Burrow (Boston), Hamill (Chicago), MacCurdy (Baltimore), Adolph Meyer (Baltimore), Tanenhill (Baltimore), and Alexander Young (Omaha). Naturally, however, the members of the New York Society were welcome at our meetings, as the members of any psycho-analytical society are at the meetings of any other, and in fact they made up the majority of the audience, for they were twenty-one to our eight. After the war, when local societies began to be established in other centres, the American Association gradually evolved, as I had intended it should, into a comprehensive Federation in which all the local societies could unite for a common purpose.

"May meetings" is a phrase that has a different connotation in America from what it has, or used to in the old Exeter Hall days, in England. It is the month when travelling becomes more agreeable and when the freshness of summer makes a swift appearance. The occasion is naturally used for all sorts of conferences and congresses, and I know it best in connection with annual medical ones. For purposes of convenience for those who travelled great distances, we arranged that the Psycho-Analytical Association should meet on the day before the American Psychopathological Association which, in its turn, met the day before the American Neurological Association and in whatever place the latter had decided on. They were hectic days for me, since in addition to business matters and scientific discussions, public and private, I was given to reading papers before all three bodies.

Chapter Eleven

Return to London: Wartime

ON my return to London, late in 1913, I was fully aware of the hopelessness of pursuing any further academic career there—even if there were no other reason, my association with psycho-analysis would alone settle that matter—and I signalised my acceptance of the fact by deciding to live and practise in a flat in Great Portland Street, outside the hallowed medical quarter; in those days no consultant could practise east of Portland Place or west of Welbeck Street. I was to be, if not an outsider, certainly a very irregular person. It was manifest that I was "obsessed with sex", if not worse, and in those days the conception of sex simply did not exist in scientific circles, as Havelock Ellis had long ago found out to his cost. My former friends received me with politeness, but without intimacy. Harry Campbell told me roundly I should be ostracised if I stayed in London. The sharpness of the remark somewhat shocked me, but I am prone to giving people the benefit of the doubt and I took it that he was giving me a friendly warning to prepare me for possible affronts. It was not very long, however, before I received indubitable evidence that he was spreading disreputable stories about me which he must have known to be untrue. I had liked him and been an intimate friend of his, but now I was bound to conclude that the harsh epithet Victor Horsley had applied to him years before was not quite so misplaced as I had supposed. But I was beginning to learn that proximity to sexual ideas has the power of evoking the worst in man as well as the best.

With Trotter the situation was complex. Although I had paid him brief annual visits since we separated five years before, there had been little opportunity for real talks, and I now remarked a decided change in him, both towards myself and in general. He welcomed me cordially, talked freely and as interestingly as ever on all sorts of topics, but nevertheless made me feel that a new barrier had grown up between us which I was not to transgress; we were no longer to share our lives, our hopes, and aspirations. He did not invite me to visit him, nor did he ever visit me except occasionally for medical purposes. That was, it is true, a general attitude of his, but still it was new towards me. It naturally caused me some pain, or rather a sense of deprivation, and yet it became intelligible to me. In the first place, he was now on the staff of University College Hospital, with a rapidly growing consulting practice, and he had a wife and child. He certainly had none of the bourgeois ambitions that these words might imply, and they relate to something more subtle. He himself said rather brutally to me once that he had "decided to choose security in life", but what he meant to convey, I think, was his perception that he could accomplish more in life, and give of what he had to give to his fellow-man, by functioning in the world of reality as he found it, rather than by indulging in revolutionary and impracticable phantasies. His coolness towards me really betokened his repudiation of that part of himself. Years later, when my increasing maturity reassured him that I was not likely to commit myself to any sort of wildness, he drew closer to me, but it was never "glad confident morning" again. Another more personal motive was perhaps an even stronger ground for his attitude. He was possessive and very jealous indeed; he opened his heart only to those he could consider his disciples. When I became interested in psycho-analysis he confessed to me that his jealousy of my interest in Freud's work was coming between us. Having little or no propensity to jealousy myself, I laughed at the notion of taking such a matter in a personal sense, but I am sure he was deeply affected by it. So he adapted himself to his environment; but unfortunately he was not able to accomplish the change except at the cost of considerable inhibition. Great as was his value in his surgical teaching and in his occasional inimitable addresses, so pregnant with thought and admirably couched, the world lost much when he exchanged freedom for security.

My position on this return to London might seem to be rather forlorn and without prospect, but I did not feel it so myself. At peace within, and with a sense of great activity, I was not even lonely. I might have few friends in my native land, but I had many good ones in various other countries; and the low esteem in which I was probably held here was counterbalanced by the international reputation I had won in wide professional circles. I soon had a few interesting patients, and was able to pay my way almost from the start. So I settled down to work.

The first thing to be done was to get into touch with others interested in psycho-analysis, to consolidate their interest and develop their technical knowledge. To that end I at once—over-hastily as it turned out—founded a Psycho-Analytical Society, on October 30th, 1913. It was a hardy undertaking, since I had not yet fully comprehended the gulf that lies between "being interested" in psycho-analysis, often transitorily, and possessing a serious understanding of all its implications.

I have already said something about the beginnings of this society and have now to describe its teething troubles. The oldest member, David Forsyth, attended very few meetings, and then found excuses for staying away; his personal jealousy of myself was already beginning to manifest itself. Eder, the secretary, who I naturally assumed would know more than I could about local conditions in respect of psycho-analysis, kept introducing new members whom I accepted on his recommendation, but they were not always of a satisfactory kind. Two of them, for example, Maurice Nicoll and Constance Long, soon became ardent followers of Jung, and Eder himself, whose wife was at the time being analysed by Jung, was before long powerfully influenced in the same direction. The opposition took the usual form of doubt about the existence of infantile sexuality, particularly in its relation to incestuous impulses, and every endeavour was made to reinterpret the concrete data of the unconscious into Jung's cloudy generalities and thus discount their emotional significance. More and more time at the meetings was taken up, or rather wasted, in this fashion, and progress in psycho-analytical knowledge itself came almost to a standstill.

After a year or two of patient discussion, I came to the decision that nothing more could be accomplished in this way. I then proposed that we suspend the meetings and try the effect of more private individual discussions on our aim of achieving some agreement, or at least some understanding of our differences. For the main trouble with Eder was that he obstinately refused to admit that there was any noticeable difference between Freud and Jung. He was evidently drawn in both directions and was unwilling to admit the nature, or even the existence, of the unconscious conflict within himself that was responsible for his muddled attitude. I arranged to spend a couple of evenings a week working through our clinical material together so as to get clear about the matters at issue. But Eder, when obstinate, like so many people with that unfortunate failing, could be incredibly stupid, and at times I was driven to despair at the wall of blank misunderstanding he presented. I am a good arguer and able to keep an issue well defined, but a person in that mood can of course evade any issue, however sharp. His wife was very often present, and even she got ashamed and tried also to explain my simple points to him. In the end we were beginning to make some impression, but about that time he joined the R.A.M.C. and left for Malta and Palestine. There he had leisure to think things over, and as soon as he could—I think in 1920 or 1921—went to Budapest for analytic work with Ferenczi. This cleared everything up and he became a steady psycho-analyst.

In the meantime, however, my promising Society was broken up for the time being. Many of its members had been dispersed in war activities, and there seemed to be no point in trying to resuscitate it in the circumstances then obtaining. My annoyance with Eder, which after all my patience I think was natural if unreasonable, culminated when he retained his position as secretary of the Society even when he had finally to admit that he was at variance with its fundamental principles and aims. I still think he behaved wrongly in doing so. It forced me ultimately—as soon as the war was over—to dissolve the Society and reconstitute it immediately with an improved membership; in doing so I made a change in its title, substituting "British" for "London".

In other ways, however, we made much progress during the war. Psycho-analysis was already widely talked about, in both medical and non-medical circles, and the startling frequency of what was then called shell-shock presently brought the whole question of medical psychology into the foreground. My *Papers on Psycho-Analysis* was published at the end of 1912, the first book on the subject in the English language, followed a year later by another one, *Treatment of the Neuroses*, and the sales testified to a widespread interest; a second edition of the *Papers* was called for during the war. On all sides people wanted to know more about these strange theories. Much of the interest was serious and restrained; some was merely funny. I will record two instances of the latter. A doctor in Essex wrote to me expressing his interest in this new treatment and his desire to acquire a knowledge of the technique of it if I would be good enough to impart it: for this purpose he could call on me "any Tuesday afternoon". I wonder what he would have said had he learned of the six years' curriculum our Institute was to establish a few years later. Then an American gentleman called on me once to discuss the main principles of psycho-analysis. I gave him a short, but as I thought lucid, exposition, to which he listened thoughtfully. He then made the devastating remark: "That's all very interesting. And are you interested in palmistry too?"

A month or so before the war a great International Congress of Medicine met in London. Incidentally, my friends from the United States were charmed at finding there various notices put up that referred to "Foreigners *and* Americans", which I assured them represented a characteristic British attitude—though unfortunately one only imperfectly reciprocated in their country. At the Congress Professor Janet used the important occasion to make a slashing and satirical attack on Freud and his work. Delivered with his inimitable theatrical skill, it made a visible impression, especially on those in the audience who were disposed to accept his assertions without criticising them. With my practice in such debates, however, it was easy for me to demonstrate to the audience not only Janet's profound ignorance of psycho-analysis but also his lack of scruple in inventing, in the most unfair way, men of straw for his ridicule to play on. He feebly excused himself by saying he could not read German, but in the *Journal of Abnormal Psychology* I published my comments on his address, and I feel sure his reputation for objectivity has never been the same since. He was one of many medical psychologists—Morton Prince and Havelock Ellis were others—who felt that their achievements, substantial enough in themselves, were threatened by the new discoveries Freud was making, and who could not rise above the jealousy they, rather naturally, felt. Just then it was fashionable to discount Freud by speaking of his immense debt to Janet's work, and Janet himself on this occasion had depicted Freud's achievements as consisting of nothing more than taking over and distorting his own conclusions. Nothing could have been farther from the truth. During his stay in Paris in 1885 Freud had not heard of Janet's existence, and although in his first book, the *Studien*, he had made a passing polite reference to Janet's first one, actually he never took his work very seriously and had certainly not acquired any of his own conclusions from it.

In the four war years I read papers before various societies, including the British Medical Association, Royal Society of Medicine, British Association for the Advancement of Science, British Psychological Society, etc. The meetings of the last two, held at Manchester and Durham respectively, remain especially in my memory. They were miniature congresses, where one had satisfactory opportunities of meeting people of standing and of discussing in a personal and informal way matters that in public debate lead only to blind opposition. One of my papers advanced a psychological theory of what was popularly called shell-shock, whose frequency was causing serious concern to the authorities. Opponents of Freud's sexual theory of the neuroses were making great play with the condition, asserting that here before our eyes was a neurotic complaint with certainly no sexual causation. The interesting thing was that a little later two friends of mine on the Continent, quite independently both of each other and of myself, put forward an identical explanation of the condition, and this has since been widely accepted.

Another of my writings had a less happy fate. It was one of those I wrote on the psychology of war-like impulses and the motives that lead to war. I had been asked to write it by a Swiss periodical that was maintaining a precarious attitude of neutrality, its sympathies being really with the Allies. *The Times* did me the honour of devoting an irate leader to the matter; I suppose there was a lull in more serious topics at the moment. I was accused of sustaining the enemy by my action, the flattering implication being that my brilliant article would cause so many copies of the periodical to be sold that its owners, gratuitously assumed to be Germans, would net an amount of foreign exchange that would enable them to prolong the war! A good example of "war mentality". Even Scotland Yard, who interviewed me, were at first not sure that I had not contravened some technical ordinance, though they soon decided otherwise.

During the war a certain number of enemy scientific periodicals were allowed to be imported through neutral countries, chiefly for university libraries, and I was fortunate enough to get permission from the Home Office to obtain in this way regular copies of the psycho-analytical periodicals published abroad. Somehow the censor never noticed that my name continued to appear throughout the war as associate editor of a periodical published in Germany, perhaps a unique occurrence for a British subject. The information thus obtained enabled me to keep *au courant* with the advances made abroad in psycho-analysis, and at the end of the war I read a paper summarising them which produced a considerable impression.

So far I have said nothing about how the war itself affected me. It had not taken me by surprise, since I was one of that small group (outside official circles) with a keen enough interest in foreign affairs and with enough knowledge of German tendencies to feel the inevitability of a clash. It would not be long feasible, I had seen, to cope with German lunges and *coups* by diplomatic measures only, nor would she restrain herself sufficiently to make that possible. Nevertheless, such a long time had elapsed since a major European war that the average person had grown up in the belief that such things no longer happened. When a French general, on being asked if a major war would ever take place again, responded: "Will it ever rain again?" he was regarded as a cynical professional. Assuredly most of the English-speaking world, isolated from the Continent, could not bring themselves to believe in the likelihood of such a calamity. I think a farm labourer I talked to in Somerset the first year of the war was typical in that respect. His son had just been killed at the Front, and he mournfully remarked to me: "None of us in these parts wanted any war." The pathos of this comment on life from that old man so helplessly caught up in world events made a deep impression on me.

The same bewilderment extended across the Atlantic. I remember my old chief at Toronto, Dr. Clarke, writing to ask me what I thought had brought about the war, since he couldn't understand the necessity for it. I impishly replied, and afterwards regretted I had done so: "It was because someone couldn't endure the snub from Berchtold that his predecessor had from Berchtold's predecessor, Aerenthal." What was in my mind was impatience that so few people took the trouble to inform themselves about vital foreign affairs. Incidentally, I thought at the time, and most historians of the war have come to the same conclusion, that if any individual could be singled out to have the most responsibility for its outbreak imputed to him, it would be Graf Berchtold. But it did not then cross my mind that in years to come I should pay him a courtesy visit in his castle in Moravia. I found a charming old gentleman, eager to talk of his great fondness for England, hampered by the shaking palsy that had afflicted him, but not apparently at all weighed down by the thought of what he had done to the world.

When war broke out, I was plunged into a quandary about my own course of action. Men were needed in endless numbers and I was free and unattached. On the one hand, I reflected that I represented in England a peculiar advance in knowledge, of whose future importance to the community I was convinced, and that it would be a long time—as indeed later events showed—before I could be replaced in this function; I was like a sentry at a post. On the other hand, the words: "England hath need of thee" exercised a potent spell. So before long I offered my services. The Medical Board, apparently unimpressed by my physique, advised me not to press my claim to be enlisted, expressing the opinion that I was of more use in my present work than I probably should be in the trenches—a piece of insight with which I secretly concurred. So I had to content myself with a G.R. armband, a token of voluntary enlistment, which only people with an uneasy conscience ever actually wore. Later on came conscription, and I was re-examined on two or three occasions, but was each time judged unfit for actual service.

By then I was aware of the increasing strain that was being placed on the patriotism of doctors—at all events specialists. The R.A.M.C. before the First World War (fortunately not after it) had been recruited from that part of the profession who put adventure or an easy life before interest in their scientific activities; I had had a considerable experience of them in my coaching days, and a very jolly lot they were. They naturally were not highly esteemed by the rest of the profession, and they seemed to know it, for when war broke out they came into their own and got a good deal of their own back. It was not merely that to them doctors were simply doctors, all of a heap with no discrimination, so that if half a dozen doctors were wanted anywhere the first half-dozen on the list were sent there—with such an attitude one could not quarrel, since this wasteful attitude to promiscuous fodder characterised that war throughout—but they at times seemed to go beyond that in actively seeing to it that round pegs got into square holes, never into round ones. One heard of gynaecologists being put in charge of ophthalmic wards in Egypt, while distinguished ophthalmic surgeons saw to the brothels of Cairo—with their morbidic products. Sir Victor Horsley, whose investigations of the numerous head and nerve injuries of the war would have been of priceless value, was sent as a captain to Mesopotamia, where he died of sunstroke. In the Second World War, much greater concern was displayed about placing men where their particular talents were of most use. I cannot account for such progress in intelligence; it is by no means what experience has led one to expect from those in authority, but it is the more gratifying for that.

Naturally I tried to see in what other way I could be of service. To be on special medical duty during air raids was in those days not an onerous matter. It mainly consisted in standing by when the police inspector telephoned to say: "Hostile action by the enemy is expected over London," and waiting for the sonorous announcement that: "Normal conditions are re-established." The police have become less formal since then. Not long ago I rang them up to complain that, so far from keeping to the twenty-mile limit in Regent's Park, cars were using it as a speedway to north London at one in the morning, averaging some forty miles an hour. The inspector sympathetically expressed his agreement in the words: "Yes, they do 'op it a bit at that time, sir."

The only opening for serious war work in London was the hospital for shell-shock that was being established at Palace Green, Kensington. I applied to join the staff, but to my surprise was rejected. On investigation I found this was due to the action of Mr. Sidney Holland (later Lord Knutsford), the treasurer of the London Hospital and at that time by far the most influential person in the hospital world in London. So I called on him. He said he had been told I was the best qualified person for such work, but also that I had years ago been asked to resign from the West End Hospital, and that he could not be disloyal to another hospital committee by accepting someone whom they had thought unsuitable for hospital staff work, whatever their reasons may have been. In this attitude he was adamant, being unmoved even by the consideration of the national needs, and so I had once more to retire into private life—this time for good. I thought, and still think, that his attitude contained just those elements of dogmatism and unreason which provoke so much protest on the part of those who have to submit to them when they are associated with tyrannical power.

The greater part of my practice in those years was with officers suffering from some form of war neurosis. This meant continued discussion, not to mention arguments, with army medical boards. Early in the war the very existence of neuroses, whether related to the war or otherwise, was ignored or openly denied, all cases being ascribed either to malingering or to concussion of the brain. When, however, recruits in England began to exhibit symptoms indistinguishable from those arising in men who had been blown up or buried alive, the respectable way of developing the neuroses which the pundits called concussion of the brain, then even the R.A.M.C. had to think of revising its ideas. My main difficulty was to secure adequate extensions of the time allowed for such a slow treatment as psycho-analysis necessarily is. To grant merely another six weeks meant that the patient spent a good deal of his time in fretting with anxiety about his next board instead of on exploring the sources of his condition. On the whole, however, I was not dissatisfied with the results that could be obtained even in these unfavourable circumstances, and it was both important and interesting work.

The situations were often extremely pathetic, as indeed they mostly are in neurotic conflicts. There comes to my mind, for instance, a naval officer of forty who consulted me in the very first days of the war. He had just been appointed captain of a battleship, but could not face taking up his duties for a most extraordinary reason. He had a crick in the neck, a slight rheumatic symptom which few people escape at one time or another. This obsessed him so much that his whole attention was devoted to it, and to wondering whether he could feel it again if he moved his head, and so when engaged in conversation, or even in the moment of issuing a command, his attention would altogether wander and he would become dumb. He wept as he told me his bitter shame at failing his Service when the very day had come for which he had been training all his life. The naval authorities refused to grant him any leave, comprehensibly enough from their point of view, and I never saw him again. Even more anxious was the case of a man in a responsible civil position who had to decide whether to join the army or to obtain exemption. He said he was reasonably brave, but that there was one thing in war he could not possibly face. I naturally asked him what it was, but he was unable to mention the horrible idea. After some encouragement he told me that, while he was prepared to endure the other terrors and horrors of trench warfare, he would be seized with uncontrollable panic if another soldier, squeezing past him in a narrow trench, happened inadvertently to—tread on his big toe. That part of his body was invested with an indescribable sensitiveness in his mind: it was the holy of holies. I have never met a more striking contrast between what Freud terms "real fear"—i.e. fear of actual dangers in the outer world—and the anxiety of a phobia; there can be no doubt which of the two is the more dreadful.

Then there was an extremely brilliant officer in the Intelligence Service who was paralysed with depression and a crushing sense of inferiority. After six months I so restored him to health that he got married with the happiest omens, but not long afterwards the medical board decided that Palace Green was the proper place for him. After a couple of months there, deprived of all treatment and of all hope of consolidating his cure, he escaped one night. His wife feared suicide and came to me for help. She gave me his revolver to keep (which I did till the next war) so as to exclude the most obvious method; we knew he could not obtain poison in war-time; he was an excellent swimmer; and we began to hope things would yet go well. But the next morning he was found outside a London terminus with his chest crushed; he had laid himself across a rail before an express train. Opponents have often asserted that many, or perhaps, most, patients who consult psycho-analysts commit suicide, but that is the nearest instance that has come within my experience.

One of my patients was a highly placed gentleman whose position was such that he was informed of all the transactions of the War Cabinet, the most secret knowledge possible in wartime. His trust in me was, I need hardly say, justified, and the following story is the first and only time I shall repeat anything of what he told me. At the time of the submarine crisis in 1917, when Britain—largely unknown to itself—was faced with starvation and defeat, Mr. Lloyd George had to make an important public speech in which he could not avoid making some statement on the situation. A Cabinet meeting was held to consider what hope or reassurance he could hold out to the country. Unfortunately there was none. The naval reports were as gloomy as the food controller's. So, after vainly searching for light in any direction, the Prime Minister tossed his mane and said: "I have it." Whereupon he narrated a bawdy story that had a forcible ending and then added: "So that's what I shall say; submarines be buggered!" The day of the speech came and the country heard to its relief and somewhat to its surprise, that the danger was passing, since the submarine menace was being mastered. Luckily for us, the "Welsh wizard" was exercising second sight, for within a few weeks means were at last found to counter the peril.

Although I accomplished a good deal of scientific work during the four years of the war, I either lacked the necessary strength of mind or else had too much of a social conscience to devote my attention entirely to it, which in the circumstances would doubtless have been the most useful thing to do. That was what Freud did. He would glance through the newspaper, toss it aside with the condemnation "*scheusslich*" (horrible) and go on with his work. But for my part I found it too distracting. I followed daily events in meticulous detail, checked the calculations and estimates of Hilaire Belloc and other military writers in every way I could, and took a profound interest in both the military and the political issues. I was thus impelled to read all manner of books on strategy, the theory of war, and above all the history of the various European countries involved. I certainly acquired in this way a vast amount of interesting information, which I have been glad to possess, but I am sure I should have achieved more in life had I not been fascinated by such a large variety of its aspects. One lives but once, it is true, and to be deeply interested in all life offers is a good way of living, even if it somewhat limits the extent of one's personal contribution to the common weal.

My productive work was now also becoming increasingly hampered by ill-health. A painful form of rheumatoid arthritis had shown itself at the early age of twenty-eight, but after eight years of being only a nuisance it developed into a serious affliction, attacking my spine, many nerves, and most joints and muscles in the body. I observe that most autobiographers disdain any reference to bodily disorders, as if they were above such mundane impediments. Well, I think I have fought mine bravely enough and certainly have never given in to them, but I do not feel they need be hidden as if they were the shameful inferiority they betoken in Butler's *Erewhon*. Indeed, were it not for my knowledge of how boring such topics are to other people, I would confess to the wish that friends could have had some idea of the pains I endured and the affliction under which I laboured: so hard is it to dispel the childhood belief that sympathy has the power of relieving pain! I was to have far worse times in later years, but even in those earlier days during the war I remember the pain from neuritis being bad enough to make it impossible for six months at a time to use a pen or hold a telephone receiver. I tried, of course, to get at the source of the trouble. Vaccines made from my own germs or other peoples' had no effect. My body was so healthy that it was hard to think of any septic focus. On the off-chance of improving the condition of the post-nasal cavity I had an operation on the septum of the nose, but it had no more effect than subsequent hopeful removals of many teeth, the tonsils, and the appendix. This operation was just before Christmas 1914, and I spent the holiday convalescing at Lyme Regis, where I had the experience late one night of helping to bring in sailors rescued from the battleship *Formidable* that had been torpedoed in the Channel.

It is hard now to remember the optimistic forecasts about the duration of the First World War. The Kaiser's promise to lead his troops home before Christmas was equalled by the general belief in England that it could be only a matter of months. Kitchener staggered both the military and political leaders by predicting a three-years' war, and actually my own amateur prediction of between four and five years proved nearer the truth. Hanns Sachs told me later of the consternation a letter of mine produced among his friends in Vienna when in the autumn of 1916 I calmly announced that we were about half-way through the war! The other extreme was reached by a young teacher friend who asked me in August 1914 if I thought the war could last for months. She was from an enemy country and was on holiday when war broke out, and when I answered "yes" she exclaimed: "But that's impossible, I have to be back in school by October." So much for the self-centredness of the young!

Another prediction, which I published in the middle of the war, was much commented on afterwards, though nowadays it would evoke no surprise. I gave psychological reasons for supposing that Great Britain would make desperate efforts after the war to re-establish the Gold Standard, even at the cost of massive unemployment and social discontent. It took some years before those in authority were willing to perceive the innate connection between these two things, though since then it has become a platitude.

It was possible to maintain a regular correspondence with Freud and other "enemy" friends throughout the war. One simply asked a friend in a neutral country—and in that war there were many such—to forward the letter, which was, of course, censored before it left this country.

Although I am by nature a very sociable being, my devotion to work has precluded my leading a social life except on a limited scale, so that this autobiography will differ from most in not scintillating with the names of interesting people "I have met". And in those war years social life was in any event greatly restricted. Once a month or so I used to dine with a group of men who had been medical students with me at Cardiff. We would discuss the prospects of the war, relate our own experiences (the others were all in the R.A.M.C.), and at times remind ourselves of bygone days. Then I was a guest at two or three family centres where unusual people used to gather, poets, writers, Bohemians, Socialists, and non-Bloomsbury intelligentsia. Among them was Litvinov, later the Soviet Foreign Minister.

A most interesting person in this collection was D. H. Lawrence. I probably met him first through the Eders, though his wife—the sister of the famous German ace Baron von Richthofen—was the bosom friend of Otto Gross's wife, a lady I had known well in my Munich days. He was already showing signs of tuberculosis, for which he had been exempted from war service, and had hoped to receive benefit for it by living in Cornwall. To his anger they had been expelled from that sea-girt county because of his wife's extraction, and he was rather at a loose end in London. He dominated every company with his eager assertive manner, his vital—all too vital—personality, and his penetrating intelligence. Even then he was planning the post-war expeditions he carried out later—the colony in New Mexico and similar schemes. He pressed me hard to join him in these plans, which to my more sober way of thinking seemed decidedly hare-brained. I had already some experience of utopian colonies that were to be examples to a stupid world—Van Eeden's in Holland and others in America—and I was obliged to hurt his feelings by refusing. It was very plain to me as a psychologist that Lawrence, with his obvious lack of balance, was the last person with whom it would be possible for anyone to co-operate for long. All that he wanted was "disciples", and I have always been much too independent to play that part. Still, it was stimulating to hear him deliver himself on every subject under the sun: naturally in a monologue, for Lawrence could not tolerate much real conversation. I remember, for instance, his giving me an original explanation of why we were bound to win the war. It was that the Germans had no true leader; the Kaiser was only a mountebank. With his blue eyes flashing and his red beard bristling, he declaimed: "That posturing ape, with his winged helmet, keeps telling his people what a fine fellow he is and what noble followers they were. A real leader would not speak of himself or his followers; he would simply command: 'There is the enemy, strike.'" I am afraid, however, that he saw through the Kaiser so well partly because his own personality contained similar elements.

The relations between Lawrence and his wife would make a chapter in themselves, and others have often described something of them. They were both impelled by mischievous demons to goad each other to frenzy. When this culminated in a sadistic orgy there was again peace for a time, but it was not always so. I recollect being aroused late one night by a panic-stricken female bursting into my flat and begging for refuge because her husband was intent on murdering her. I administered a cold douche by replying: "From the way you treat him, I wonder he has not done so long ago." The talk that followed did her, I hope, some good; it at least gave her some insight into the dark forces that drove them into such tempestuous situations. After all, she lived with him to the end and survived him, so some elements of wisdom and self-control must have played their part. And she was a charming as well as an intelligent woman.

Early in the war an amateur psychologist, Lucy Hoesch-Ernst, whom I had met at various times in Germany and America, wrote to say I could have the use of her bungalow in Sussex for the duration of the war. She was a stormy petrel. A member of a prominent Rhineland family, she became a pacifist and strongly anti-German; naturally she did not escape the attentions of the police in her homeland. After the war she again wandered forth and ultimately became a British subject. Well, the "bungalow" turned out to be a disused railway carriage that had been dumped with others on the beach near Shoreham and formed the nucleus of the later "bungalow town" there. Unlike most such "rashes" in Sussex, with the notorious Peacehaven pre-eminent among them, this one could at least be seen from nowhere except the sea. I bought a motor-cycle and, after five minutes' teaching, embarked on the journey to visit it. There was one mild visit to a ditch, but the rest went off well; after all, I had been a very expert cyclist in my time. The week-end habit easily developed, and I soon came to look forward to my weekly dip in the sea and a night passed with the roar of the shingle. After a year or two, however, I found I no longer had the habitation to myself. Soldiers training in the neighbourhood were appropriating it, and soon the doors and windows disappeared. What soldiers do with such articles I have never been able to find out.

After this taste of freedom from town life, I began to wish for a little spot of my own in the country. The sequel I have narrated in the first chapter of this book. How I came in 1916 to secure the little cottage, which from the local name of the paddock attached I christened The Plat, has its psychological interest.

I had meant to spend only two or three hundred pounds, but liked the look of it so much that I offered four hundred against the eight which the owner wanted for it. In looking over the rooms I had made a curious observation. The reason why the man wanted to sell was because his wife had heart attacks, which necessitated their spinster daughter of about forty cycling five miles and back to fetch a doctor. Now, in her room I noticed a receipt of her subscription to a society devoted to reform of the divorce laws. It seemed odd that such a person should be interested in a topic so remote from her life, and it occurred to me that it was probably an expression of her unconscious hostility to her mother (the wish to separate the parents). If so she would be doubly anxious lest her repressed wishes be fulfilled during her desperate dashes for the doctor, and I thought it likely she would work on her father's feelings as soon as I left. My calculation was apparently justified, for in a couple of days I had a letter reducing the figure to six hundred pounds, an offer which I accepted and have always been glad of, for I soon came to love my little home.

A home needs a mistress and I was in the mood to find one. Marriage-making friends had for some time been offering their services, but in vain. It was irrational, but something in me strove against marrying an Englishwoman; it seemed so commonplace. Then towards the end of the year I met at a small party a brilliant young Welsh musician, Morfydd Owen. The third time we met, I proposed to her. A day or two later I rang up an old school friend I hadn't seen for some time and told him I had some news for him. He replied: "I can guess it; you are going to marry Morfydd Owen." Astonished, I asked him how he knew, since no other friends did. He said he had known her for some time and had had the thought that if we two ever met we should fall in love with each other; it had come to his ears that we had met recently, so he assumed his expectation was correct. An example of intuition that with many people would rank as second sight.

Such events occur only when there is a deep affinity, based beyond doubt on profound emotions emanating from early impressions from childhood, and it was not hard for me to recognise various associations linking her with my young mother. That was not very relevant consciously, since she was enough of a fascinating and remarkable personality to stand on her own merits. It has been said of her that she was the most gifted musician Wales had ever produced, which is saying much, but it was certainly true of her generation. After graduating at the University of Wales she entered, full of honours and scholarships, the Royal Academy of Music, where she swept all before her and was made an Associate Professor at the early age of twenty-four. She was equally distinguished as pianist, singer, and composer, though of course it is in this last capacity that her name will live. I will say no more of her artistic career here; it is narrated in a biography with which I prefaced a four-volume selection from her works that I published after her death.

I will not speak here of the happiness of that marriage nor of its difficulties that had to be overcome. It is not to be counted on that genius of such an order should go hand-in-hand with a completely harmonious personality, nor does this often happen. Singularly mature, and with unerring integrity of soul in all that concerned her art, Morfydd's mental evolution had not proceeded evenly in all directions. Her attachment to her father was so great that she had misgivings at "deserting" him for anyone else. Her faith and devotion, so admirable when related to her country and her people, were also unfortunately attached to very simple-minded religious beliefs, and it was at first a great grief to her that I did not share them. This had also its practical inconveniences, since she wished to attend her Church services, and even Sunday School, on the Sabbath, whereas I had long been in the habit of devoting that day to worship of the country. As time went on, however, love began to tell, and her ideas broadened. As may be imagined, my notion of adjustment in such matters consists in persuading the other person to approach my view of them, and that is what gradually and painlessly happened.

Our happiness grew more and more complete, but after eighteen months it came to an abrupt end. We were paying a summer visit to my father in Wales, and I was looking forward to taking her over my familiar Gowerland; though a native of the same county, she had never visited that beautiful peninsula. On the way down I wanted to buy her a box of chocolates, which for some reason she declined; it was poignant to reflect later that it would probably have saved her life. Life and great issues are always at the mercy of meaningless trivialities. Soon after arriving she fell obscurely ill, and it was a couple of days before it became plain that there was an appendicitis, which was going on to form an abscess. An operation was urgently indicated. I spent four or five hours at the telephone trying to reach Trotter; communications late in 1918 were poor, both by telephone and by rail. He advised me to secure a local surgeon and not risk the delay of waiting till he could come the next day; it was, of course, a simple operation. She did not do well, however, and after a few days became delirious with a high temperature. We thought there was blood poisoning till I got Trotter from London. He at once recognised delayed chloroform poisoning. It had recently been discovered, which neither the local doctor nor I had known, that this is a likelihood with a patient who is young, has suppuration in any part of the body, and has been deprived of sugar (as war conditions had then imposed); in such circumstances only ether is permissible as an anaesthetic. This simple piece of ignorance cost a valuable and promising life. We fought hard, and there were moments when we seemed to have succeeded, but it was too late.

The grief I then had to endure was the most painful experience of my life, though it did not persist indefinitely as a later similar experience has. Life lost most of its value, or at least savour. The acuteness of the pain had the effect of bringing out all the gentleness and kindliness in my nature. I felt that with such possibilities of pain in the world it behoved everyone, or at all events those who knew of them, to be as kind as they could be to their fellows. If only mankind could learn that lesson! Nature sees to it that misfortune, sickness, and grief provide all the suffering in the world that the sternest moralist could demand for our improvement, so that the senseless additions we make to it by cruelty are truly superfluous. At least I was spared one agony. I did not have the insuperable task of having to reconcile this tragedy with a belief in a benevolent Deity. How I pitied Morfydd's father, a devout believer, in that struggle! Poor man, death took from him his wife and all his children, his darling daughter and two sons, within the space of a year. Even his religion broke under the strain. After all, the belief in God owes much of its value to the expectation that He will protect and comfort in critical situations, particularly those affecting our loved ones. If, on the contrary, He deals the chief of these a frightful blow, for which His omnipotence makes Him by definition responsible, then one is faced with the predicament of accepting His conduct, which would involve a disloyalty to the loved one, or of repudiating Him. When the human love reaches a very high order no ordinary religious belief will vie with it.

For myself, I was simply dazed as at an incredible event. It was impossible to think of going back to what had been our home. So I wandered about spending a few days with various friends, with the Trotters in London, with Bernard Hart at the famous shell-shock hospital at Maghull, with the Flugels at their farm in a remote corner of Yorkshire.

I remember it was on one of these train journeys that a soldier just back from France told me he thought the war would soon be over. I had been looking to the great American offensive that was being arranged for the following spring, and so was incredulous, but he assured me he had often seen the Germans give way in battle but never in the fashion they were doing now. I made a note of it and then a few weeks later I was puzzled to see that British cavalry were advancing beyond the Rupel Pass into Macedonia. This seemed to contradict all previous experience in the war and was explained only by the news that came presently about the giving way of Bulgaria. Even so, the main war looked like lasting a good while longer, until the October *pourparlers* made it plain that Germany also was at the end of her tether.

To me, as to many other people, the form taken by the end of the war seemed profoundly unsatisfactory. It was not merely the natural sense of being thwarted by the absence of a spectacular victory with an unambiguous German rout. From my knowledge of the psychology of militarism, and of German militarism in particular, I felt sure that such a victory, with the hoped-for "march on Berlin", provided the only chance of seriously discrediting aggressive militarism in German eyes. One can of course sympathise with the advice Foch proffered that no further victory could give him more complete domination over the enemy than the actual terms of the armistice did give, so that the loss of still more lives would be unjustifiable, and also with the frightful state of exhaustion that could contemplate only relief from the continuous slaughter and could not face the effort of further thought for the future. All the same, it was more than a pity, and I was full of foreboding for the future. It was almost at once evident that the military clique were going to succeed in saving their prestige by the device of the "civilian stab in the back" legend, and few Englishmen, knowing the truth about the military situation, ever learned how extraordinarily successful this legend proved to be in Germany. But from November 11th, 1918, I never wavered in my conviction that Germany would rise again, reassemble her forces, and attack us once more in the hope of catching us in a state of complacent unpreparedness. So it proved. For us the Great War was finally over; for the Germans the first round had been fought.

After three weeks I had resumed work—after all, there was nothing else to be done. Patients naturally expressed their resentment at the interruption by finding opportunities to flick my still unbearably raw wound; psycho-analytic treatment does not bring out the most charming aspects of human nature. But I was responding with resignation. Since there could be no further happiness for me, nothing more mattered personally, so I could devote the whole of my energies to helping other people. There was some relief in that thought: nothing more could hurt me—so I then thought—and life would be well worth living through being useful to others. But the pain itself lasted without the slightest diminution for more than a year.

Armistice night, which in happier days I had looked forward to spending with old friends, came and went. I stared at it, and at the German howitzers lining the Mall, but for me, as for so many others, it meant the end of an old world rather than the beginning of a new one.

Epilogue

AN unfinished scientific treatise or a historical work—even, conceivably, a play or a novel—can be completed by another hand. But nothing of this sort can be attempted with an autobiography, for it owes all its character and value to the outlook and personality of the author. It is therefore only the factual record, and not the rounded portrayal, of my father's life that I shall try to complete by a summary of events from 1918 to his death in 1958. The task is the easier because the story of Ernest Jones is essentially that of psycho-analysis, and its development, in which of course he played an essential part, is fully chronicled in his three-volume biography of Freud.

Indeed—and this illustrates the relationship between the two men—my father's decision to write a definitive life of Freud, a labour which he knew must consume most or all of his own last years, accounts for the unfinished state of this book. He had started to write his autobiography in 1944, and made a manuscript draft of eleven chapters. Then a difficulty presented itself. The book would lose in value and integrity unless it frankly described the disagreements and rifts which accompanied the growth of psycho-analysis and the shortcomings of some well-known figures. To present these from his own angle might seem unduly subjective. Yet the facts, of which he had an unrivalled knowledge, were a part of scientific history. He decided, therefore, to embark on a work centred, not on his own experiences, but on psycho-analysis and its founder.

In 1957, with the biography of Freud written and published, he returned to the present book. Increasing illness, however, forced him to realise that he could never finish it. He felt that its main interest would lie in the early chapters, particularly in their picture of the medical world at the beginning of this century; so he decided not to extend the manuscript, but to revise and in places rewrite it, and to complete to his satisfaction a book that could be published with some such title as *Early Memories* (though he had originally chosen the title *Free*

Associations for his autobiography). This was to consist of eight chapters of the manuscript, and thus to include his first meeting with Freud and his entry into the world of psycho-analysis.

In the event, my father revised only seven chapters. Indefatigable to the last, he dictated a new opening sentence of Chapter Eight, but was not satisfied with it; and the last matter which he tried to discuss with me, when he had less than a day to live, was the form of this sentence.

I hope that readers will agree that there is much of interest in all eleven chapters of the book as it now stands; for I thought it right to publish the last four from the manuscript, with only the minimum of obvious corrections.

The story breaks off at the death of Ernest Jones's first wife, Morfydd. It is certain that Chapter Twelve, had he written it, would have expressed the sudden—and lasting—joy that he found in his second marriage. This took place at Zurich in October 1919, during his first visit to the Continent after the war-time break. My mother, *née* Katharina Jokl, was born at Brünn (now Brno, in Czechoslovakia), had lived since early childhood in Vienna, and had studied in Switzerland. When she and my father met—they were introduced by Hanns Sachs, who is mentioned in this book—they were engaged in three days and married within three weeks.

It is not exceptional for a man to make two successful marriages; rather more rarely is a second marriage a love match in the best and deepest sense of the words. The happiness which my father found in almost forty years of life with my mother was of a quality far more often envied than attained. His affection for and gratitude to her were only strengthened by time. I can only affirm, and cannot express as he would have, the degree to which he loved and valued her as a wife, as an unfailing support in times of strain, and as an essential help in his work, especially in preparing the Freud biography.

The marriage, as he often said, brought him luck at once. Psycho-analysis struck firm and healthy roots in this country when the British Psycho-Analytical Society, founded in 1919, replaced the earlier London Society. Ernest Jones's practice increased, and before long he was refusing patients and passing them on to colleagues, whose numbers also grew. His income, too, expanded, and at his wife's urging he left off coaching and similar donkey-work. In 1921 he moved from his Great Portland Street flat and took a Crown lease of a house in York Terrace, Regent's Park, which was his home until the Second World War. He was able, much sooner than he can have imagined on his return from Canada in 1914, to take a consulting-room in the traditional street of specialists and become once more a Harley Street man, if of an unconventional sort.

A daughter, Gwenith, was born in 1920; her death from pneumonia at the age of seven was the great sorrow that my parents had to endure. I was born in 1922, my sister Nesta in 1930, and my brother Lewis in 1933.

Even as a child I was aware of the prodigious amount of work my father got through. For years he saw ten or eleven patients a day. His hours were too long for the Harley Street house where he had his consulting-room; so one patient came to York Terrace before breakfast and others on Saturday morning.

But of course this was not the end of Ernest Jones's day, and his practice was only part of his work. The leadership, and a good deal of the detailed work, of the Society fell on his shoulders. He was the type of man—reliable and unfailingly punctual in whatever he promised, quick-thinking, unafraid of decisions, fluent with tongue and pen—to whom work naturally gravitates. He was President of the British Society from 1920 to 1940, and took the chair at scientific meetings and at committees. He founded the Society's Training Commission, which used to meet at York Terrace and whose work he guided, as also he did that of the London Psycho-Analytic Clinic, which he founded in 1924.

Ernest Jones was active in advancing the status as well as the development of psycho-analysis. With Edward Glover he defended its interests on a special committee set up by the British Medical Association, which met from 1926 to 1929. His tact and firmness were largely responsible for the favourable result, for he was one of the sub-committee of three which drew up the report.

In the wider forum of public opinion, too, he made himself the advocate of the new science—the Huxley, it was often said, to Freud's Darwin. In 1928 he wrote a short book, *Psycho-Analysis*, for Benn's Sixpenny Library; it sold widely, was translated into many languages, and must have given a grounding in the subject to millions of people. Jones and Sir Cyril Burt succeeded, a few years later, in overcoming the taboo on psycho-analysis at Broadcasting House, and gave a series of talks, which were afterwards published. When invited, Ernest Jones also gave public lectures and wrote articles in the general press.

He did not, however, allow the work of popularisation to divert him from making important contributions to psycho-analytic theory. A complete list of his writings in psycho-analytic journals would fill several pages. Most of them are collected in book form as *Papers on Psycho-Analysis* and *Essays in Applied Psycho-Analysis*. The best known of his books were *On the Nightmare* and *Hamlet and Oedipus*, an expansion of the study of Hamlet which had been among his earliest essays.

In the International Psycho-Analytic Association, Ernest Jones was accorded the same outstanding position and gave the same untiring service as in Britain. Freud's dislike of official responsibility created an obvious need for a kind of chief administrator, and Jones was uniquely qualified by his standing, his diplomatic skill, and his first-hand knowledge of professional conditions alike on the Continent, in Britain, and in the United States. He was President of the Association from 1920 to 1924 and again from 1932 until 1949. This involved a vast amount of correspondence, frequent meetings and journeys, and responsibility for preparing, as well as presiding over, the biennial Congresses.

Throughout the years between the two wars, moreover, Jones was editor of the *Journal* and the International Psycho-Analytical Library. The latter published more than fifty books, all of which he had to scc through the press.

When he retired from the Presidency, he was made honorary President of the Association for life. It became a tradition for the first paper at each Congress to be read by Ernest Jones. He carried out this duty for the last time in Paris in 1957.

Psycho-analysis suffered its heaviest blow when the Nazis took power, in Germany and later in Austria. Jones advised and helped the German Society in a delaying action aimed at the ultimately hopeless task of preserving its freedom and integrity. Most of the German analysts had to emigrate, either because it was the only way to continue their work or because they were

Jews. My father applied himself to the wearying job of overcoming the barriers, professional and bureaucratic, that stood in the way of their acceptance in this country. Thanks to his persistence and ingenuity, fifty German or Austrian analysts found refuge in this country, either permanently or on their way to America. Some of them, no doubt, owe their lives to him.

Many readers will know—a full account is given in my father's life of Freud—how he flew to Vienna when the Nazis invaded Austria. In conditions of turmoil and danger (he was under arrest for some hours), he saved much of the assets and archives of psycho-analysis and made the arrangements for Freud to come to London.

All this left scant time for recreation; but Ernest Jones entered into his hobbies with the same thoroughness as his work. First among these was skating. He practised hard at rinks in London and on winter holidays in Switzerland, and was no mean performer. Characteristically, he found that there was no satisfactory book for people who wanted to take up figure-skating, and wrote one. He was delighted when someone who knew him as a psycho-analyst remarked: "There's a good book on skating by a man of your name."

He was a keen chess-player and enjoyed playing over the games in world championship matches. Only a chess-playing psycho-analyst could have written Ernest Jones's essay on the strange American genius, Paul Morphy. In later life he was always engaged in about a dozen games of correspondence chess, some of which seemed to last almost as long as a psycho-analysis.

To the end of his life my father was a zestful traveller. He prepared for each day's sightseeing as thoroughly as in the youthful journeys described in this book; my mother and I often emerged worn out from a tour of a castle or a cathedral, with my father elated at having enlarged the knowledge of the official guide on several points of architecture and history.

He had always planned to retire to the Sussex cottage (mentioned in this book), which was enlarged in 1935. The war, and damage to the London house in the air raids, hastened the move. The word "retire", however, must be used in a very qualified way, for Ernest Jones was fitted for anything but inactivity. Some patients still came to him despite war-time difficulties, as indeed they did to the end of his life. One Minister of Information proposed to make use of Jones's psychological knowledge, but was replaced before anything was settled. My father, as he writes sardonically, "accepted the post of salvage officer"; as a matter of fact, he was also medical officer in the local Home Guard.

After the war, the psycho-analytic societies in Britain and elsewhere resumed full activity, but Jones declined to carry his former responsibilities any longer. He devoted himself wholeheartedly to writing the biography of Freud which, he estimated, would take ten years of hard work—in fact, it took rather less, although the first volume had to be largely re-written when a trunkful of letters was discovered after the death of Freud's widow. Anyone who has even glanced at those three stout volumes, which embody both a detailed narrative of Freud's life and a survey of his thought, can see what a formidable task was thus tackled by a man in his seventies, living in the country away from reference books, and without outside secretarial help. It was mastered by means of a system which only my parents really understood, and which involved distributing papers among tall pyramids of wire baskets, of the sort you see in a supermarket.

The work was nearing its end when the time came for the celebration of the centenary of Freud's birth. For this, Ernest Jones had to prepare the lectures which are published as his last book, *Four Centenary Addresses*. He had accepted an invitation to the United States, now the home of the greater part of the psycho-analytic profession. At this point, his health betrayed him. Of this I shall write in some detail, for my father was strongly of the opinion that bodily matters have their place in a biography, and he would complain when reading *The Times*: "People never seem to die *of* anything."

He had by nature an unusually strong and tenacious constitution, and this essential sturdiness was not diminished either by years of rheumatic suffering or by a tendency to bronchial trouble. His first serious illness was a coronary thrombosis in October 1944. It was fairly severe and he was in bed for six weeks, but he made a remarkable recovery and in later years exerted himself in ways that confounded all predictions.

The emergency that arose in 1956 was an operation for the

removal of a growth in the bladder. It was successful; and a fortnight after it, when he should normally have been convalescing, he flew to America with my mother and carried out a heavy programme (only slightly shortened) of lectures, banquets, interviews, and television appearances in various cities. For the actual date of the centenary he was back in London to lecture and to unveil a plaque on the house where Freud died.

The condition which had caused this alarm seemed to have been eradicated, but a year later, in June 1957, my father suffered a second coronary attack. It was milder than the first; nevertheless, after that he was never in good health. In August, while in Paris for his last Congress, he had a haemorrhage in the eye. In October he was gravely ill with what at first looked like a gastric complaint. He recovered slowly and partially, and was up and dressed for Christmas and for his seventy-ninth birthday, but he was much weakened. Early in the new year he was in bed again.

The coronary had laid a false trail, and it was thought that a failing heart was responsible for the illness; but, as my father's condition grew worse, cancer of the liver was diagnosed. He knew that death was not far, and faced it with the keen regret of one who has greatly loved life, but entirely without fear, and of course without any change in the view of the universe which he has expressed in this book.

My mother had been his devoted nurse throughout the illness, but in the last phase he was taken by ambulance to his old hospital, University College. He died on February 11th, 1958.

Ernest Jones was cremated, without ceremony other than tributes by his colleagues, at Golders Green, where his ashes are preserved close to those of Sigmund Freud.

